Exploiting Earnings Volatility

An Innovative New Approach to Evaluating, Optimizing, and Trading Option Strategies to Profit from Earnings Announcements

BRIAN JOHNSON

DEDICATION

To my former derivative students, whose desire to learn and
seemingly limitless supply of insightful questions fueled my enduring
fascination with options and inspired many new research ideas.

DISCLAIMER

Information in this book and in the accompanying spreadsheets is provided solely for informational and general educational purposes and should not be construed as an offer to sell or the solicitation of an offer to buy securities *or to provide investment advice*. Option trading has large potential rewards, but also large potential risk. You must be aware of the risks and be willing to accept them in order to invest in the options markets. Do not trade with money you cannot afford to lose.

CONTENTS

INTRODUCTION

Brian Johnson, a professional investment manager with many years of trading and teaching experience, wrote his first book, *Option Strategy Risk / Return Ratios: A Revolutionary New Approach to Optimizing, Adjusting, and Trading Any Option Income Strategy* in 2014. It has been one of the top-selling option books and it has received outstanding reviews by the option trading community.

His new book, *Exploiting Earnings Volatility*, introduces an innovative new framework for evaluating, optimizing, and trading option strategies to profit from earnings-related pricing anomalies. Leveraging his extensive background in option-pricing and decades of experience in investment management and trading, Brian Johnson developed this inventive approach specifically to design and manage option earnings strategies.

These revolutionary new tools can be applied to any option earnings strategy on any underlying security. In an *Active Trader* article titled "Modeling Implied Volatility," Mr. Johnson introduced a formula for aggregating discrete volatility measures into a single metric that can be used with conventional option pricing formulas to accurately model implied volatility before and after earnings announcements. The practical application of this formula has profound implications for option trading and strategy development.

Exploiting Earnings Volatility is written in a clear, understandable fashion and explains how to use this revolutionary approach to 1) solve for the expected level of earnings volatility implicitly priced in an option matrix, 2) calculate historical levels of realized and implied earnings volatility, 3) develop strategies to exploit divergences between the two, and 4) calculate expected future levels of implied volatility before and after earnings announcements.

Furthermore, *Exploiting Earnings Volatility* also includes two Excel spreadsheets. The Basic spreadsheet employs minimal input data to estimate current and historical earnings volatility and utilizes those estimates to forecast future levels of implied volatility around earnings announcements.

The Integrated spreadsheet includes a comprehensive volatility

1

model that simultaneously integrates and quantifies every component of real-world implied volatility, including earnings volatility. This powerful tool allows the reader to identify the precise level of over or undervaluation of every option in the matrix and to accurately forecast future option prices and option strategy profits and losses before and after earnings announcements.

The Integrated spreadsheet even includes an optimization tool designed to identify the option strategy with the highest level of return per unit of risk, based on the user's specific assumptions.

Written specifically for investors who have familiarity with options, this practical guide begins with a detailed review of volatility, the single most important (and often misunderstood) component of option pricing. The aggregate implied volatility formula is fully explained in Chapter 2, which also includes graphical examples to communicate the mathematical relationships visually and intuitively.

Chapter 3 includes a detailed step-by-step guide to using the Basic spreadsheet to calculate historical and implied levels of earnings volatility and to forecast future levels of implied volatility before and after earnings announcements.

The next chapter provides a conceptual and mathematical explanation of "True Greeks," accurate measures of risk and return sensitivity that reflect the real-world behavior of options. New option Greeks that are specific to earnings announcements are also introduced in this chapter. The Integrated spreadsheet calculates "True Greek" values for individual options and for option strategies.

Building on the above foundation, Chapter 5 includes a trade example that uses actual market data and analytical results from both spreadsheets to design a unique option strategy to exploit earnings-related pricing and volatility anomalies.

After illustrating the capabilities of the spreadsheets in a real-world trade example, Chapters 6 through 8 explain every module of the Integrated spreadsheet tool and how to best use this spreadsheet in practice: how to import the data, enter user specifications, solve for volatility parameters, and optimize and evaluate option strategies. The data for a single underlying security and its option matrix with actual prices are used in both spreadsheets and throughout these chapters to demonstrate the process traders would employ in a real-world environment.

The next chapter includes another real-world trading example with actual market data, which illustrates how the analytical tools in this book can be used in different market environments. The final chapter examines practical considerations and prospective applications of these innovative new tools.

This book introduces a new analytical framework that may sound complicated at first, but is really quite intuitive. Formulas are provided to ensure an accurate mathematical description of the analytical framework. The formulas presented in the book are limited to basic high-school algebra, so they should be accessible to most readers. However, for those readers who still have nightmares about high-school algebra, important mathematical relationships are also explained intuitively and depicted graphically.

Most important, *you will not need to perform any of these calculations manually. Exploiting Earnings Volatility* includes a link to Excel spreadsheets that perform all of the calculations described in the book. In addition, the Integrated spreadsheet functions are all automated and accessible via

"push-button" macros.

All of the formulas in the book are presented in Excel format to make it easier for readers who would like to experiment with these tools in their own Excel spreadsheets.

The unique price and volatility behavior of options before and after discrete earnings announcements is an enigma to most option traders, even to many professional option traders. The aggregate volatility formula is relatively simple, but it has profound implications. When integrated with a real-world volatility model, it offers unparalleled insights into earnings volatility, price behavior, option strategy construction, and prospective value-added opportunities.

1 - VOLATILITY REVIEW

Option pricing before and after earnings announcements is *highly inefficient* and the mechanics of calculating the corresponding implied volatility values is a mystery to most market participants. As a result, for traders with the proper tools and an understanding of earnings volatility, option earnings strategies represent one of the best and most reliable sources of value-added opportunities in the option market. Even better, these opportunities occur every quarter and there are hundreds of individual stocks that have options with sufficient liquidity to exploit these opportunities.

Until now, there has never been a consistent, objective framework for evaluating and constructing option earnings strategies that simultaneously models every aspect of volatility, including earnings effects. This book will provide the tools you need to objectively evaluate and develop option earnings strategies on any underlying stock, in any market environment. However, before I introduce these new tools, we need to examine volatility and how volatility affects option values. The key to understanding option valuation is the asymmetrical payoff function. Portions of the following crucial section also appeared in my first book: *Option Strategy Risk / Return Ratios*.

Asymmetrical Payoff Functions

Call and put options have asymmetrical payoff functions. This sounds complicated, but is actually relatively straightforward. A call option gives the owner or buyer the right, but not the obligation, to purchase the underlying asset at the strike price on or before the expiration date. For now, let's keep things simple and ignore the fact that many options can be exercised prior to expiration. This will allow us to focus our attention on what happens at option expiration.

4

The following example (depicted in Figure 1.1 below) should help illustrate the concept of asymmetry. If we purchased a one-year call option on IBM with a strike price of $100, we would only choose to exercise the call option if the price of IBM was above the $100 strike price (in the money) on the expiration date.

If the price of IBM was $110 on the expiration date, the payoff would be $10. The payoff is also called the intrinsic value and represents the value of exercising an in-the-money option at expiration. In this case, we could purchase IBM for the $100 strike price and immediately sell it at the market price of $110 for a payoff of $10. If the market price of IBM was $120 on the expiration date, the payoff would be $20. For every dollar the price of IBM rose above the strike price of $100, the payoff of the call option would increase by $1. As a result, the slope of the payoff function above the strike price is positive 1.0 (one dollar increase in payoff for every one dollar increase in the price of IBM).

If the price of IBM was below the $100 strike price (out of the money) on the expiration date, we would choose not to exercise the option and it would expire worthless. In that scenario, the payoff would be zero – although we would incur a loss on the trade.

It is important not to confuse payoffs and profits. Payoff functions (not profit and loss functions) should be used to determine the value of options. It would not matter how much the price of IBM dropped below $100; the call option would expire worthless and the payoff would still be zero. All options that are out of the money on the expiration date expire worthless and therefore have an intrinsic value and payoff of zero. As a result, the slope of the payoff function below the strike price is zero (zero change in the payoff function for a one dollar increase in the price of the underlying security).

Note the discrete change in the slope of the payoff function that occurs at the strike price. The slope of the lite-colored kinked payoff function is zero when the price of the underlying stock (IBM) is below the strike price ($100) and the slope of the payoff function line is plus 1.0 when the price of the stock is above the strike price. This payoff function is asymmetric and this asymmetry creates value for the call option.

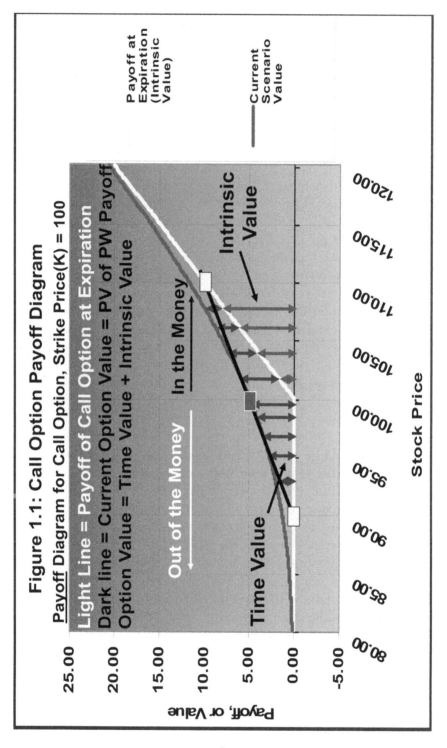

Figure 1.1: Call Option Payoff Diagram

Volatility, Asymmetry, & Option Values

The value of an option represents the present value of its probability-weighted future payoffs. What does that mean? Let's use the IBM call option payoff function from Figure 1.1 again to work through a simple example. First, let's assume that the stock price of IBM today is $100 and that one year from today, there were only two possible states of the world: the price of IBM would either increase by 10% (+ $10) or the price of IBM would decrease by 10% (- $10). In other words, one year from today there would be a 50% probability of IBM closing at $90 and a 50% probability of IBM closing at $110.

The payoffs in those two hypothetical scenarios would be $0 and $10, respectively (see lite-colored boxes in Figure 1.1 above). Given that the two possible payoffs of $0 and $10 both had a 50% probability of occurring, the average payoff one year from today would be $5 = [(50% x $0) + (50% x $10)]. To determine the value of the call option today, we would technically need to discount the probability-weighted payoff of $5 back to the present using a proxy for the risk-free interest rate.

However, as I write this, short-term interest rates are approximately zero and have been near zero for several years. Even more important, discounting the expected future payoff would complicate our example unnecessarily and shift our focus away from our primary objective: understanding the effects of asymmetric payoff functions and volatility on option values.

To summarize the hypothetical option valuation example, IBM is currently trading at $100. If there was a 50% probability of IBM increasing or decreasing by 10% in one year, the value of a one-year call option with a strike price of $100 would be $5 (ignoring discounting).

Now let's calculate the value of the same call option holding all values constant, except for the expected level of volatility. Let's assume the expected level of volatility for the next year increases from 10% to 20%. The stock price of IBM today would still be $100 and one year from today, there would only be two possible states of the world: the price of IBM would either increase by 20% (+ $20) or the price of IBM would decrease by 20% (- $20). One year from today there would now be a 50% probability of IBM closing at $80 and a 50% probability of IBM closing at $120.

The payoffs in those two hypothetical scenarios would now be $0 and $20, respectively. Given that the two possible payoffs of $0 and $20 both had a 50% probability of occurring, the average payoff one year from today would now be $10 = [(50% x $0) + (50% x $20)].

As is evident in this simple example, option prices are a direct function of the expected level of volatility. As the expected level of volatility increases, the values of both call and put options also increase. The reason is asymmetry. Increasing volatility magnifies the value of asymmetry. Decreasing volatility diminishes the value of asymmetry.

Volatility Assumptions & Conventions

Volatility is a measure of price dispersion and is typically expressed as a one standard deviation (SD) *annualized* percentage price change in the underlying security based on a log-normal return distribution. Figure 1.2 depicts the normal and log-normal price distributions of a $100 non-dividend paying stock, one year into the future. The assumed risk free interest rate was 0.25% and the annual standard deviation was 25%. The future stock price is shown on the independent x-axis and the probability is shown on the dependent y-axis. The percentages were calculated in increments of $1 and Microsoft Excel connected the probabilities using a smooth curve. The normal distribution is represented by the dashed line and the log-normal distribution is depicted by the solid line.

First, note that the normal distribution is symmetric and is centered (approximately) at the current stock price of $100. The symmetry of a normal distribution leads to a very significant problem when valuing options: negative prices for the underlying security. In practice, there is no upper bound on stock prices (provided there are investors who are willing to pay more for the stock), but stock prices cannot drop below zero. As a result, it is not practical to use normal distributions when pricing options.

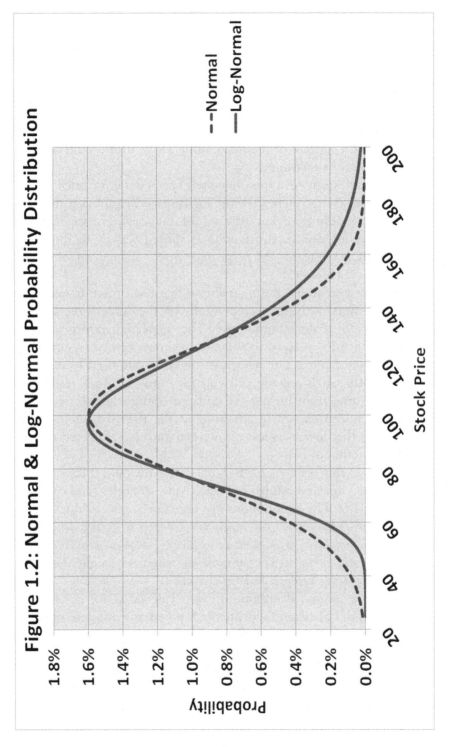

Figure 1.2: Normal & Log-Normal Probability Distribution

The Black Scholes Option Pricing Model (BSOPM) assumes that the returns of the underlying security are distributed log-normally, which means that the natural log of the ending price divided by the beginning price (ending price/beginning price) are distributed normally. Prices derived from a log-normal distribution cannot drop below zero, but are not limited in how much they can increase. The resulting log-normal distribution in Figure 1.2 appears to be skewed to the right: the left tail of the distribution looks truncated relative to the right tail of the distribution.

This would seem to imply that the expected future price of the underlying security is higher for the log-normal distribution than for the normal distribution, but that is not the case. Notice that the center of the log-normal distribution is shifted slightly to the left – just enough to ensure the expected price change of the two distributions are identical.

That brings up an interesting question that few option traders fully appreciate: what is the expected return of the underlying security under the BSOPM assumptions? The expected return of the underlying security is equal to the rate of return earned by investing at the risk-free interest rate, which is the same rate used to discount future payoffs when valuing call and put options. As a result, the expected returns from buying call and put options are also equal to the rate of return earned by investing at the risk-free interest rate. This implies that investors are risk-neutral and that expected returns are not a function of risk.

As I write this, one-year US T-bill rates are only 0.15%, which indicates that expected returns for underlying securities (and calls and puts) under BSOPM assumptions are effectively zero in the current environment. *That means that option prices implicitly assume an expected return of approximately zero for all stocks on earnings announcement dates.* This assumption will become very important when we begin designing directional option strategies in later chapters.

The above return distributions were calculated for a one-year holding period. However, there are obviously many different options, all with varying amounts of time remaining until expiration. The industry convention is to express volatility in annual terms, regardless of the time remaining until expiration for a given option.

This yields two important benefits. First, the annualized volatility estimate can be used directly in the BSOPM and binomial option models. Even more important, the resulting annualized volatilities are directly comparable across all variables: time, underlying security, strike price, time to expiration, option type, etc. This further elevates the importance of volatility relative to other option metrics.

Volatility versus Time

Just because volatility is expressed in annual terms does not mean that it cannot be used to calculate expected price changes for other periods. Volatility is a function of the square root of time. The following formula can be used to calculate the expected future price of an underlying security under the simplifying assumptions of a 0% risk-free rate and a 0% dividend yield:

$$S_T = S_0 * EXP(N * \sigma * (TD/252)^{0.5})$$

S_T = Stock Price T years into the future
S_0 = Stock Price today (Zero years into the future)
EXP represents the Excel function e raised to a power,
e = 2.718281828
N = Number of standard deviations (can be positive or negative)
σ = **Annualized volatility**
TD = Number of trade days remaining
252 = Approximate number of trading days in calendar year

You will note that the number of trade days (TD) was used in the above formula, instead of the number of calendar days. All of the formulas in this book use trade days, as do all of the spreadsheets. The improved precision of trade days is required to accurately quantify the impact of earnings volatility.

Now let's use the above formula to forecast a hypothetical negative one standard deviation price for a $100 stock, 42 trading days in the future, assuming an annual volatility of 25%.

$$S_T = S_0 * EXP(N * \sigma * (TD/252)^{0.5})$$
$$S_T = 100 * EXP(-1 * 0.25 * (42/252)^{0.5})$$
$$S_T = 100 * EXP(-1 * 0.25 * (0.408248))$$
$$S_T = 100 * EXP(-0.102062) = 90.29$$

The resulting price of $90.29 represents a 9.71% decline from the initial stock price of $100. If we repeat this calculation for a range of time periods (measured in trade days), we can construct the graph in Figure 1.3, which depicts the positive and negative one standard deviation percentage price changes as a function of the number of trading days. The initial price of the non-dividend paying stock was $100; the assumed risk free interest rate was 0.00% and the annual standard deviation was 25%.

The number of trading days is shown on the independent x-axis and the percentage price change is shown on the dependent y-axis. The negative one SD percentage price changes are represented by the dashed lower line and the positive one SD percentage price changes are depicted by the solid upper line. The circle on the lower dashed line represents the percentage price change for the hypothetical negative one SD move over 42 trade days (approximately two months).

The ability to forecast expected price changes for a given level of annualized volatility is a critical element of option trading and is especially crucial for option earning strategies. It should be one of the main tools in your option trading toolbox. I use this formula on a daily basis.

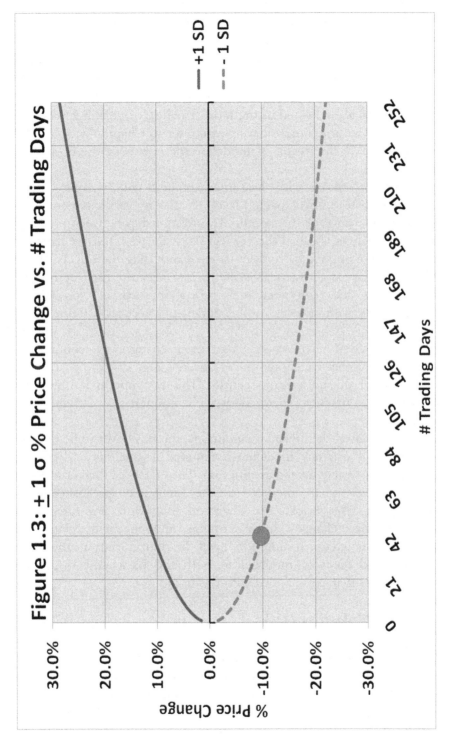

Figure 1.3: ± 1 σ % Price Change vs. # Trading Days

Constant and Continuous

The BSOPM assumes that volatility is constant. Unfortunately, this is not true in practice. In reality, market participants typically assume that volatility will increase or decrease over time and these assumptions are reflected in the term structure of volatility, which is also called the horizontal skew. Please refer to Chapter 7 for a more comprehensive discussion of modeling the effects of the horizontal skew.

Even for options with the same expiration date, volatility is not constant. Instead, the expected level of volatility varies as a function of the strike price of the option. The relationship between volatility and strike prices is called the vertical skew. Please refer to Chapter 7 for a more comprehensive discussion of modeling the effects of the vertical skew. The vertical skew exists because the log-normal distribution does not accurately reflect the market's probability expectations with respect to the underlying security's future price changes.

The BSOPM also assumes that price changes are continuous, which means that we should never observe large discrete changes in the price of the underlying security. This assumption is obviously violated in practice, particularly when quarterly earnings are announced.

Despite all of the invalid assumptions, the BSOPM can be used in practice, but volatility modeling is required to quantify and correct the effects of every invalid assumption. The effects of the vertical and horizontal skews are modeled in the Integrated spreadsheet that accompanies this book. The analytical framework for integrating discrete price changes from earnings announcements into the BSOPM's volatility assumptions will be introduced in the next chapter and are also modeled in both the Basic and Integrated spreadsheets that are included with this book.

Implied Volatility (IV)

Until now, I have ignored the fact that the term "volatility" can be used to describe several different concepts, all of which are relevant to this book. The first is implied volatility, which is a measure of expected or forward-looking volatility.

Option values are determined by only a handful of variables: the stock price, the strike price, the time to expiration, the risk-free interest rate, and the expected level of volatility (and dividends, which we will ignore for now). What is unique about the expected level of volatility relative to the other variables?

Do we know an option's current stock price with certainty? Yes, it is observable on our broker platforms. What about the strike price and time to expiration? Certainly, both are used to describe the option. Do we know the risk-free interest rate that corresponds to the time to expiration of the option? Well, this confuses some traders, but US Treasury Bill yields are typically used as a proxy for the risk-free interest rate. US T-Bills are highly liquid and their yields are also quoted on broker platforms in real time.

Do we know the expected level of volatility? Unfortunately, we do not – at least not directly. However, since we know the values of the other variables that are required to calculate the value of an option and we also know the market price of the option, we can use an option valuation formula, such as the Black Scholes Option Pricing Model (BSOPM), to solve for the *implied volatility* (IV).

Do you see why this is called implied volatility? Implied volatility is the expected level of volatility *implied by* or embedded in the price of the option. In other words, IV represents the market's estimate of the future level of volatility of the underlying security, as determined by the price of the option.

If we know the option price, we can solve for the corresponding implied volatility. Similarly, if we know the expected level of volatility, we can solve for the price of the option. The relationship between the price of an option and the expected level of volatility of the underlying security is completely deterministic, but it does require an option valuation model, which relies on a given set of assumptions.

To keep things simple, we will focus on the BSOPM in this book, but we will include dividend adjustments for practical purposes. We will also discuss the binomial model, which is a discrete version of the BSOPM; properly constructed, the binomial model's option values converge to the BSOPM's option values as the number of intervals used in the binomial model increases. The spreadsheets that accompany this book also use the BSOPM and binomial models, but are not limited by their unrealistic and simplistic volatility assumptions.

Now, let's find the implied volatility of the hypothetical one-year IBM call option that we explored earlier in this chapter (depicted in Figure 1.1). You will recall that the stock and strike prices were both $100, the time to expiration was one year, and the assumed risk-free interest rate was 0%. If the value of the call option was $5, what would be the implied volatility? You will recall from the earlier valuation example that an expected level of future volatility of 10% resulted in a call option value of $5 = [(50% x $0) + (50% x $10)]. As a result, an option price of $5 would imply an expected level of volatility of 10%.

If the value of the call option was $10, what would be the implied volatility? In the earlier example, we found that an expected level of future volatility of 20% resulted in a call option value of $10 = [(50% x $0) + (50% x $20)]. Therefore, an option price of $10 would imply an expected level of volatility of 20%.

Remember that we need to implicitly or explicitly use an option valuation model to calculate implied volatility. In this example, you should note that *we did not use BSOPM* to solve for implied volatility. Instead, we used the very simple symmetric binomial (two-state) model described earlier that had only two possible future stock prices, both of which were a function of the current stock price and the expected future level of volatility. If we had used the BSOPM, we would have arrived at a different value for implied volatility.

Implied volatility is arguably the most important option pricing variable; it is synonymous with the price of an option, but unlike price, it is directly comparable across time, underlying securities, option types, strike prices, and expiration dates. It is impossible to evaluate option prices without modeling implied volatility.

However, as explained earlier, using the BSOPM to calculate implied volatility assumes that volatility is constant and that price changes in the underlying security are continuous. Instead, due to the periodic release of important quarterly earnings data and forward guidance, stocks experience large discrete price changes after every quarterly earnings announcement.

Modeling the expected price dispersion due to earnings announcements requires a new type of implied volatility called *implied earnings volatility*. Instead of using option prices to solve for implied volatility, the analytical framework presented in the following chapter will formally document the mathematical relationship between implied volatility, "normal" (or non-earnings) volatility, and earnings volatility.

This formula will allow us to use option prices and the corresponding implied volatilities to solve for each option's normal implied volatility and the overall level of implied earnings volatility for all options on a given stock. This will provide the foundation for an intuitive new approach for designing option strategies to exploit earnings volatility.

Historical Volatility

The second volatility concept that we will need is historical volatility, which is a measure of past or backward-looking volatility. Practitioners use past levels of price volatility as a means of forecasting future levels of price volatility, which are then used to forecast option prices. To be useful as an estimate of implied volatility, historical volatility must be expressed in the same units as implied volatility. In other words, historical volatility must represent an annualized volatility of the historical log returns of the underlying security.

To calculate the annualized historical volatility of a return series, annualize the root mean squared daily log returns of the underlying security.

To calculate the annualized historical volatility:

1. Calculate the ratio of the daily closing prices (closing price/previous closing price).

2. Calculate the natural log of the daily price ratios (from step 1).

3. Square the log returns (from step 2).

4. Calculate the average of the squared log returns (from step 3).

5. Calculate the square root of the average of the squared log returns (from step 4).

6. Annualize the root mean squared (RMS) log returns (from step 5).

While I did use the term standard deviation before, you should note that we *did not and should not* use the formula for standard deviation to calculate historical volatility. Standard deviation measures the deviation *around the mean or average value of a data series,* while the root mean squared return measures the deviation *around zero.*

You will recall that the expected daily return for all assets is approximately zero under the BSOPM assumptions, which is consistent with the root mean squared (RMS) calculation. The standard deviation calculation implicitly assumes that the expected daily return equals the average daily return, which can significantly understate volatility, especially for small data sets.

The hypothetical example in Figure 1.4 illustrates the potential magnitude of the problem of using standard deviation as a measure of historical volatility. The twelve daily returns are listed in the first column, all of which equal 2.02%. The natural log of one plus the daily returns is provided in the next column, followed by the squared log returns in column three.

Daily Return	Log Return	Log Return Squared	Dev from Mean Squared
2.02%	2.00%	0.04%	0.0017%
2.02%	2.00%	0.04%	0.0017%
2.02%	2.00%	0.04%	0.0017%
2.02%	2.00%	0.04%	0.0017%
2.02%	2.00%	0.04%	0.0017%
2.02%	2.00%	0.04%	0.0017%
2.02%	2.00%	0.04%	0.0017%
2.02%	2.00%	0.04%	0.0017%
2.02%	2.00%	0.04%	0.0017%
2.02%	2.00%	0.04%	0.0017%
2.02%	2.00%	0.04%	0.0017%
2.02%	2.00%	0.04%	0.0017%
Period	RMS	SD	
Daily	2.00%	0.00%	
Annual	31.75%	0.00%	

Figure 1.4: Historical Volatility

Each of the log returns equals 2.00%, which means that the mean or arithmetic average of the log returns also equals 2.00%. Therefore, the daily deviations from the mean must all equal zero, as does the standard deviation (SD) around the mean. Using the standard deviation formula, we would have calculated a historical volatility of 0.00% for a security that was moving in price by 2.02% per day.

Unlike the standard deviation formula, the root mean squared (RMS) formula provides an accurate and representative historical volatility measure and is not affected by the average level of volatility. The daily RMS for the hypothetical example was 2.00% (steps 1-6). You will recall that volatility is a function of the square root of time. We can use this fact to calculate an annualized historical volatility from the daily historical volatility.

If we assume there are 252 trade days per calendar year, we multiply the daily volatility value of 2% by the square root of 252 to arrive at the annualized historical volatility (see formula below).

Annual Volatility = Periodic Volatility * ((252/TD) ^ 0.5)
TD = Number of trade days used to calculate the periodic log return series

Annual Volatility = Periodic Volatility * ((252/TD) ^ 0.5)
Annual Volatility = 2.00% * ((252/1) ^ 0.5) = 31.75%

If we determined that the resulting historical volatility of 31.75% was a fair and unbiased estimate of future volatility, we could use the value of 31.75% as a forecast of the future level of annualized volatility in the BSOPM to estimate the value of an option on the underlying security.

As we saw with implied volatility, there is also a corresponding measure of historical volatility due to earnings announcements, which is called *historical earnings volatility*. Instead of performing the RMS calculation on a series of sequential daily returns, we use the RMS formula on the daily returns history from past earnings announcements.

Specifically, we calculate the historical daily earnings returns using the closing price for the first trade day immediately following the earnings announcement and the closing price for the previous trade day, which will immediately precede the earnings announcement. In other words, we use the closing prices immediately before and after the earnings announcement to calculate historical returns due to earnings. The resulting historical earnings returns will still be daily returns, because they will always be measured using closing prices over a span of one trading day.

Realized volatility

Using the price of an option in conjunction with an options valuation model (such as the BSOPM), we can calculate the implied volatility of the option, which represents the market's estimate of future price volatility. We can also calculate historical volatility, which can also be used to estimate future price volatility. Why would we need two estimates of volatility? Because the market's estimate of future volatility is frequently wrong.

If we could come up with a more accurate estimate of future volatility than the market's implied volatility estimate, then we could design option strategies to exploit our insight and earn excess returns. We will look at actual strategies later, but for now, let's assume that the market's annualized implied volatility estimate was only 50%, but the annualized historical volatility was 100%.

In this hypothetical example, it would appear that the market's implied volatility estimate is too low. Since volatility is synonymous with price, option prices would also be too low. In other words, if we believe our annualized future volatility estimate of 100% is more accurate than the market's implied volatility estimate of 50%, then options must be cheap or undervalued and should be purchased.

How could we profit from such a trade? Let's ignore directional price changes and focus on volatility. If we purchased undervalued options at the market's implied volatility of 50% and the market's implied volatility estimate of 50% converged to our future volatility estimate of 100%, then the prices of our options would increase and we would earn an excess return.

What if the market's implied volatility estimate (50% annualized) never changed, but our expected future level of volatility (100% annualized) proved to be correct? What would this mean and how would it affect our strategy? It would mean that we were ultimately correct and the *realized volatility* experienced over the holding period (the time we held the strategy) was equal to our future volatility forecast, which was based on *historical volatility*.

In this scenario, we would expect to earn an excess return because the *realized volatility* experienced over the holding period was greater than the market's *implied volatility*, despite the fact that the market's estimate of implied volatility did not change. Why did we earn an excess return? Because option payoff functions are asymmetric and the undervalued options we purchased benefited from a higher than expected level of volatility.

Since our annualized volatility estimates were derived from log returns, if we want to compare the realized volatility to the annualized levels of historical or implied volatility, we need to calculate the log of the realized volatility as well. Specifically, we need to calculate the natural log of the realized ending price divided by the realized beginning price (realized ending price/realized beginning price). However, the resulting realized volatility would not be annualized; it would be unique to the length of the holding period. How do calculate the *expected* level of future volatility for a specific holding period? We can use the following formula to convert an annualized volatility to the expected volatility for a holding period of any length.

Holding Period Volatility = Annualized Volatility * ((HPD/252) ^ 0.5)
HPD = Number of trade days in holding period

If we assume a holding period of ten trading days and an annualized volatility of 100%, then the expected level of volatility for ten days would be:

Holding Period Volatility = Annualized Volatility * ((HPD/252) ^ 0.5)
Holding Period Volatility = 100% * ((10/252) ^ 0.5)
Holding Period Volatility = 100% * (0.1992) = 19.92%

If we assume a holding period of 10 trade days and an annualized volatility of only 50%, then the expected level of volatility for 10 days would be:

Holding Period Volatility = Annualized Volatility * ((HPD/252) ^ 0.5)
Holding Period Volatility = 50% * ((10/252) ^ 0.5)
Holding Period Volatility = 50% * (0.1992) = 9.96%

In the continuation of our earlier example above, the market was implicitly expecting a price movement of 9.96% over the holding period, which corresponds to an annualized implied volatility of 50%. We assumed that the realized volatility would instead be consistent with the annualized historical volatility of 100%, which would result in a realized price change of 19.92%, far exceeding the market's estimate, which would have allowed us to profit from buying options at too low a price.

To make this example more accessible, I avoided a discussion of the Greeks, which will be explained more fully in a later chapter. However, for those of you with a working knowledge of the Greeks, when implied volatility is too low (50%) and we expect implied volatility to increase and/or we expect realized volatility to exceed implied volatility, we would want to construct a strategy with positive Vega to profit from the expected increase in implied volatility and positive Gamma to benefit from a higher than expected level of realized volatility.

Vega represents the change in the value of an option or option strategy for an instantaneous 1% increase in implied volatility, holding all of the other variables constant. Gamma reflects the curvature of the option price function. More specifically, Gamma equals the change in Delta for an instantaneous $1 increase in the price of the underlying security, holding all of the other variables constant. While that is the definition of Gamma, it is not very intuitive, which is why I refer to the curvature or convexity of the option price function instead.

All long option positions have positive Gamma, which means they benefit from realized changes in the price of the underlying security. What does "long" mean? It means the investor purchased the option, which gives the buyer the right but not the obligation to exercise the option. Conversely, a short position means the investor sold the option (without previously owning it), which means the *seller* has the obligation to sell (call) or buy (put) the underlying security at the specified strike price. Why do long option positions benefit from realized volatility? Because of asymmetry and asymmetry is the source of positive Gamma.

As was the case for the other volatility concepts presented earlier, there is an earnings component to realized volatility as well, which we will call *realized earnings volatility*. Since earnings are typically announced after the market closes or before the market opens, we will calculate realized earnings volatility for the one day holding period beginning at the close immediately before the earnings announcement and ending at the close on the following trade day. As was the case with historical earnings volatility, realized earnings volatility will always be calculated over a period of one trading day.

Let's repeat the realized volatility calculation above for a one-day holding period associated with a single earnings announcement. If we had an annualized historical earnings volatility of 100%, the corresponding level of earnings volatility over a one-day holding period would be:

Holding Period Volatility = Annualized Volatility * ((HPD/252) ^ 0.5)
Holding Period Volatility = 100% * ((1/252) ^ 0.5)
Holding Period Volatility = 100% * (0.0630) = 6.30%

If we had an annualized implied earnings volatility of only 50%, the corresponding level of earnings volatility over a one-day holding period would be:

Holding Period Volatility = Annualized Volatility * ((HPD/252) ^ 0.5)
Holding Period Volatility = 50% * ((1/252) ^ 0.5)
Holding Period Volatility = 50% * (0.0630) = 3.15%

As you can see from this example, it does not matter whether we are talking about volatility or earnings volatility. For every volatility concept, there is a corresponding earnings volatility counterpart.

However, to exploit anomalies in earnings volatility, we first need the tools to calculate implied, historical, and realized earnings volatility. The following chapter will explain the mathematical relationship between implied volatility, normal volatility, and earnings volatility. This intuitive formula will lay the groundwork for innovative new spreadsheet tools that will offer unparalleled insights into option earnings strategies that can be optimized to provide the highest level of expected returns per unit of risk.

2 - THE AGGREGATE IV FORMULA

For many years, I avoided trading options on individual stocks and focused almost exclusively on index and futures options. There were two principal reasons for my reluctance to trade stock options: 1) I did not feel that I had any advantage in implementing option strategies on individual stocks and 2) I did not have the requisite tools to accurately evaluate and model stock option strategies around earnings announcements.

It frustrated me to know that I was missing out on the profit opportunities from an entire class of options, so several years ago I researched the subject further and eventually derived the mathematical formula that precisely quantifies the behavior of implied volatility (IV) before and after earnings announcements. This breakthrough provided the market edge that I was lacking in individual stocks and formed the foundation for the toolset needed to calculate option pricing and true-risk metrics for stock options that incorporated earnings effects.

I first introduced the formula in my June 2011 *Active Trader* article titled "Modeling Implied Volatility." The article explained that implied volatility on individual stocks can be broken down into two components: earnings volatility and "normal" or non-earnings volatility. The aggregate implied volatility formula provides a means of correctly combining both components into a single, precise aggregate implied volatility value that can be used in conventional option valuation models. Unfortunately, while the aggregate implied volatility formulas are accurate, the approach I outlined in the *Active Trader* article for modeling "normal" volatility was not precise enough to use for strategy construction purposes.

Over the past few years, I designed a new comprehensive volatility model that can be used in conjunction with the aggregate implied volatility formula to simultaneously model both normal and earnings volatility for every option in a matrix. The comprehensive volatility model and attendant strategy optimization and analysis tools are included in the Integrated spreadsheet that accompanies this book.

The aggregate implied volatility formula will be explained fully in this chapter using *hypothetical examples*. In addition, several graphs will be used to help you visualize the mathematical relationships and to provide a more intuitive understanding of the behavior or implied volatility around earnings announcements. The remainder of the book will explain how to apply the formula in practice using *real-world strategies with actual market data.*

The aggregate implied volatility formula that appears in this chapter is mathematically equivalent to the original aggregate implied volatility formula that appeared in the 2011 *Active Trader* article, but I rearranged a few of the terms to make the formula more intuitive. In this chapter, I will present three algebraically equivalent versions of the formula that solve for aggregate implied volatility, earnings volatility, and normal volatility, respectively. Finally, I will include numerical examples, for those of you who would like to verify that you are applying the formula correctly.

For this example, we will assume that the annualized earnings volatility equals 180% and the annualized normal volatility equals 30%. Why the huge disparity between earnings volatility and normal volatility? As I explained earlier, the BSOPM assumes that price changes are continuous, which implies that the distribution of information that affects stock prices is also released continuously. This is obviously not the case and one of the most glaring exceptions is periodic earnings announcements.

Public companies report earnings quarterly. When reporting earnings, senior corporate executives also conduct conference calls where they disclose new information about the future prospects of the company in the form of forward guidance. The release of new financial data and the new insights gained from forward guidance immediately alter investors' expectations regarding future earnings, growth rates, and ultimately value, which can create large discrete changes in the price of the stock.

In the following calculation examples, we will also assume there is exactly one (1) earnings trading day and eleven (11) normal trading days remaining until expiration of the option. Therefore, the option would have a total of twelve (12) trading days remaining until expiration. We will use the first and most intuitive version of the formula to solve for the aggregate implied volatility.

I use the term aggregate implied volatility because it aggregates earnings volatility and normal volatility into a single implied volatility value. Aggregate implied volatility is synonymous with implied volatility, which means that it is directly comparable to the implied volatility calculated by your broker or research platform and it can be used in conventional option pricing and risk models, including the BSOPM.

Intuitively, the formula simply asserts that the aggregate implied volatility is a weighted average of earnings and normal volatility and the respective weights are proportional to the number of earnings and normal trading days remaining until expiration of the option. If we know any two of the three volatility terms, we can solve for the third.

The first section of the formula below calculates the weights and the second section uses those weights to solve for the aggregate implied volatility.

NTD_E = Number of Earnings Trading Days
NTD_N = Number of Normal Trading Days
W_E = Earnings Volatility Weight
W_N = Normal Volatility Weight

$W_E = NTD_E/(NTD_E + NTD_N)$
$W_E = 1/(1 + 11) = 8.3333\%$

$W_N = NTD_N/(NTD_E + NTD_N)$
$W_N = 11/(1 + 11) = 91.6667\%$

By definition, the weights will sum to 100%. The aggregate implied volatility is completely explained by earnings and normal volatility, and the sum of the earnings and normal trading days remaining will always equal the total number of trading days remaining until expiration.

As a result, the weight assigned to earnings volatility equals the number of earnings trading days (1) divided by the total number of trading days remaining until expiration (12). Similarly, the weight assigned to normal volatility equals the number of normal or non-earnings trading days (11) divided by the total number of trading days (12).

IV = Aggregate Implied Volatility (Annualized)
V_E **= Earnings Volatility (Annualized)**
V_N **= Normal Volatility (Annualized)**

IV = $((W_E*(V_E{\wedge}2))+(W_N)*(V_N{\wedge}2)){\wedge}0.5$
IV = $((8.3333\%*(180\%{\wedge}2))+(91.6667\%)*(30\%{\wedge}2)){\wedge}0.5$
IV = $(35.25\%){\wedge}0.5$
IV = 59.37%

I stated above that aggregate implied volatility is a weighted average of earnings and normal volatility, but that was an oversimplification. As you can see from the above formula, the *squared* aggregate implied volatility is a weighted average of the *squared* earnings volatility and the *squared* normal volatility.

To find the squared aggregate implied volatility, we square the earnings volatility (180%^2) and multiply it by the earnings weight (8.3333%). We then square the normal volatility (30%^2) and multiply it by the normal weight (91.6667%) and add both volatility terms together. Finally, we calculate the square root of the squared aggregate implied volatility (35.25%) to find the aggregate implied volatility (59.37%).

So, what does this mean? It means that if the annualized earnings volatility was 180% and annualized normal volatility was 30%, the aggregate implied volatility would equal 59.37%. It is important to note that the *aggregate implied volatility formula is not an approximation*. If we knew the earnings and normal volatility with certainty (as we do the number of earnings and normal trading days) and the earnings and normal volatilities conformed to the assumed BSOPM log-normal distribution, the aggregate implied volatility formula would yield the exact value of implied volatility derived from option pricing theory (for European options).

Technically, changes in the optimal path-dependent early exercise of American options would not be precisely captured by the aggregate implied volatility formula, but in practice, these negligible deviations would be swamped by the magnitude of earnings events. The BSOPM does not even consider the value of optimal early exercise of American options.

I concede that we do not know earnings and normal volatility with certainty, but I will explain practical ways to estimate those values in later chapters. For now, let's focus on the implications of this formula. We can observe the price of any option, which means that we can also calculate the real-time implied volatility. If we can estimate the normal or earnings volatility, we can solve for the remaining volatility term.

We can then use the above formula to determine how the implied volatility of any option will change as time passes. In other words, the formula allows us to use our estimates of earnings and normal volatility to calculate the future values of implied volatility for any option as the option ages and the number of trading days remaining until expiration declines.

Before we calculate future implied volatility values, we need to review the alternative versions of the aggregate implied volatility formula that allow us to solve for earnings volatility and normal volatility. The earnings and normal volatility weight calculations are the same for all versions of the formula, so the weight formulas and calculations were not repeated below.

IV = Aggregate Implied Volatility (Annualized)
V_E **= Earnings Volatility (Annualized)**
V_N **= Normal Volatility (Annualized)**

$V_E = (((IV^2)-(W_N*(V_N^2)))/W_E)^{0.5}$
$V_E = (((59.37\%^2)-(91.6667\%*(30\%^2)))/8.3333\%)^{0.5}$
$V_E = (324\%)^{0.5}$
$V_E = 180\%$

$V_N = (((IV^2)-(W_E*(V_E^2)))/W_N)^{0.5}$
$V_N = (((59.37\%^2)-(8.3333\%*(180\%^2)))/91.6667\%)^{0.5}$
$V_N = (9\%)^{0.5}$
$V_N = 30\%$

To find the squared earnings volatility, we first square the implied volatility (59.37%^2) and subtract the squared normal volatility (30%^2) multiplied by the normal weight (91.6667%). We divide the difference by the earnings weight (8.3333%) to find the squared earnings volatility (324%). Finally, we calculate the square root of the squared earnings volatility (324%) to find the earnings volatility (180%).

The process for using the implied volatility and earnings volatility to calculate the normal volatility is the same. If you know any two volatility terms, you can use the formula to solve for the third. The numerical values in the preceding formulas were rounded for display purposes, but I used the actual values in the calculation to avoid loss of precision.

Volatility Weights vs. Time (Single Option)

Now that we have applied the aggregate implied volatility formula to an option on a single date, let's calculate how the volatility weights change as they approach and pass the date of the earnings announcement. To do so, we will use the same assumptions from the previous static example: 180% earnings volatility, 30% normal volatility, one earnings trading day, and eleven normal trading days. We will assume the values of the volatility components remain constant, but the number of trading days will decrease as time passes.

We will also need to know when the earnings announcement will occur. In this example, earnings will be announced after the market closes, when two trading days remain until option expiration. The first of those trading days immediately following the announcement will be the earnings trading day by definition. The first normal trading session following earnings is when the new earnings information is processed by the market participants. Their resulting sales and purchases stimulate the forces of supply and demand throughout the trading day to arrive at a new post-earnings equilibrium price for the underlying stock.

The second of the two post-earnings trading days will be a normal trading day. Let's use this hypothetical example to evaluate how the earnings and normal volatility weights would change over time.

NTD_E = **Number of Earnings Trading Days**
NTD_N = **Number of Normal Trading Days**
W_{EN} = **Earnings Volatility Weight (N Trading Days before Earnings)**

$$W_E = NTD_E/(NTD_E + NTD_N)$$
$$W_{E10} = 1/(1 + 11) = 8.3\% \text{ (as calculated earlier)}$$
$$W_{E9} = 1/(1 + 10) = 9.1\%$$
$$W_{E8} = 1/(1 + 9) = 10.0\%$$
$$W_{E7} = 1/(1 + 8) = 11.1\%$$
$$W_{E6} = 1/(1 + 7) = 12.5\%$$
$$W_{E5} = 1/(1 + 6) = 14.3\%$$
$$W_{E4} = 1/(1 + 5) = 16.7\%$$
$$W_{E3} = 1/(1 + 4) = 20.0\%$$
$$W_{E2} = 1/(1 + 3) = 25.0\%$$
$$W_{E1} = 1/(1 + 2) = 33.3\%$$
$$W_{E0} = 1/(1 + 1) = 50.0\%$$
$$W_{E-1} = 0/(0 + 1) = 0.0\%$$

We could use the analogous weight formula to calculate the corresponding normal volatility weights, but we know the earnings and normal volatility at a given point in time must add to 100%, so we can simply subtract the earnings weights from 100%.

WE10 represents the earnings volatility weight ten trading days before earnings. As explained above, two additional trading days will occur following earnings and then the option will expire. As a result, ten days before earnings the option will have a total of twelve trading days remaining until expiration: one earnings trading day and eleven normal trading days. We calculated the value of WE10 in the initial static example and that value is rounded above to one decimal place.

Every day before the release of earnings is a normal or non-earnings trading day. Therefore, for every day that passes before the release of earnings, we reduce the number of normal trading days by one day. This also reduces the number of total trading days by one day. During this period approaching earnings, the numerator (the number of earnings trading days) will remain constant and the denominator (the total number of trading days) will decline by one day for each day that elapses.

This means that the relative weight of earnings volatility increases and the relative weight of normal volatility decreases. The earnings volatility weight will increase from the initial value of 8.3% (ten days before earnings) to 50% (immediately before earnings). During the same period, the normal volatility weight will decrease from 91.7% to 50%.

The day after earnings are announced, the number of earnings trading days will decline by one day and the number of normal trading days will remain constant. As a result, the numerator will decline from a value of one trading day to a value of zero trading days, which explains why the earnings volatility weight will fall from 50% to 0% one day after earnings are announced. The normal volatility weight will obviously increase from 50% to 100%. The earnings and normal volatility weights for this example are provided in table format in Figure 2.1.

Figure 2.1: Volatility^2 % Weight vs. Time (2 TD Post)		
# TD Before Earnings	Earnings Volatility^2 Percentage Weight	Normal Volatility^2 Percentage Weight
10	8.3%	91.7%
9	9.1%	90.9%
8	10.0%	90.0%
7	11.1%	88.9%
6	12.5%	87.5%
5	14.3%	85.7%
4	16.7%	83.3%
3	20.0%	80.0%
2	25.0%	75.0%
1	33.3%	66.7%
0	50.0%	50.0%
-1	0.0%	100.0%

The same earnings and normal volatility weights are depicted graphically in Figure 2.2. The independent x-axis represents the number of trading days before earnings. The dependent y-axis depicts the volatility weights. The earnings volatility weights are shown by the solid line; the dashed line illustrates the normal volatility weights. Remember, in the aggregate implied volatility formula, the volatility weights are applied to the *squared* volatility values, not to the volatility values.

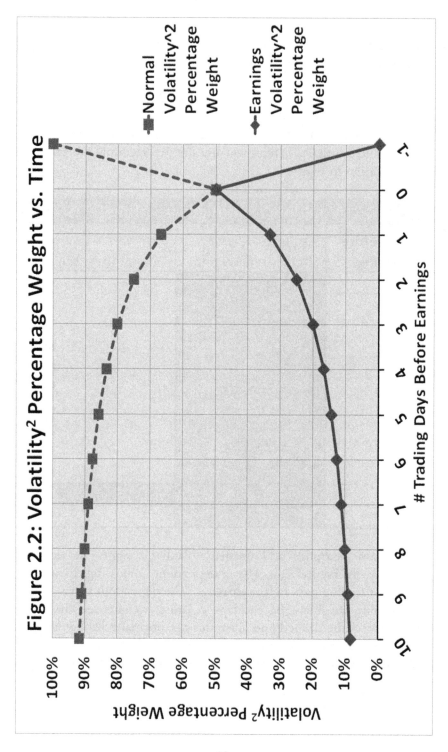

Figure 2.2: Volatility² Percentage Weight vs. Time

As you can see from the volatility values in Figure 2.2, the change in the volatility weights over time is not linear. This is due to the daily change in the *denominator* of the weight calculation.

Volatility Weights vs. Time (Multiple Options)

On the date of the earnings announcement, the option in the preceding example had two days remaining until expiration. We calculated the volatility weights beginning ten trading days before earnings and ending one day after earnings. Let's repeat the same volatility weight example for options with the following number of trading days remaining *after* the earnings announcement: 1, 2, 7, 12, 17, 21, 42, 126, 252, and 504.

The number of trading days for the last three options is consistent with option expiration dates occurring six months (126 trading days), one year (252 trading days), and two years (504 trading days) in the future. How would the weight calculation potentially be different for these three options? Unlike the options with fewer than 63 trading days remaining until expiration, the six month, one year, and two year options would all experience *multiple earnings trading days*. Two for the six month option, four for the one year option, and eight for the two year option.

To keep things simple at this stage, the hypothetical volatility weight and implied volatility examples in this chapter assume one trading day for all options, regardless of their expiration date. The Basic spreadsheet introduced in the next chapter uses several simplifying assumptions to reduce the amount of input data required from the user. As a result, *the Basic spreadsheet also assumes one earnings trading day for all options.* The Integrated spreadsheet requires more data, but is far more sophisticated and powerful than the Basic spreadsheet. It does not use simplifying assumptions and it uses the actual number of earnings trading days for every option in the matrix.

The earnings volatility weights for options with a range of trading days remaining after earnings (1, 2, 7, 12, 17, 21, 42, 126, 252, and 504) are shown in Figure 2.3. The shaded values in the second column represent the earnings weights for the same option that we evaluated earlier (Figures 2.1 and 2.2). What conclusions can we draw from the data? The most obvious result is that the effect of earnings volatility is much greater for shorter options – those with fewer

33

trading days remaining until expiration. This makes sense if we think about the formula.

$$W_E = NTD_E / (NTD_E + NTD_N)$$

The denominator of the earnings volatility weight formula would be smaller for shorter-term options, which would increase the relative importance and weight of earnings volatility. *The earnings weight would be higher and would increase at a more rapid rate for short-term options relative to long-term options.* Given that earnings dates are known in advance, these weights can be calculated precisely.

As we computed earlier, the earnings volatility weight for the option with *two* trading days remaining after earnings increased from 8.3% (ten trading days before earnings) to 50% (on the announcement date). The corresponding earnings volatility weight for an option with *seven* trading days remaining after earnings would have only increased from 5.9% to 14.3%. This is a dramatic reduction in the impact of earnings volatility for a very small (5 day) increase in the number of trading days. Given the assumption of one earnings trading day for all options, the earnings volatility weight for all options drops to 0% one day after earnings.

The earnings volatility weights for the ten different options described earlier are presented in Figure 2.3, which assumes one earnings trading day for all options. Even though we will not relax this assumption until we begin using the Integrated spreadsheet in later chapters, I provided Figure 2.4, which will allow you to see the effect of using the actual number of earnings trading days on the earnings volatility weights for the same ten options. Finally, the earnings volatility weights for all ten options are depicted graphically in Figure 2.5, which assumes one earnings trading day for all options.

In Figure 2.5, the independent x-axis represents the number of trading days before earnings. The dependent y-axis depicts the earnings volatility weights. The earnings volatility weights for each option are illustrated by a different line. They earnings volatility lines appear in the same order as the legend on the right-side of the graph.

Figure 2.3: Earnings Volatility^2 Percentage Weight (1 ED)

# TD Before Earnings	# Trading Days (TD) After Earnings									
	1	2	7	12	17	21	42	126	252	504
10	9.1%	8.3%	5.9%	4.5%	3.7%	3.2%	1.9%	0.7%	0.4%	0.2%
9	10.0%	9.1%	6.3%	4.8%	3.8%	3.3%	2.0%	0.7%	0.4%	0.2%
8	11.1%	10.0%	6.7%	5.0%	4.0%	3.4%	2.0%	0.7%	0.4%	0.2%
7	12.5%	11.1%	7.1%	5.3%	4.2%	3.6%	2.0%	0.8%	0.4%	0.2%
6	14.3%	12.5%	7.7%	5.6%	4.3%	3.7%	2.1%	0.8%	0.4%	0.2%
5	16.7%	14.3%	8.3%	5.9%	4.5%	3.8%	2.1%	0.8%	0.4%	0.2%
4	20.0%	16.7%	9.1%	6.3%	4.8%	4.0%	2.2%	0.8%	0.4%	0.2%
3	25.0%	20.0%	10.0%	6.7%	5.0%	4.2%	2.2%	0.8%	0.4%	0.2%
2	33.3%	25.0%	11.1%	7.1%	5.3%	4.3%	2.3%	0.8%	0.4%	0.2%
1	50.0%	33.3%	12.5%	7.7%	5.6%	4.5%	2.3%	0.8%	0.4%	0.2%
0	100.0%	50.0%	14.3%	8.3%	5.9%	4.8%	2.4%	0.8%	0.4%	0.2%
-1	0.0%	0.0%	0.0%	0.0%	0.0%	0.0%	0.0%	0.0%	0.0%	0.0%

Figure 2.4: Earnings Volatility^2 Percentage Weight (Actual ED)

# TD Before Earnings	# Trading Days (TD) After Earnings									
	1	2	7	12	17	21	42	126	252	504
10	9.1%	8.3%	5.9%	4.5%	3.7%	3.2%	1.9%	1.5%	1.5%	1.6%
9	10.0%	9.1%	6.3%	4.8%	3.8%	3.3%	2.0%	1.5%	1.5%	1.6%
8	11.1%	10.0%	6.7%	5.0%	4.0%	3.4%	2.0%	1.5%	1.5%	1.6%
7	12.5%	11.1%	7.1%	5.3%	4.2%	3.6%	2.0%	1.5%	1.5%	1.6%
6	14.3%	12.5%	7.7%	5.6%	4.3%	3.7%	2.1%	1.5%	1.6%	1.6%
5	16.7%	14.3%	8.3%	5.9%	4.5%	3.8%	2.1%	1.5%	1.6%	1.6%
4	20.0%	16.7%	9.1%	6.3%	4.8%	4.0%	2.2%	1.5%	1.6%	1.6%
3	25.0%	20.0%	10.0%	6.7%	5.0%	4.2%	2.2%	1.6%	1.6%	1.6%
2	33.3%	25.0%	11.1%	7.1%	5.3%	4.3%	2.3%	1.6%	1.6%	1.6%
1	50.0%	33.3%	12.5%	7.7%	5.6%	4.5%	2.3%	1.6%	1.6%	1.6%
0	100.0%	50.0%	14.3%	8.3%	5.9%	4.8%	2.4%	1.6%	1.6%	1.6%
-1	0.0%	0.0%	0.0%	0.0%	0.0%	0.0%	0.0%	0.8%	1.2%	1.4%

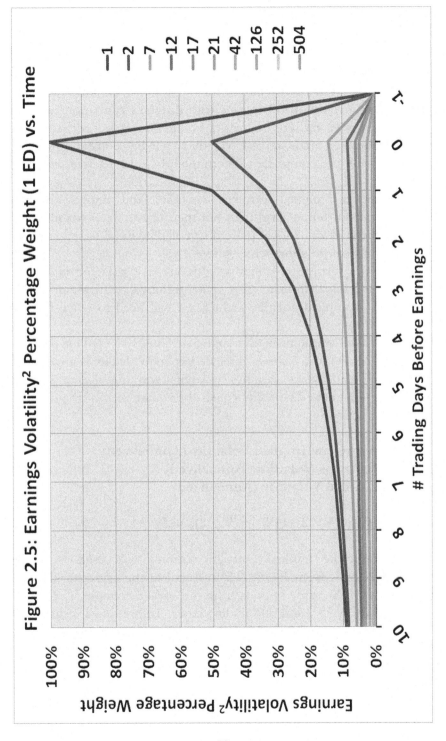

Figure 2.5: Earnings Volatility^2 Percentage Weight (1 ED) vs. Time

Aggregate IV vs. Time

In the above examples, we assumed that the earnings volatility and normal volatility remained constant. This assumption allowed us to focus on the relative magnitude and pattern of earnings volatility weights for a selection of options with different expirations as they approached and passed the earnings announcement date. If we assume earnings and normal volatility remain constant, implied volatility will be completely determined by the relative volatility weights.

In practice, implied earnings volatility and implied normal volatility do not remain constant, but their day-to-day variability will be dominated by the known pattern of volatility weights approaching earnings, at least for short-term options.

While the relative volatility weights are a key factor in option earnings behavior and are also quite intuitive, we are ultimately interested in implied volatility, which we will need to solve for the value of an option.

As you will recall from the aggregate implied volatility formula (repeated below), the *squared* aggregate implied volatility is a weighted average of the *squared* earnings volatility and the *squared* normal volatility. The implied volatility equals the square root of the squared implied volatility.

IV = Aggregate Implied Volatility (Annualized)
V_E = Earnings Volatility (Annualized)
V_N = Normal Volatility (Annualized)

$$IV = ((W_E*(V_E\char94 2))+(W_N)*(V_N\char94 2))\char94 0.5$$

The aggregate implied volatility formula was used with the earnings weights from Figure 2.3 to calculate the aggregate implied volatilities for the same options from our earlier example (1, 2, 7, 12, 17, 21, 42, 126, 252, and 504 trading days). The results are shown in tabular format in Figure 2.6 and in graphical format in Figure 2.7. The weights used in the implied volatility calculations assume one earnings trading day for all options, regardless of the time remaining until expiration.

In Figure 2.7, the independent x-axis represents the number of trading days before earnings. The dependent y-axis depicts the aggregate implied volatilities. The implied volatilities for each option are illustrated by a different line. The implied volatility lines appear in the same order as the legend on the right-side of the graph.

It should be no surprise that we see the same pattern in implied volatility that we observed in the earnings volatility weights approaching the earnings announcement. The implied volatility of the option with one trading day remaining after earnings increases from 61.3% ten trading days before earnings to 180% on the announcement date (Figure 2.6). The increase in implied volatility can be completely explained by the relative increase in the earnings volatility weight relative to the normal volatility weight. Why does the IV equal 180% on the earnings announcement date? Because the earnings volatility equals 180% and the earnings volatility weight equals 100%. On the earnings date, there is only one trading day remaining and it is an earnings trading day by definition. Therefore the implied volatility must be equal to the earnings volatility for that option.

The implied volatility of the option with two trading days remaining after earnings increases from 59.4% ten trading days before earnings to 129.0% on the earnings announcement date. The corresponding implied volatilities for an option with seven trading days remaining after earnings are only 52.5%% and 73.5%. The increase in implied volatility over the same ten days is much more muted for longer-term options. The implied volatility for a two-month (42 trading days) option increases by only 1.8% (40.6% - 38.8%).

Given the assumption of one earnings trading day for all options, the earnings volatility weight for all options drops to 0% one day after earnings, which has a predictable crushing effect on implied volatility. The implied volatility of the option with two trading days remaining until expiration drops from 129% on the earnings date to 30% one day later. Why 30%? Because normal volatility equals 30% and the normal volatility weight equals 100%. As we discovered with earnings volatility weights, the effect of earnings volatility on the implied volatility of short-term options is much greater than the effect on long-term options.

Figure 2.6: Aggregate Implied Volatility (Annualized) (1 ED)

# TD Before Earnings	# Trading Days (TD) After Earnings									
	1	2	7	12	17	21	42	126	252	504
10	61.3%	59.4%	52.5%	48.3%	45.5%	43.8%	38.8%	33.6%	31.9%	31.0%
9	63.6%	61.3%	53.6%	49.0%	46.0%	44.2%	39.0%	33.7%	31.9%	31.0%
8	66.3%	63.6%	54.8%	49.7%	46.5%	44.6%	39.1%	33.7%	32.0%	31.0%
7	69.6%	66.3%	56.1%	50.6%	47.0%	45.0%	39.3%	33.7%	32.0%	31.0%
6	73.5%	69.6%	57.6%	51.5%	47.6%	45.5%	39.4%	33.7%	32.0%	31.0%
5	78.4%	73.5%	59.4%	52.5%	48.3%	46.0%	39.6%	33.8%	32.0%	31.0%
4	84.9%	78.4%	61.3%	53.6%	49.0%	46.5%	39.8%	33.8%	32.0%	31.0%
3	93.7%	84.9%	63.6%	54.8%	49.7%	47.0%	40.0%	33.8%	32.0%	31.0%
2	106.8%	93.7%	66.3%	56.1%	50.6%	47.6%	40.2%	33.9%	32.0%	31.0%
1	129.0%	106.8%	69.6%	57.6%	51.5%	48.3%	40.4%	33.9%	32.0%	31.0%
0	180.0%	129.0%	73.5%	59.4%	52.5%	49.0%	40.6%	33.9%	32.0%	31.0%
-1		30.0%	30.0%	30.0%	30.0%	30.0%	30.0%	30.0%	30.0%	30.0%

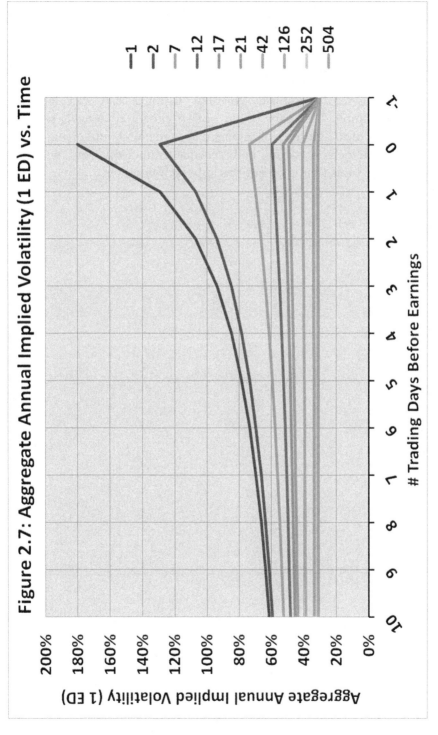

Figure 2.7: Aggregate Annual Implied Volatility (1 ED) vs. Time

You might find the graph of the implied volatilities in Figure 2.7 even more intuitive than the table in Figure 2.6. If you are an experienced option trader, you will recognize this pattern of implied volatility that we see repeated before and after every quarterly earnings announcement.

The aggregate implied volatility formula can calculate the aggregate implied volatility of any option, on any underlying security, regardless of the number of trading days remaining until expiration. It is an extremely powerful and versatile framework, but we need interactive tools to implement this approach in practice.

3 - THE BASIC SPREADSHEET

It is now time to move from theory to practice. This chapter provides a step-by-step explanation of how to use the first of two spreadsheets that accompany this book: the Basic spreadsheet. I designed the Basic spreadsheet to be accessible by a wide range of users. To minimize potential compatibility issues, I did not use macros in this spreadsheet. In addition, the Basic spreadsheet uses some simplifying assumptions to reduce the amount of input data required from the user, but still estimates historical and implied earnings volatility and uses those estimates to forecast future levels of implied volatility around earnings announcements.

Please be aware that both spreadsheet tools have important limitations. Unlike $1000 per year option analytical platforms that control and supply all input data, the user is responsible for entering and verifying all of the input data in both spreadsheets. While I included some data-validation rules to prevent obvious input errors, the algorithms in these spreadsheets are complex and highly sensitive to erroneous data. *As a result, inaccurate or invalid input data will generate misleading volatility estimates and possible spreadsheet errors.*

To eliminate any additional costs for the reader, I designed both spreadsheets to use the free version of Solver that is included with Microsoft Excel. Unfortunately, the free version of Solver has significant size and speed limitations and its solution algorithms are not as sophisticated as those in commercial optimization packages. I set up the spreadsheet optimization problems to work as well as practicable with the free version of Solver, but you may still experience varying degrees of success with Solver on certain problems. However, you may be able to improve upon your initial results by rerunning Solver and/or by slightly modifying Solver's solution parameters.

The purpose of this chapter is to explain how to *use* the Basic spreadsheet, not how to construct the Basic spreadsheet or how to perform every intermediate calculation. If you have an interest in the intermediate calculations, please review the formulas in the spreadsheet cells. Any formulas or simplifying assumptions that materially affect volatility estimates or prospective investment decisions will be explained in detail.

The Basic spreadsheet contains several individual tabs. The tabs will be referenced by name. References to a cell or groups of cells on a given tab will use the following column-row format: (A1:A20), which indicates the cells in Column A from row 1 to row 20, inclusive.

There will be two tabs in the Basic spreadsheet that are very straightforward and will not be discussed in detail. The first is the "Holidays" tab, where you will enter the dates of exchange holidays (B3:B24) that will be used by the day-count algorithms to calculate the number of trading days throughout the Basic spreadsheet. The other tab that will not be discussed extensively is the "Saved" tab. It is not used directly in any calculations; instead, it is provided as a convenient location to copy and paste data from other tabs that you might want to use again in the future.

As you proceed through this chapter, keep in mind that our goal in using the Basic spreadsheet is to estimate historical and implied earnings volatility and to use those estimates to forecast future levels of implied and realized earnings volatility.

Historical Earnings Volatility

Just as we use historical volatility to evaluate implied volatility and to forecast future realized volatility, it makes sense to use historical *earnings* volatility to analyze implied earnings volatility and to predict future earnings realized volatility. As I explained in the 2011 *Active Trader* article, "The earnings volatility level is specific to each company. Factors that make estimating earnings more difficult, such as earnings variability, rapid earnings growth, and cyclicality, all tend to increase earnings volatility. Also, high P/E ratios magnify the price response to earnings surprises, which also increases earnings volatility."

Furthermore, many factors that affect a company's earnings tend to persist over time: management, marketing, capital structure, product lines, competitors, cyclical earnings patterns, and earnings growth rates. In addition, the same institutional analysts tend to cover the same companies from quarter to quarter and from year to year. While there is obviously some turnover, many shareholders own the same stocks for extended periods and traders also tend to focus on the same stocks over time. As a result, we have the same investors, traders, and analysts forecasting the same company's earnings every quarter. It should be no surprise that historical earnings return data is one of our best sources of information about future earnings returns.

We will use actual market data in this chapter and throughout the remainder of the book. The Basic and Integrated spreadsheets use data for Under Armor (UA) that was available as of the close on July 23, 2014. The purpose of this chapter is to explain how to use the Basic spreadsheet, not how to evaluate a specific trade. However, as you proceed through this chapter, consider the implications of the UA data for constructing an option earnings strategy. In Chapter 5, we will use Basic and Integrated spreadsheets to design the optimal option earnings strategy for UA immediately preceding its July 24, 2014 pre-open earnings announcement.

For both spreadsheets, *user inputs are limited to cells with white text and dark shaded backgrounds*. All of the other cells contain formulas, which should not be modified in any way. Editing formula cells would compromise the functionality of the spreadsheets and invalidate the resulting calculations. All tables and graphs in this section are located on the "HistoricalEV" tab of the Basic spreadsheet.

Figure 3.1 includes a table of the historical earnings data and summary statistics for UA. Figure 3.2 depicts the same historical earnings data for UA graphically. The historical rates of return (calculated from the close immediately preceding earnings to the close on the next trading day) for the twelve previous UA earnings announcements are entered in cells B3:B14. The Basic spreadsheet uses these returns to calculate the summary statistics and to generate the earnings return graph.

The (natural) log returns for the twelve historical earnings events are calculated in cells C3:C14. As explained earlier, option models generally assume a log-normal return distribution and log returns must be used in the calculation of earnings volatility to preserve the integrity of the aggregate implied volatility formula. The next two columns contain intermediate calculations, so let's focus on the summary statistics at the bottom of the table in Figure 3.1.

To profit from earnings announcements, we must be able to forecast directional price changes due to earnings, identify overstated or understated levels of implied earnings volatility, or both. The summary statistics are designed to provide insight into both directional price changes and the expected level of earnings volatility.

Rows 15 through 20 contain summary statistics related to the directional return forecasts. Row 16 reports the results of a linear regression that uses the twelve previous historical earnings returns to forecast the expected log-return for the next earnings announcement. The return forecast for the July 24, 2014 earnings release is 6.24% (B16), which corresponds to the intercept term at time zero. The slope of 0.53% (D16) indicates that UA earnings returns have been gradually increasing over time. The R squared (E16) of 0.04 reveals that the explanatory power of the regression is quite low.

Additional directional statistics for UA are reported in rows 18 to 20 and are based on the linear regression estimate (6.24% in Cell C18), the median log-return (3.11% in Cell C19), and the mean log-return (2.41% in Cell C20). The next column calculates the ratio of these return values to the root-mean-squared error (D18:D20). The resulting calculation yields a Z-score, which can be used to forecast the probability of a positive earnings return on the next earnings date. The linear regression estimate, the median, and the mean historical earnings returns all suggest that the next earnings return will be positive for UA with corresponding probabilities of 77% (E18), 64% (E19), and 61% (E20), respectively. We will use this directional information when we design an option earnings strategy for UA in Chapter 5.

In addition to a directional return forecast, we also need to calculate the annualized historical earnings volatility for UA. This will help us forecast the future *realized* level of earnings volatility as well as give us some insight into the appropriate level of implied earnings volatility.

The daily root-mean-squared-error (RMSE) of the historical log returns for UA was 8.62% (C22). This equates to an annualized earnings volatility of 136.76% (D22). We will be able to use the annualized historical earnings volatility to estimate the expected future earnings volatility for UA. In addition, we will also be able to use our annualized earnings volatility forecast in the aggregate IV formula. The daily and annualized standard deviation (SD) around the mean earnings return is also provided (C23:D23), but as explained earlier, the RMSE provides a superior estimate of volatility versus the standard deviation.

Earnings Quarter	Post-Earnings % Change (Close to Close)	Post-Earnings LN Return: Next TD	LN Squared	Dev from Mean Squared
	Figure 3.1 Historical Earnings Volatility Table			
-1	-7.38%	-7.67%	0.5878%	1.0153%
-2	22.92%	20.64%	4.2586%	3.3221%
-3	-4.76%	-4.88%	0.2379%	0.5310%
-4	12.21%	11.52%	1.3271%	0.8300%
-5	1.32%	1.31%	0.0172%	0.0121%
-6	5.69%	5.53%	0.3063%	0.0976%
-7	-6.51%	-6.73%	0.4531%	0.8356%
-8	9.11%	8.72%	0.7601%	0.3980%
-9	5.20%	5.07%	0.2570%	0.0707%
-10	-5.26%	-5.40%	0.2920%	0.6104%
-11	5.03%	4.91%	0.2408%	0.0624%
-12	-4.02%	-4.10%	0.1683%	0.4242%
	Linear Regression	Intercept	Slope	R Squared
	6.24%	6.24%	0.53%	0.04
	Earnings Statistics	LN ROR	ROR/RMSE	Pr(ROR>0)
	Linear Regression	6.24%	0.72	77%
	Median	3.11%	0.36	64%
	Mean	2.41%	0.28	61%
	Earnings Statistics	Earnings ROR	Annualized Volatility	
	Root Mean Square %Change	8.62%	136.76%	
	Sigma Around Mean	8.27%	131.30%	

HistoricalEV / ImpliedEV / EVvsTime / Holidays

I always like to study relationships visually as well as numerically. Human beings excel at pattern recognition and it is often possible to identify relationships visually that are not otherwise apparent. Figure 3.2 is a graph of the historical log-returns for the twelve previous UA earnings events. The independent x-axis represents the earnings quarter and the vertical y-axis depicts the one-day earnings return. The red-line is a trendline that Excel generates automatically based on the historical log-return data.

Do you notice anything in the graph that you did not see in the numerical data? The one item that jumped out at me was that the variability of the earnings returns had increased recently. In other words, it had become increasingly difficult for investors and analysts to forecast the earnings for UA in recent quarters. If that trend continued, the historical earnings volatility estimates calculated by the spreadsheet would be too low. Hold that thought. We will revisit the volatility forecast again in Chapter 5.

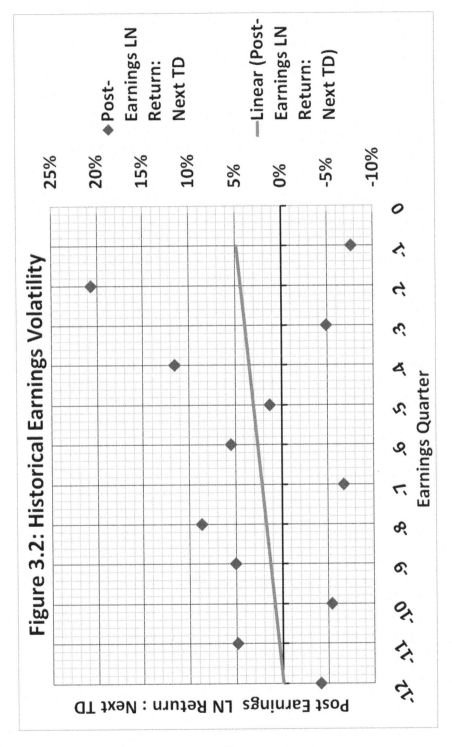

Figure 3.2: Historical Earnings Volatility

Before we explore how to use the Basic spreadsheet to calculate implied earnings volatility, we need to revisit the source of the historical earnings return data in Figures 3.1 and 3.2. As you would imagine, it would be quite cumbersome to personally track the earnings dates for every stock and to manually calculate the quarterly return data. I recognized this immediately when I began to use this approach to design and trade option earnings strategies.

As a result, I subscribed to OptionSlam.com, one of the premier providers of historical earnings data and filtering tools. While writing this book, I advised OptionSlam.com on their filtering methodology and I requested several site enhancements, including the ability to access historical earnings data for backtesting purposes.

After publication, I plan to work closely with the team at OptionSlam.com to integrate some of the analytical concepts from this book, which will further enhance their filtering tools and volatility statistics. Please see the resource section at the end of this book for additional information on OptionSlam.com, including a discounted subscription offer for *Exploiting Earnings Volatility* readers.

Figure 3.3 is an OptionSlam.com screenshot of the historical earnings return data for UA as of July 1, 2014. This page illustrates a recent OptionSlam upgrade that allows traders to screen for stock candidates and examine each candidate's earnings data *as of a user-specified date in the past*. In other words, the historical earnings screen and the historical earnings statistics for each company show the results we would have seen had we run the screener on a specified analysis date in the past.

We can use this feature to backtest our earnings strategies, without being influenced by seeing the actual earnings data that occurred after the historical analysis date. This tool allows us to evaluate our investment process using actual market data *before* we commit capital to our strategies. I never trade any strategy without first testing and evaluating its performance historically. Without this feature, it would have been impossible to evaluate historical earnings candidates objectively.

There are three main sections on the OptionSlam.com screenshot in Figure 3.3. Working from left to right, the first section provides the earnings date, the pre-earnings close, and the after-hours percentage price move (close to open).

The middle section reports the open, high, low, close, and one-day percentage change *for the first trading session following earnings*. Both the one-day *closing* and *maximum* percentage returns are provided. For purposes of calculating the earnings volatility, we are interested in the *closing* percentage return, which is the return on the underlying stock from the close immediately preceding the earnings announcement to the close on the next trading day. The return data entered in the Basic spreadsheet (B3:B14) were taken directly from the "Closing%" column in this section.

The third section at the right-side of the page shows the mean and median *absolute* and *raw* returns for the twelve previous earnings events, which were calculated using one-day closing percentage returns. The user has the option of displaying the mean and median values for the one-day *closing* percentage returns or the one-day *maximum* percentage returns.

The mean and median values of the *absolute values* of the one-day *closing* percentage returns are useful in evaluating historical earnings volatility. The mean reduces the impact of all outliers relative to the RMSE calculation and the median further reduces the effect of outliers on the volatility estimate. The resulting mean and median values can be used as a proxy for earnings volatility, but the annualized RMSE of the log-returns that is calculated in the Basic spreadsheet should always be used when estimating earnings volatility for use in the aggregate IV formula. The RMSE of the log-returns is the only metric that is consistent with option pricing theory and the calculation of aggregate implied volatility.

The third section also provides the mean and median *raw* one-day closing returns for the twelve previous earnings events. Unlike the absolute values, the raw returns preserve the directional movement of past earnings events, which can be useful in identifying a systematic directional earnings return bias for individual stocks. On the webpage, the positive raw returns are shown in green text and the negative raw returns are displayed with red text to make it easier to identify directional trends. The mean and median values provided in the Basic spreadsheet represent the mean and median of the *raw log-returns*, which is why they differ slightly from the raw mean and median statistics calculated by OptionSlam.com.

Earnings History: Historical Earnings Statistics as of 2014-07-01

Under Armour, Inc. (UA) - NYSE [icon]   Next Earnings Date : July 24, 2014 Before Market Open ▲

UA EVR as of 2014-07-01: 2.9

Earnings Events Available: 26

Figure 3.3: OptionSlam.com Historical EV

EARNINGS DATE	PRE EARNINGS CLOSE	AFTER HOURS MOVE	PRICE MOVEMENT WITHIN ONE TRADING DAY						MEAN AND MEDIAN OF ONE DAY CLOSING MOVEMENT OF PREVIOUS 12 EARNINGS			
			OPEN	HIGH	LOW	CLOSE	CLOSING%	MAX%	MEAN	MEDIAN	MEAN RAW	MEDIAN RAW
April 24, 2014 BO	$54.44	-4.68%	$51.88	$52.31	$48.77	$50.42	-7.38%	-10.41%	7.77%	5.47%	2.47%	3.17%
Jan. 30, 2014 BO	$85.22	13.47%	$96.70	$106.65	$96.00	$104.76	22.92%	25.14%	6.77%	5.47%	1.47%	3.17%
Oct. 24, 2013 BO	$83.98	-5.94%	$78.98	$80.84	$77.34	$79.98	-4.76%	-7.9%	6.39%	5.47%	1.88%	3.17%
July 25, 2013 BO	$61.83	5.74%	$65.38	$69.55	$65.34	$69.38	12.21%	12.48%	5.44%	5.23%	0.79%	0.72%
April 19, 2013 BO	$55.67	3.95%	$57.87	$58.44	$55.28	$56.41	1.32%	4.97%	5.73%	5.23%	0.28%	-0.35%
Jan. 31, 2013 BO	$48.13	4.21%	$50.16	$51.94	$50.00	$50.87	5.69%	7.91%	5.75%	5.23%	-0.68%	-2.42%
Oct. 25, 2012 BO	$56.62	-4.52%	$54.06	$55.50	$52.01	$52.93	-6.51%	-8.14%	6.17%	5.23%	-1.1%	-2.42%
July 24, 2012 BO	$48.38	6.86%	$51.70	$55.00	$51.70	$52.79	9.11%	13.68%	5.47%	5.11%	-1.91%	-2.42%
April 20, 2012 BO	$48.25	-1.57%	$47.49	$51.43	$47.06	$50.76	5.2%	6.59%	6.11%	5.14%	-1.27%	-2.42%
Jan. 26, 2012 BO	$38.74	-1.91%	$38.00	$38.63	$36.28	$36.70	-5.26%	-6.35%	5.86%	4.9%	-1.02%	-1.54%
Oct. 25, 2011 BO	$38.15	-2.72%	$37.11	$41.74	$37.03	$40.08	5.03%	9.38%	7.63%	5.39%	0.74%	-1.54%
July 26, 2011 BO	$39.29	0.5%	$39.50	$41.08	$37.35	$37.72	-4.02%	-4.96%	7.84%	6.3%	1.62%	-0.76%

Implied Earnings Volatility (Dynamic)

In addition to calculating historical earnings volatility, we are also interested in calculating the implied earnings volatility that immediately preceded previous earnings dates. If implied volatility is the expected level of volatility *implied by* or embedded in the price of the option, then *implied earnings volatility* represents the expected level of *earnings* volatility *implied by* or embedded in the price of the option.

While we can calculate the implied volatility directly from the price of an option, we have to be more creative in solving for the implied earnings volatility (IEV). You will recall that the aggregate implied volatility represents a weighted average of two distinct sources of volatility: earnings volatility and normal or non-earnings volatility. The "ImpliedEV" tab of the Basic spreadsheet uses the aggregate IV formula and implied volatility data immediately before and after earnings to solve for the implied earnings volatility (IEV). Before examining how the spreadsheet solves for the IEV, let's review the steps required to use this tab and examine the results.

To use the "ImpliedEV" tab to solve for the implied earnings volatility preceding a past earnings date:

1. Enter the analysis date (C2), which will always be the date immediately preceding the earnings announcement.

2. Enter an initial "seed" estimate of the annualized implied earnings volatility (C3).

3. Enter the expiration dates for the at-the-money (ATM) options that you plan to use to estimate the IEV (B5:B15).

4. Enter the implied volatility for each ATM option immediately preceding earnings (F5:F15).

5. Enter the implied volatility for each ATM option at the close of the next trading day (J5:J15).

6. Use Solver to determine the IEV that best explains the changes in the ATM implied volatilities.

It is important to note that the ATM IVs in columns F and J will probably be derived from options with different strike prices. The expiration dates will be the same, but we are interested in the at-the-money IV and the price of the underlying security will undoubtedly change when earnings are released. The IV of the option with the strike price closest to the closing price of the underlying security should always be used for this calculation. Using the ATM IVs minimizes the effect of the vertical skew on estimation of the IEV.

Figure 3.4 includes a table of the input data and all required calculations to estimate the IEV for UA on April 23, 2014. The table includes data for eleven different option expiration dates ranging from 4/26/2014 to 1/15/2016 (B5:B15). As explained above, the input data for each option expiration date are entered in columns B, F, and J.

In addition to determining the number of earnings trading days (one by definition) and normal trading days (E5:E15), the spreadsheet calculates the estimated post-earnings ATM IV for each option expiration date (I5:I15) as well as the estimated change in the ATM IV for each option expiration date (K5:K15). The actual change in the ATM IV for each option is also provided (L5:L15).

Solver uses its solution algorithm to find the value of IEV that best explains the change in ATM IV across all options. Solver found that an annualized IEV of 143.0% (C3) best explained the observed changes in the ATM IVs due to the April 23, 2014 UA earnings event. The root-mean-squared-error was 1.73% (M3), which is a measure of the average difference between the estimated changes in the ATM IVs and the actual changes in the ATM IVs. The estimation errors for each option expiration date are provided in cells M5:M15.

		Mean & σ	126.8%	14.9%									0.3304%
		Analysis Date	4/23/2014	This analysis is ALWAYS performed using the closing IV data immediately before and after earnings announcements									
		Market Implied EV	143.0%	9.0%		Solver Estimation of Historical Market Implied Earnings Volatility					Min=>	1.73%	0.3304%

Figure 3.4: Historical Market Implied Earnings Volatility (Dynamic)

Option Expiration Date	Total Calendar Days	Total Trade Days	Total Normal Days	Aggregate IV of ATM Option	Implied Earnings Volatility	Implied Normal ATM IV	Estimated Post Earnings ATM IV	Actual Post Earnings ATM IV	Estimated Post Earnings ATM IV Change	Actual Post Earnings ATM IV Change	ATM IV Change Error	ATM IV Change Error Squared
4/26/2014	3	2	1	105.0%	143.0%	40.1%	40.1%	39.8%	-64.9%	-65.2%	0.3%	0.0006%
5/3/2014	10	7	6	66.0%	143.0%	40.9%	40.9%	38.6%	-25.1%	-27.4%	2.3%	0.0538%
5/10/2014	17	12	11	54.7%	143.0%	37.5%	37.5%	39.6%	-17.2%	-15.1%	-2.1%	0.0446%
5/17/2014	24	17	16	49.2%	143.0%	36.0%	36.0%	39.0%	-13.2%	-10.2%	-3.0%	0.0916%
5/24/2014	31	22	21	46.8%	143.0%	36.3%	36.3%	37.7%	-10.5%	-9.1%	-1.4%	0.0184%
5/31/2014	38	26	25	44.8%	143.0%	35.6%	35.6%	36.6%	-9.2%	-8.2%	-1.0%	0.0094%
6/21/2014	59	41	40	41.4%	143.0%	35.3%	35.3%	36.9%	-6.1%	-4.5%	-1.6%	0.0258%
7/19/2014	87	60	59	38.8%	143.0%	34.4%	34.4%	35.9%	-4.4%	-2.9%	-1.5%	0.0220%
10/18/2014	178	124	123	38.6%	143.0%	36.5%	36.5%	37.6%	-2.1%	-1.0%	-1.1%	0.0110%
1/17/2015	269	186	185	38.2%	143.0%	36.8%	36.8%	38.6%	-1.4%	0.4%	-1.8%	0.0313%
1/15/2016	632	437	436	37.9%	143.0%	37.3%	37.3%	38.8%	-0.6%	0.9%	-1.5%	0.0219%

HistoricalEV / ImpliedEV / EVvsTime / Holidays / Saved

If you have never used Solver before, then you will first need to enable the Solver Add-in in your version of Microsoft Excel. This exact procedure will depend on your version of Excel. In MS Office 2010, you would use the following button sequence:

File => Options => Add-Ins => Manage Excel Add-ins => Go

This will bring up the following screen (Figure 3.5), which you can use to use to enable the Solver Add-in. You may need to browse to find the Solver Add-in. Please refer to your Excel documentation for further instructions on managing Add-ins.

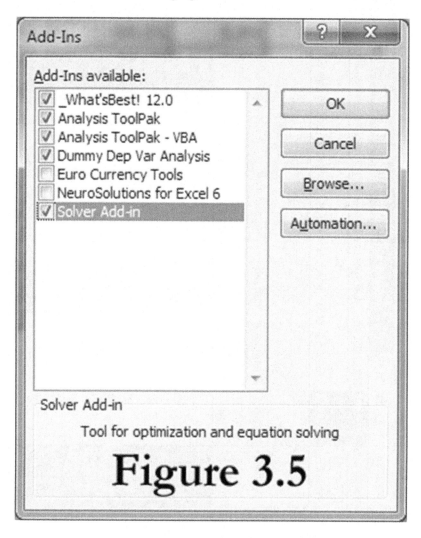

Figure 3.5

The exact button sequence to run Solver may also depend on your version of Excel. In MS Office 2010, the following sequence will bring up the Solver problem description associated with the current spreadsheet tab: Data => Solver

On the "ImpliedEV" tab, this should bring up the Solver problem specification depicted in Figure 3.6. If Solver does not retrieve the problem specification, then you will need to set the objective cell (M3) to "Min" and set the changing variable cells to C3. Use the Add button to enter the single constraint in the image below. Finally, the "Make Unconstrained Variables Non-Negative" should be checked and the Solving method should be "GRG Nonlinear." To run Solver, press the "Solve" button.

Figure 3.6: Solver

A comprehensive discussion of optimization theory and tools is beyond the scope of this book, but here is a very brief explanation of what Solver is doing in this problem. Solver is using its nonlinear solution algorithm to find the value of the IEV (the variable cell: C3) that minimizes the value of the RMSE (the objective cell: M3), subject to satisfying the constraint that the IEV (C3) must be greater than or equal to zero. In other words, Solver is solving for the annualized implied earnings volatility that best explains the observed decline in implied volatilities after earnings.

Now that I have explained how to use the "ImpliedEV" tab of the Basic spreadsheet, how does it work? It should be no surprise that the aggregate IV formula is the key. Specifically, the "ImpliedEV" tab uses the version of the aggregate IV formula that allows us to solve for the normal IV, given the implied IV and the earnings volatility.

The following example reproduces the calculation of the estimated post-earnings ATM IV (H5) for the option with two trading days remaining until expiration (Row 5). The spreadsheet repeats the sample calculations below for every option in the spreadsheet.

NTD_E = **Number of Earnings Trading Days**
NTD_N = **Number of Normal Trading Days**
W_E = **Earnings Volatility Weight**
W_N = **Normal Volatility Weight**

$W_E = NTD_E/(NTD_E + NTD_N)$
$W_E = 1/(2) = 50\%$

$W_N = NTD_N/(NTD_E + NTD_N)$
$W_N = 1/(2) = 50\%$

V_E = **Earnings Volatility = 142.9894% (C3) (Solver value)**
IV = **Implied Volatility = 105% (F5) (IV before earnings)**
V_N = **Normal Volatility**

$V_N = (((IV^2)-(W_E*(V_E^2)))/W_N)^{0.5}$
$V_N = (((105.0\%^2)-(50\%*(143\%^2)))/50\%)^{0.5}$
$V_N = (16.04\%)^{0.5}$
$V_N = 40.05\%$ **(I5)**

Remember, the Basic spreadsheet relies on the simplifying assumption that all options have only one earnings trading day. As a result, after earnings are released, all remaining days are assumed to be normal trading days. After earnings, the assumed earnings weight will drop to 0% and the normal volatility will equal the observed implied volatility.

If we assume that the normal volatility remains unchanged on the first trading day following the earnings release, we can use the aggregate implied volatility formula and Solver to solve for the implied earnings volatility that best explains the observed changes in ATM IVs. The resulting IEV estimate of 143% (C3) results in an estimated normal volatility of 40.05% (I5). That value is an estimate of the *observed* implied volatility value the day after earnings, which equals 39.8% (J5): a difference of less than 0.3% (M5).

To recap, we entered the analysis date, the expiration dates, and the at-the-money implied volatilities before and after earnings. Solver did the rest, solving for the implied earnings volatility that was embedded in the at-the-money option prices immediately before the earnings announcement.

Implied Earnings Volatility (Static)

This chapter has demonstrated how to use the "HistoricalEV" and "ImpliedEV" tabs of the Basic spreadsheet to solve for the historical earnings volatility from past earnings events and how to estimate the implied earnings volatility immediately (IEV) preceding past earnings announcements. However, to identify and exploit earnings volatility opportunities, we also need to estimate the implied earnings volatility (IEV) embedded in *current* option prices.

The "EVvsTime" tab of the Basic spreadsheet performs the required calculations that allow us to use Solver to estimate the IEV based on current implied volatility levels. It also uses the resulting IEV estimate to calculate future implied volatilities approaching the earnings announcement.

To use the "EVvsTime" tab to solve for the implied earnings volatility at any point in time:

1. Enter the beginning analysis date (C2), which will always be before the next earnings date.

2. Enter the ending analysis date (D2), the final forecast date for

future implied volatilities.

3. Enter the next earnings date (C3), which will always be the date of the close immediately preceding the earnings announcement.

4. Enter an initial "seed" estimate of the annualized implied earnings volatility (C4).

5. Enter the expiration dates for the at-the-money (ATM) options that you plan to use to estimate the IEV (C6:C15).

6. Enter the implied volatility for each ATM option on the analysis date (G6:G15).

7. Use Solver to determine the IEV that best explains the current ATM implied volatilities.

Figure 3.7 includes a table of the input data and all required calculations to estimate the IEV for UA on July 14, 2014. I selected an arbitrary analysis date approximately ten days before the earnings announcement that occurred on July 24, 2014. We will use Solver to solve for the IEV on the beginning analysis date (July 14, 2014) and we will use the resulting IEV estimate to calculate the future equilibrium implied volatilities from the beginning to the ending analysis dates. The table in Figure 3.7 includes data for nine different options expiring from 7/26/2014 to 1/15/2016 (C6:C14). Since we are interested in estimating the IEV, all of the options should expire *after* the earnings announcement.

As explained above, the input data for each option are entered in columns C and G. In addition to determining the number of earnings trading days (one by definition) and the number of normal trading days (F6:F15), the spreadsheet calculates the implied normal ATM IV for each option (I6:I15) based on the assumed IEV (C4). The deviations from the average normal ATM IV for each option are shown in column J (J6:J15).

Solver uses its solution algorithm to find the value of IEV that minimizes the RMSE, which is a proxy for the average difference between the implied normal ATM IV across all options. Solver found that an annualized IEV of 137.4% (C4) minimized the average difference between the normal ATM IVs across all options on July 14, 2014.

Figure 3.7: Implied Earnings Volatility (Static)

	Beginning Analysis Date	Ending Analysis Date						Implied Normal ATM IV	Deviation: Average Normal ATM IV	Squared Deviation from Avg. Normal IV
1										
2	7/14/2014	7/31/2014								
3	7/23/2014	Next Earnings Date (AMC)						31.5%	1.13%	0.01%
4	137.4%	Assumed Annualized Earnings Volatility								
5	Option Expiration Date	Total Trade Days	Earnings Days	Total Normal Days	Aggregate IV of ATM Option	Implied Earnings Volatility	Implied Normal ATM IV	Average Normal ATM IV	Squared Deviation from Avg. Normal IV	
6	7/26/2014	9	1	8	55.4%	137.4%	33.1%	1.5%	0.0%	
7	8/2/2014	14	1	13	47.2%	137.4%	30.8%	-0.8%	0.0%	
8	8/9/2014	19	1	18	43.5%	137.4%	30.8%	-0.7%	0.0%	
9	8/16/2014	24	1	23	40.8%	137.4%	30.3%	-1.3%	0.0%	
10	8/23/2014	29	1	28	40.0%	137.4%	31.4%	-0.2%	0.0%	
11	8/30/2014	34	1	33	38.7%	137.4%	31.2%	-0.4%	0.0%	
12	10/18/2014	68	1	67	34.5%	137.4%	30.4%	-1.1%	0.0%	
13	1/17/2015	130	1	129	34.4%	137.4%	32.3%	0.8%	0.0%	
14	1/15/2016	381	1	380	34.3%	137.4%	33.6%	2.1%	0.0%	
15	0	0	0	0						

61

The root-mean-squared-error was 1.13% (J4), which is a measure of the average difference between calculated normal ATM IVs and the average normal ATM IV (I4). At-the-money options are used to eliminate the effects of the vertical skew and to allow an "apples-to-apples" comparison. The estimation errors for each option are provided in cells J6:J15.

The exact button sequence to run Solver may depend on your version of Microsoft Excel. In MS Office 2010, the following sequence will bring up the Solver problem description associated with the current spreadsheet tab: Data => Solver

On the "ImpliedEV" tab, this should bring up the Solver problem specification depicted in Figure 3.8.

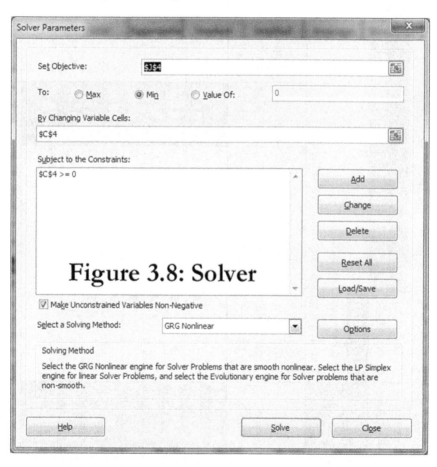

Figure 3.8: Solver

If Solver does not retrieve the problem specification, then you will need to set the objective cell (J4) to "Min" and set the changing variable cells to C4. Use the Add button to enter the single constraint in the image below. Finally, the "Make Unconstrained Variables Non-Negative" box should be checked and the Solving method should be "GRG Nonlinear." To run Solver, press the "Solve" button.

In this case, Solver is solving for the annualized implied earnings volatility on July 14, 2014 that minimizes the average difference between the normal ATM IVs and the average normal ATM IV across all options.

As was the case before, the aggregate IV formula is the key to these calculations. The "ImpliedEV" tab also uses the version of the aggregate IV formula that allows us to solve for the normal IV, given the implied IV and the earnings volatility on a given analysis date.

The following example reproduces the calculation of the estimated post-earnings ATM IV (I6) for the option expiring on 7/26/2014. On July 14, 2014, that option had nine trading days remaining until expiration (Row 6). The spreadsheet repeats the sample calculations below for every option in the spreadsheet.

NTD_E = **Number of Earnings Trading Days**
NTD_N = **Number of Normal Trading Days**
W_E = **Earnings Volatility Weight**
W_N = **Normal Volatility Weight**

$W_E = NTD_E / (NTD_E + NTD_N)$
$W_E = 1/(9) = 11.1111\%$
$W_N = NTD_N / (NTD_E + NTD_N)$
$W_N = 8/(9) = 88.8889\%$

$V_E = 137.3808\%$ **(C4) (optimal Solver value)**
IV = Implied Volatility on Analysis Date = 55.4% (G6)
V_N = **Normal Volatility**

$V_N = (((IV^2)-(W_E*(V_E^2)))/W_N)^{0.5}$
$V_N = (((55.4\%^2)-(11.1111\%*(137.3808\%^2)))/88.8889\%)^{0.5}$
$V_N = (10.9362\%)^{0.5}$
$V_N = 33.07\%$ **(I6)**

All of the tabs in the Basic spreadsheet rely on the simplifying assumption that all options have only one earnings trading day. The Basic spreadsheet could be modified to calculate the actual number of earnings days, but I wanted to keep this spreadsheet as simple as possible. The "EVvsTime" tab of the Basic spreadsheet uses the aggregate implied volatility formula and Solver to solve for the implied earnings volatility that minimizes the average deviation between calculated normal ATM IVs and the average normal ATM IV. Without knowing the precise shape of the horizontal normal volatility skew, this is an effective technique for estimating the implied IEV.

The Integrated spreadsheet does calculate the actual number of earnings days and simultaneously estimates the vertical skew, the horizontal skew, and the implied earnings volatility. This will eliminate all simplifying assumptions, which will improve the accuracy of the estimates and greatly expand our ability to design and optimize strategies. However, this functionality will come at a cost. The Integrated spreadsheet is significantly more complex and requires more input data. That is why I provided both the Basic and Integrated spreadsheets with this book, to ensure the analytical framework is as accessible and practicable as possible for readers with varying backgrounds and experience levels.

To summarize, we entered the analysis dates, the earnings date, the expiration dates, and the at-the-money implied volatilities. Solver did the rest, solving for the implied earnings volatility on the analysis date, which allowed us to calculate the implied normal volatilities for each ATM option.

The resulting IEV estimate of 137.4% (C4) represents the market's forecast of the UA earnings volatility on the next earnings date (July 23, 2014). In other words, 137.4% was the expected level of implied earnings volatility embedded in UA's ATM option prices on July 14, 2014.

Forecasting Implied Volatility

We now know the implied normal volatilities for each ATM option and the implied earnings volatility, which applies to all of the ATM options that expire after earnings. If we assume that the earnings and normal volatilities remain constant, we can use the aggregate IV formula to forecast the implied volatilities for all of the ATM options as they approach the earnings announcement. To forecast the implied volatilities, the only remaining values that we need to calculate are the daily volatility weights, which are solely determined by the number of normal and earnings trading days remaining on each date. These calculations were explained in detail in Chapter 2.

In the section above, we calculated the volatility weights and the implied normal volatility (33.07%) for the ATM UA option expiring on 7/26/2014, which had nine trading days remaining on the analysis date of July 14, 2014. As calculated earlier, the initial earnings volatility weight was 11.1111% and the normal volatility weight was 88.8889%. At the close of the last trading day before the earnings release on July 23, 2014, the earnings and normal volatility weights were both 50%. On that date, there was exactly one normal and one earnings day remaining until expiration. As a result, the forecasted implied volatility was 99.92% (see calculation below).

NTD_E = **Number of Earnings Trading Days**
NTD_N = **Number of Normal Trading Days**
W_E = **Earnings Volatility Weight**
W_N = **Normal Volatility Weight**

$W_E = NTD_E/(NTD_E + NTD_N)$
$W_E = 1/(2) = 50.0\%$

$W_N = NTD_N/(NTD_E + NTD_N)$
$W_N = 1/(2) = 50.0\%$

IV = **Aggregate Implied Volatility (Annualized)**
V_E = **Earnings Volatility (Annualized)**
V_N = **Normal Volatility (Annualized)**

$IV = ((W_E*(V_E{}^\wedge 2))+(W_N)*(V_N{}^\wedge 2))^\wedge 0.5$
$IV = ((50\%*(137.3808\%^\wedge 2))+(50\%)*(33.07\%^\wedge 2))^\wedge 0.5$
$IV = (99.8355\%)^\wedge 0.5$
$IV = 99.92\%$

We can repeat these calculations for every one of the ATM options, on every trading day leading up to the earnings announcement. The resulting implied volatilities for all of the UA ATM options are shown in Figure 3.9. The independent x-axis shows the analysis date.

Analysis date "1" represents the initial analysis date of July 14, 2014. Analysis date "8" represents the last trading day before the earnings release: July 23, 2014. The dependent y-axis corresponds to the annualized implied volatility. The daily forecasted implied volatilities are shown with separate lines for all nine ATM UA options. The lines are shown in order of the shortest-term option to the longest-term option (top to bottom).

As explained previously, the earnings volatility will have the greatest effect on options that expire shortly after the earnings date. This is due to the greater weight of the earnings volatility relative to the normal volatility, which magnifies the impact of the outsized earnings volatility on implied volatility. If you attempt to replicate the implied volatility calculations, always remember that the volatility weights are multiplied by the *squared annualized volatilities*, not the actual annualized volatilities.

Experienced option traders will immediately recognize the shape of the implied volatility curves in Figure 3.9. We have all seen the familiar pattern of implied volatility spikes and crashes that occur like clockwork every quarter, but we can now forecast those quarterly implied volatility changes in advance. But how accurate are those forecasts?

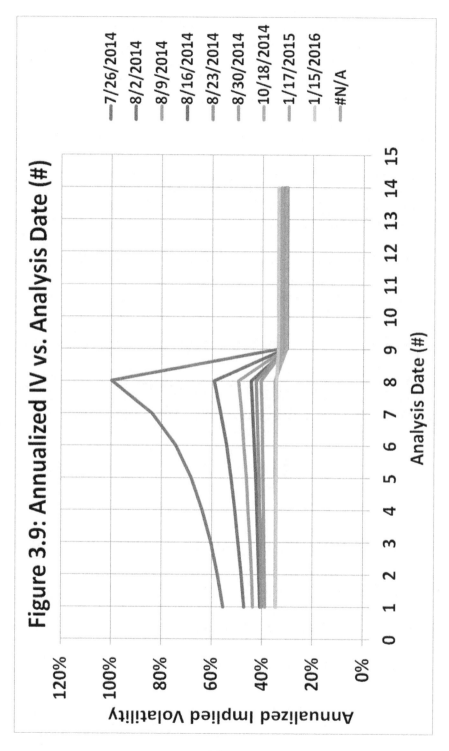

Figure 3.9: Annualized IV vs. Analysis Date (#)

The Basic spreadsheet uses some simplifying assumptions and is a crude tool, but it is still very effective at forecasting the future pattern of implied volatilities. Figure 3.10 includes a table with the forecasted ATM IVs, the actual ATM IVs, and the forecast errors for the nine ATM UA options from the previous example. The ATM UA IV forecasts in the table are for the close on the last trading day before the release of earnings: July 23, 2014. The ATM IV forecasts were made using the ATM IV data on the analysis date (July 14, 2014), seven trading days before the earnings announcement.

Let's look at an example. The IV forecast for the ATM UA option expiring on 7/26/14 was 99.9% and the actual ATM IV was 97.6%. The resulting forecast error was only 2.3%. Given that this forecast was made seven trading days earlier, when the ATM IV was only 55.4%, this is remarkably accurate. In fact, this was the largest of the forecast errors. The next largest error was 1.4%. The root-mean-squared-error (RMSE) was 1.1%, and the average error was only 0.8%.

Figure 3.10: UA 7/23/14 ATM IV Forecast Accuracy

Option Expiration	Forecast ATM IV	Actual ATM IV	Forecast Error
7/26/2014	99.9%	97.6%	2.3%
8/2/2014	59.2%	59.1%	0.1%
8/9/2014	49.4%	48.6%	0.8%
8/16/2014	44.4%	44.1%	0.3%
8/23/2014	42.4%	41.7%	0.7%
8/30/2014	40.4%	39.0%	1.4%
10/18/2014	34.9%	34.7%	0.2%
1/17/2015	34.5%	33.4%	1.1%
1/15/2016	34.3%	34.1%	0.2%

The above example was not "cherry-picked" to identify an unusually accurate forecast. As I explained earlier, the aggregate IV formula is not an approximation. While the implied earnings volatility and the implied normal volatilities can obviously change from day to day, the aggregate implied volatility formula is consistent with option pricing theory and will always accurately aggregate the two sources of volatility into the correct value of implied volatility.

Conclusion

Using the three analysis tabs in the Basic spreadsheet (HistoricalEV, ImpliedEV, and EVvsTime), we can now calculate historical earnings volatility, past levels of implied earnings volatility, and the current levels of implied earnings and normal volatility. We can even forecast future levels of implied volatility with a reasonable degree of accuracy.

These new capabilities will allow us to make informed decisions regarding earnings volatility, normal volatility, and implied volatility for all of our option earnings strategies. In addition, our improved understanding of these volatility relationships will help us identify new strategies and better manage our existing strategies. However, before we can explore this new frontier in strategy development, we need to explore the implications for the Greeks, specifically the "True Greeks."

4 - TRUE GREEKS

The Basic spreadsheet introduced in the last chapter helps us understand and quantify the effects of earnings volatility more accurately than ever before, but the Integrated spreadsheet goes much further. The Integrated spreadsheet includes a comprehensive volatility model that *simultaneously integrates and quantifies every component of real-world volatility*, including earnings volatility. That is what will allow us to calculate the True Greeks.

The Black Scholes Option Pricing Model (BSOPM) was revolutionary when it was introduced and it is still a remarkable tool, but every one of its underlying assumptions is violated in practice. To mention a few, price changes are not continuous, returns are not distributed log-normally, and volatility is not constant. Furthermore, the formulas for the traditional Greeks (Delta, Gamma, Vega, Theta, and Rho), which were developed using stochastic calculus, are derivatives of the BSOPM formula. As a result, the traditional values of Delta, Gamma, Vega, Theta, and Rho rely on the same invalid assumptions as the BSOPM, which means that values calculated with the conventional Greek formulas are biased and are inconsistent with the actual price behavior of options.

In addition, the conventional Greeks assume that when one variable (like the price of the underlying stock) changes, all of the other variables (such as implied volatility) remain constant. That is definitely not the case. Every change in the price of an underlying security results in a corresponding change in implied volatility, and that change in implied volatility can be modeled and predicted with a reasonable degree of accuracy.

The comprehensive volatility model in the Integrated spreadsheet captures each component of real-world volatility and simultaneously estimates every volatility parameter required to model the volatility structure of the entire option matrix. It then uses the aggregate IV formula to accurately combine all volatility components into a single implied volatility value, which is used to model and simulate the true behavior of option prices in real-world market environments. This functionality allows us to discard all of the unrealistic and limiting BSOPM assumptions and to calculate True Greeks that reflect the actual behavior of option prices.

For readers who devote the time to understanding and mastering the Integrated spreadsheet, the payoffs will be significant. The Integrated spreadsheet will allow you to calculate the relative value of every option in a matrix and to quantify every component of volatility, including earnings volatility. The Integrated spreadsheet will combine this information with your specific volatility and price forecasts to simulate accurate scenario values and to identify the optimal options earnings strategy. Finally, the Integrated spreadsheet will provide the True Greeks and expected profit distribution for your strategy and display the results graphically.

We will begin to explore how to use the Integrated spreadsheet in Chapter 6, but we need to examine the True Greeks now, because we will use them to evaluate our first option earnings strategy example in the next chapter.

What are the Greeks?

Before we investigate the True Greeks in detail, let's take a brief step back and look at the Greeks in general. What are the Greeks and how are they used? The calculations and derivations of traditional Greeks are based on stochastic calculus, which is a specialized field of mathematics that is beyond the grasp of most traders. The resulting Greek formulas are complex and are not very intuitive, which explains why many option traders have never attained a working knowledge of the Greeks.

While the traditional Greek formulas and their derivations are complex, calculation of the True Greeks is much more intuitive. Furthermore, reviewing the True Greek formulas and the logic behind them should help many traders better understand how to apply the Greeks in practice.

Interpreting the Greeks and the True Greeks is quite straightforward. Greeks are nothing more than price sensitivities. The odd names intimidate many option traders, but the Greeks simply measure the change in one variable (typically the price of an option), *resulting from* a specified change in one of the explanatory variables (such as the price of the underlying security). Using this working definition, Delta would represent the change in the price of an option for a one dollar increase in the price of the underlying security, holding all of the other explanatory variables constant.

So what is an explanatory variable? It is a variable that has a direct causal effect on the price or value of an option, which means that it must be one of the input variables in the BSOPM: stock price, strike price, time to expiration, annualized volatility, and the level of interest rates (if we ignore the dividend yield).

While the strike price of an option is one of the input variables to the BSOPM, there are no Greeks associated with a change in the strike price. Why? Because, the strike price of an existing option does not change. However, the remaining input variables do change and will affect the value of an option.

By calculating how much the value of an option will change in response to a change in each of the input variables, we can systematically quantify the sources and magnitudes of potential returns, which are also the sources of risk. This is not a coincidence. Risk and return are always connected; you cannot have one without the other - except very briefly in rare examples of pure arbitrage.

The remainder of this chapter is divided into six sections, one dedicated to each of the following True Greeks: True Delta, True Gamma, True Earnings Vega, True Normal Vega, True Theta, and True Rho. You will notice that the traditional Greek Vega has been split into True Earnings Vega and True Normal Vega. For the first time, the aggregate implied volatility formula introduced in this book makes it feasible to calculate these new True Greek values, giving us much more insight into volatility exposure.

Each section in this chapter will briefly define the specific Greek metric and will explain how and why the True Greek values are calculated? If you would like a more detailed description of the *traditional* Greeks (including graphical examples), please review Chapter 2 of my first book: *Option Strategy Risk / Return Ratios*.

True Delta

To illustrate how True Greeks are different from traditional Greeks, we will begin this section with a discussion of the traditional BSOPM measure of Delta, which I alluded to in the brief example above. To reiterate, Delta represents the instantaneous change in the price of an option for a one dollar increase in the price of the underlying security, holding all of the other explanatory variables constant. Instantaneous means just that, there is no change in the time to expiration. The change in price is immediate and no time elapses.

While Delta is interpreted as the change in the value of an option for a one dollar increase in the price of the underlying security, this is misleading and I will attempt to expand on this definition to avoid any confusion. The value of Delta corresponds to (or is scaled to) a one dollar increase in the price of the underlying security, but it is actually measured over an infinitesimally small change in the price of the stock and is evaluated at the current price of the underlying stock.

For those of you who are mathematically inclined and are familiar with calculus, Delta is the first derivative of the option price with respect to a change in the price of the underlying stock. Said differently, it represents the slope or sensitivity of the option price function with respect to the stock price. More specifically, it is the slope of the line tangent to the option price function at the current stock price. This is easier to see graphically. Even if you are not comfortable with mathematics, you should find that the graphical examples are intuitive.

Figure 4.1 graphically depicts the traditional BSOPM Delta for an actual call option based on actual market data. The option used in all of the Greek examples in this chapter (except for True Normal Vega), was the Under Armor (UA) $60 8/2/2014 call option at the close on July 23, 2014, the last trading day before the earnings announcement. At the time, the price of UA was $60.63, so the $60 strike price meant the call option was slightly in the money. On July 23rd, the option had one earnings trading day and seven normal trading days remaining until expiration.

The independent x-axis in Figure 4.1 represents the instantaneous change in the price of the underlying stock (UA). As a result, the value of $0.00 corresponds to the closing stock price on July 23, 2014: $60.63.

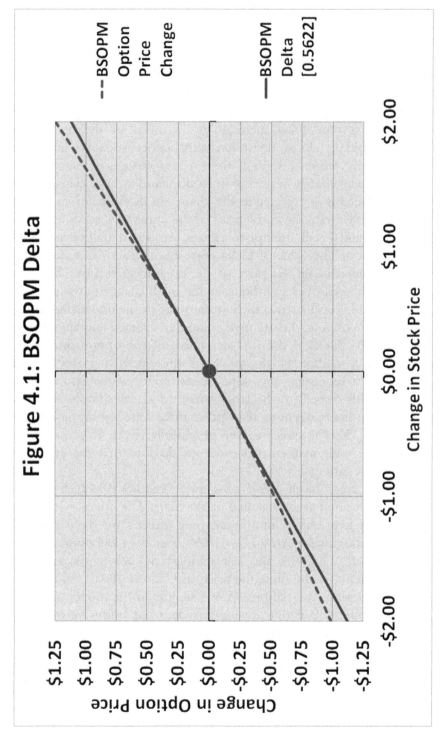

The dependent y-axis shows the instantaneous change in the price of the UA $60 8/2/2014 call option. The curved, dashed line denotes the BSOPM option price change and the straight, solid line is the line tangent to the UA call option price function at the current stock price of $60.63. The traditional measure of Delta equals the slope of that tangent line (0.5622).

In other words, the traditional measure of Delta is a linear estimate of the change in the value of the UA $60 8/2/2014 call option per one dollar increase in the value of UA. It is a linear measure of the price sensitivity of the UA call option. It indicates that the value of the call option will increase by roughly $0.56 (per share) for an instantaneous $1.00 increase in the price of UA.

For a one dollar change in the price of UA, the BSOPM value of the UA call option will *actually* increase by an amount greater than Delta and decline by an amount less than Delta. This is evident by the fact that the dashed line is above the solid line.

Delta is still the appropriate linear estimate of price sensitivity, with symmetric pricing errors due to the curvature of the option price function. Gamma will allow us to quantify the curvature of the option price function, which is a separate issue. We will concentrate on Gamma in the next section of this chapter.

For now, let's review the characteristics of the traditional Delta statistic:

1) It is measured over an infinitesimally small price change.

2) It represents the change in the value of an option *according to the BSOPM.*

3) It assumes that all *of the other explanatory variables remain constant.*

Now, let's examine how True Delta differs from the traditional measure of Delta and why those differences are important. Our calculation of True Delta also represents the slope of the option price function, but there are important differences. First, we do not measure the change in the price of the option over an infinitesimally small change in the price of the underlying security. This means that the True Delta calculation is not a derivative, which eliminates the need to use stochastic calculus. Instead, we calculate the slope of the option pricing function that passes through two discrete price levels for the underlying stock: minus one dollar and plus one dollar.

In addition, using discrete points to calculate the price sensitivity or slope function allows us to use our choice of option pricing models. We are not limited to pricing models that are continuous and differentiable, which means that we are no longer forced to use the BSOPM and all of its invalid assumptions to calculate the Greeks. This permits us to incorporate much more accurate, real-world pricing and volatility assumptions into our option pricing model. We will use this simple two-point slope methodology to calculate all of the True Greeks.

Figure 4.2 graphically depicts the True Delta for the above UA call option. The independent x-axis in Figure 4.2 represents the instantaneous change in the price of the underlying stock (UA). The dependent y-axis shows the instantaneous change in the price of the UA $60 8/2/2014 call option.

The curved, dashed line denotes the expected change in the price of the UA call option as determined by a comprehensive volatility model, not by the BSOPM. The straight, solid line is no longer tangent to the UA call price function. Instead, it passes through two discrete points that correspond to plus and minus one dollar price changes in the underlying stock (UA). The slope of the line passing through these two points gives us the value of True Delta (0.5558) – See Figure 4.2.

True Delta is still a linear estimate of the change in the value of the UA $60 8/2/2014 call option per one dollar increase in the price of UA. However, it is not a derivative of the BSOPM function. Instead, we calculate the slope from two discrete points of the option price function, which is determined by a *comprehensive volatility model* that includes all volatility components, which are estimated from the full UA option matrix.

Let's review the characteristics of True Delta:

1) It is measured over *discrete price changes* in the underlying security.

2) It represents the change in the value of an option *according to a comprehensive volatility model.*

3) It *does not* assume that all of the other explanatory variables remain constant.

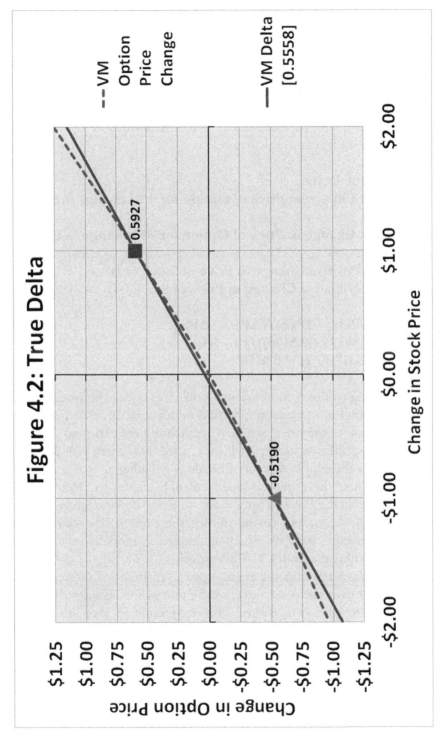

Figure 4.2: True Delta

The difference between the values of traditional Delta and True Delta in this example is small, but the errors in the traditional Greek calculations can be quite large and introduce an undesirable systematic bias. The critical issue is that the True Greeks, including True Delta, capture how option prices *actually* behave and are not constrained by artificial BSOPM pricing assumptions.

The True Delta formula below will demonstrate how all of the True Greek statistics are calculated.

D_T = True Delta
ΔPO_+ = Change in Price of Option for + $1 change in Price of Stock
ΔPO_- = Change in Price of Option for - $1 change in Price of Stock
ΔPS_+ = Positive Change in Price of Stock (+1)
ΔPS_- = Negative Change in Price of Stock (-1)

D_T = $(\Delta PO_+ - \Delta PO_-)/(\Delta PS_+ - \Delta PS_-)$
D_T = (0.5927 - (-0.5190))/(1 - (-1))
D_T = (1.1117)/(2) = 0.5558

According to the comprehensive volatility model, the price of the UA call option in our example would increase by $0.5927 for a one dollar increase in the price of UA. This includes the expected changes in implied volatility associated with the price increase in UA and also incorporates the expected level of earnings volatility.

We also use the comprehensive volatility model to calculate the price change in the UA call option due to a one dollar decrease in the price of UA. According to the model, the price of the call option would decline by $0.5190, which includes the modeled changes in implied volatility due to the UA price decline.

True Delta represents the average price sensitivity of the option. It is calculated over the price range in the underlying security of minus one dollar to plus one dollar. The numerator in the True Delta formula represents the change in the price of the option, and the denominator reflects the change in the price of the underlying stock. True Delta represents the average change in the price of the option per one dollar increase in the price of the underlying stock.

True Gamma

As explained earlier, Gamma measures the curvature of the option price function. As a result, it is the only Greek that we will examine that does not measure the price sensitivity of an option. Instead, it represents the change in *Delta*, per one dollar increase in the price of the underlying security. In our case, True Gamma will represent the change in *True Delta*, per one dollar increase in the price of the underlying security.

The traditional Gamma statistic suffers from the same flaws as the traditional measure of Delta:

1) It is measured over an infinitesimally small price change.

2) It represents the change in the value of Delta *according to the BSOPM.*

3) It assumes that *all of the other explanatory variables remain constant.*

True Gamma offers the same benefits as True Delta:

1) It is measured over *discrete price changes* in the underlying security.

2) It represents the change in the value of True Delta *according to a comprehensive volatility model.*

3) It *does not* assume that all of the other explanatory variables remain constant.

True Gamma does not measure the change in True Delta over an infinitesimally small change in the price of the underlying security. This means that the True Gamma calculation is not a derivative, which eliminates the need to use stochastic calculus. Instead, we calculate the change in True Delta using two discrete price levels for the underlying security: minus one dollar and plus one dollar.

Using discrete points to calculate the change in True Delta allows us to use our choice of option pricing models, permitting us to incorporate much more accurate, real-world pricing and volatility assumptions into our option pricing model.

Figure 4.3 depicts the True Gamma for the above UA call option graphically. The independent x-axis in Figure 4.3 represents the instantaneous change in the price of the underlying stock (UA). The dependent y-axis shows the instantaneous change in the price of the UA $60 8/2/2014 call option. The curved, dashed upper line denotes the expected change in the price of the UA call option as determined by a comprehensive volatility model, not by the BSOPM.

The straight, solid lite-colored line passes through two discrete points that correspond to price changes in the underlying stock (UA) of minus two and zero dollars. The slope passing through these two points gives us the value of True Delta *centered at a price change of minus one* (0.4813).

The straight, solid upper line passes through two discrete points that correspond to price changes in the underlying stock (UA) of zero and plus two dollars. The slope passing through these two points gives us the value of True Delta *centered at a price change of plus one* (0.6274).

You will note that the True Delta at minus one dollar (0.4813) is *less than* the initial value of True Delta (0.5558). Similarly, the value of True Delta at plus one dollar (0.6274) is *greater than* the initial value of True Delta. In other words, the True Delta of the UA call option increases as the price of UA rises and decreases as the price of UA falls. Why? Because, asymmetric payoffs benefit the owner of the option.

As the price of UA rises, the probability of exercising the call option increases. As the price of UA falls, the probability of exercising the call option declines. This forces the value of the call option to rise faster and fall more slowly than suggested by the linear estimate of True Delta.

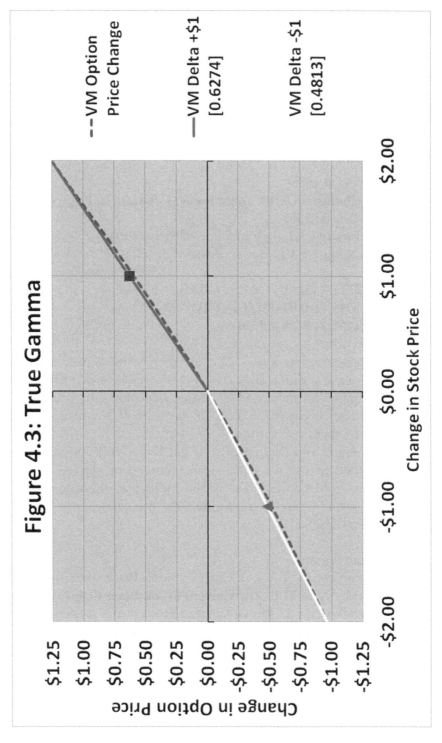

Figure 4.3: True Gamma

The True Gamma formula below is very similar to the True Delta formula. However, instead of calculating the change in price per one dollar change in the price of the underlying stock, True Gamma calculates the change in *True Delta* per one dollar change in the price of the underlying stock. Both formulas use the same discrete slope calculations.

G_T = **True Gamma**
ΔD_{T+} = **Change in True Delta for + $1 change in Price of Stock (0.6274 - 0.5558)**
ΔD_{T-} = **Change in True Delta for - $1 change in Price of Stock (0.4813 − 0.5558)**
ΔPS_+ = **Positive Change in Price of Stock (+1)**
ΔPS_- = **Negative Change in Price of Stock (-1)**

$G_T = (\Delta DT_+ - \Delta DT_-)/(\Delta PS_+ - \Delta PS_-)$
$G_T = (0.0716 - (-0.0745))/(1 - (-1))$
$G_T = (0.1461)/(2) = 0.0730$

Because of cancelling terms, we could also use the actual values of True Delta in the formula instead of the changes in True Delta. The Integrated spreadsheet does all of these calculations for you, but I will include the alternative version of the formula for readers who would like to experiment further.

The numerator and denominator of the True Greek formulas can all be modified to use the actual values instead of changes in the actual values. Note that the values of the numerator and denominator in the alternative version of the formula did not change, nor did the value of True Gamma.

G_T = **True Gamma**
D_{T+} = **True Delta $1 Above Current Stock Price (0.6274)**
D_{T-} = **True Delta $1 Below Current Stock Price (0.4813)**
PS_+ = **Stock Price $1 Above Current Stock Price (61.63)**
PS_- = **Stock Price $1 Below Current Stock Price (59.63)**
$G_T = (0.6274 - 0.4813)/(61.63 - 59.63)$
$G_T = (0.1461)/(2) = 0.0730$

The resulting calculation of True Gamma reflects the option price behavior we observe in actual market environments. The realistic option price performance is captured by True Delta, which reflects every component of volatility, including the interaction of volatility with the price of the underlying security.

True Earnings Vega

Using the True Greek discrete slope calculation framework in conjunction with the aggregate implied volatility formula allows us to calculate the *True Earnings Vega*. For the first time, we now have the tools to calculate the average change in the value of any option per 1% increase in *implied earnings volatility*. This new risk measure or Greek will provide unique insights into constructing and evaluating option earnings strategies.

The calculation of the True Earnings Vega is very similar to the procedure we used earlier to calculate True Delta. However, instead of calculating a linear estimate of the change in the price of an option per one dollar change in the price of the underlying stock, True Earnings Vega will calculate the linear estimate of the change in the price of an option per 1% increase in the annualized implied earnings volatility.

Note, we are only interested in the change in implied earnings volatility, not implied volatility. In other words, we are assuming that normal volatility remains unchanged. In this case, this is a realistic assumption. There should be no cause and effect relationship between a change in implied earnings volatility and a change in normal volatility.

Figure 4.4 graphically depicts the True Earnings Vega for the above UA call option. The independent x-axis in Figure 4.4 represents the instantaneous change in the annualized implied earnings volatility. The dependent y-axis shows the instantaneous change in the price of the UA $60 8/2/2014 call option.

The curved, dashed line denotes the expected change in the price of the UA call option as determined by a *comprehensive volatility model*, not by the BSOPM. The straight, solid line passes through two discrete points that correspond to plus and minus one dollar price changes in the underlying stock (UA). The slope of the line passing through these two points gives us the value of True Earnings Vega

(0.01335).

You are probably asking yourself why you only see one line in Figure 4.4. The reason is that the change in the value of the underlying stock for a 1% change in the implied earnings volatility is almost linear: minus 0.0133 versus +0.0134. As a result, the solid True Earnings Vega line overlies and obscures the dashed line of the option price function for the UA call option.

You might also ask, why is True Earnings Vega so small: 0.01335? The True Earnings Vega of 0.01335 indicates that the average change in the price of the UA call option is only $ 0.01335 per share, per 1% change in the annualized implied earnings volatility. The Greek examples in this chapter are expressed on a per share basis, because it is possible to compare per share Greeks directly with option prices. They are expressed in the same units and most traders find per share Greeks more intuitive.

However, in reality, the change in the value of the option position per contract (100 shares) would be $1.335, which is obviously still a small number. Why so small? First, on July 23rd 2014, the UA call option in our example had only one earnings trading day and seven normal trading days remaining until expiration. As a result, the earnings volatility weight was small relative to the normal volatility weight, which dampens the impact of the 1% change in implied earnings volatility on implied volatility.

In addition, a 1% change in implied earnings volatility (IEV) represents a very small change relative to what we actually observe in the options market. As you use the spreadsheets to calculate IEV, you will discover that annualized IEV typically exceeds 100% and can easily reach 200% to 300% for stocks with a history of volatile responses to earnings.

As a result, it is not uncommon to see 20% to 30% swings in IEV. The True Earnings Vega calculation is accurate and consistent with the traditional Vega concept, but the volatility of the explanatory variable (IEV in this case) must always be considered when applying the Greeks in practice.

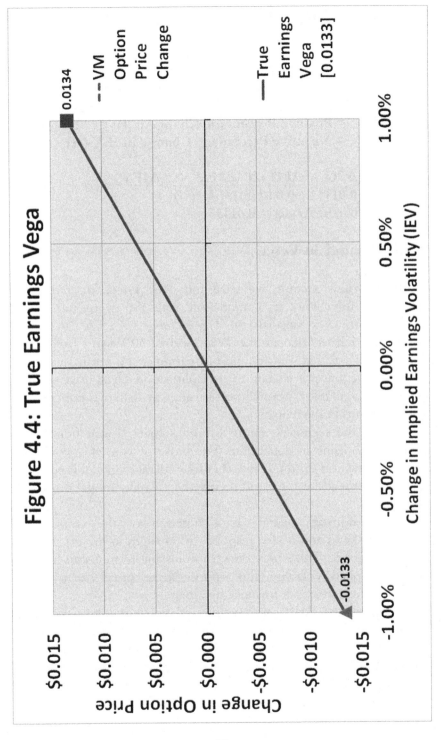

Figure 4.4: True Earnings Vega

The True Earnings Vega formula below is consistent with how all of the True Greek statistics are calculated.

EV$_T$ = True Earnings Vega
ΔPO$_+$ = Change in Price of Option for + 1% change in IEV
ΔPO$_-$ = Change in Price of Option for − 1% change in IEV
%ΔIEV$_+$ = Positive Percentage Change in IEV (+1)
%ΔIEV$_-$ = Negative Percentage Change in IEV (-1)

EV$_T$ = (ΔPO$_+$ - ΔPO$_-$)/(%ΔIEV$_+$ - %ΔIEV$_-$)
EV$_T$ = (0.0134 - (-0.0.0133))/(1 - (-1))
EV$_T$ = (0.02675)/(2) = 0.01335

True Normal 30 Vega

In the previous section, we used the True Greek discrete slope calculation framework in conjunction with the aggregate implied volatility formula to calculate the *True Earnings Vega*. We can use the same approach to calculate the True Normal 30 Vega. I have stated that implied volatility is a function of earnings and normal volatility, which is true, but it is a slight oversimplification. Even if we separate out earnings volatility, normal (non-earnings) volatility is not constant across options in the matrix.

Due to the technical nature of the subject, I will not discuss volatility modeling in detail here. For those of you who would like more information on the comprehensive volatility model used in the Integrated spreadsheet, we will review the volatility model more fully in Chapter 7.

Briefly, normal volatility is a function of the vertical and horizontal skews and it also responds to changes in the price of the underlying stock. The *vertical* skew captures the relationship between normal implied volatility and option strike prices, which were typically listed *vertically* in financial newspapers.

The *horizontal* skew captures the relationship between normal implied volatility and option expiration dates, which were typically listed *horizontally* in financial newspapers. The cause and effect relationship between the price of the underlying security and the at-the-money (ATM) normal implied volatility is also important and must be included in any volatility model.

The comprehensive volatility model in the Integrated spreadsheet uses the entire option matrix to estimate all of the required volatility parameters and applies them when calculating the True Greeks. The volatility model is particularly important to the calculation of the True Normal 30 Vega.

Why is it called the True Normal 30 Vega (TN30 Vega)? At this point, "True," "Normal," and "Vega" may be self-explanatory. It is a "True" Greek because it quantifies the *actual* price behavior of options and is not limited by the artificial BSOPM assumptions. "Normal Vega" means that it calculates the sensitivity to a 1% change in *normal* implied volatility.

So what does the number 30 signify? The number 30 represents thirty days or one month until expiration. The BSOPM assumes that changes in implied volatility are constant across all options. We already know that this is not true because of earnings volatility, but it is not even true for normal volatility.

In practice, normal volatilities are mean-reverting. In other words, extremely low and extremely high levels of normal volatility eventually revert to a more typical or average level of normal volatility. This is true for practically all securities across all markets. Due to mean reversion, the normal implied volatilities of short-term options change more than the normal implied volatilities of longer-term options. This is true regardless of the initial shape of the horizontal skew curve: positively sloped, flat, or inverted.

As a result, instead of being constrained by the limitations of traditional Vega, we *do not* need to assume that all normal implied volatilities change by the same amount when calculating the True Normal 30 Vega. Instead, we can assume a 1% change in the normal implied volatility for a one-month option, and model the estimated changes in implied volatility for all other options as a function of their time remaining until expiration.

I created such a model using daily implied volatility data for a range of expiration dates, across a broad spectrum of diverse securities. The underlying securities included stocks, ETFs, commodities, currencies, bonds, and indices. The results from the model are depicted in Figure 4.5.

Figure 4.5 graphically depicts the normal at-the-money (ATM) implied volatility (IV) multiplier versus the time remaining until option expiration. The independent x-axis represents the time remaining until option expiration (in years) and the dependent y-axis shows the ATM IV multiplier. The square, diamond, triangle, and circle highlight the x and y coordinates for option expirations of one week, one month, six months, and one year, respectively. The solid line depicts the continuous, non-linear ATM IV function for expiration dates ranging from one week to two years.

The key reference point in the diagram is the one-month option expiration (0.0833. 1.0000). The 0.0833 represents 1/12th of a year and the 1.0 signifies an ATM IV multiplier of 1.0. The multiplier tells us how much the ATM IV of the option will change for a 1% change in the ATM IV of a 30 day or one-month option. In that context, the multiplier for a one-month option must be 1.0 by definition.

The one-week option is represented by the square with a time to expiration of 0.0198 years (5 trading days/252 trading days). The multiplier of 1.5697 indicates that for a 1% change in the ATM IV of the 30-day option, the ATM IV of the one-week option will change by 1.5697%. As stated earlier, the implied volatilities of short-term options are much more volatile than the implied volatilities of longer-term options and that is evidenced by the large ATM IV multiplier for a one-week option.

Based on that premise, we should expect the ATM IV multipliers of options with expiration dates *longer* than one month to be *less than* 1.0 and that is exactly the case. The ATM IV multipliers for the six-month and one-year options are 0.2406 and 0.2194, respectively. For a 1% change in the ATM IV of a 30-day option, the ATM IV of the six-month and one-year option will only change by 0.2406% and 0.2194%, respectively.

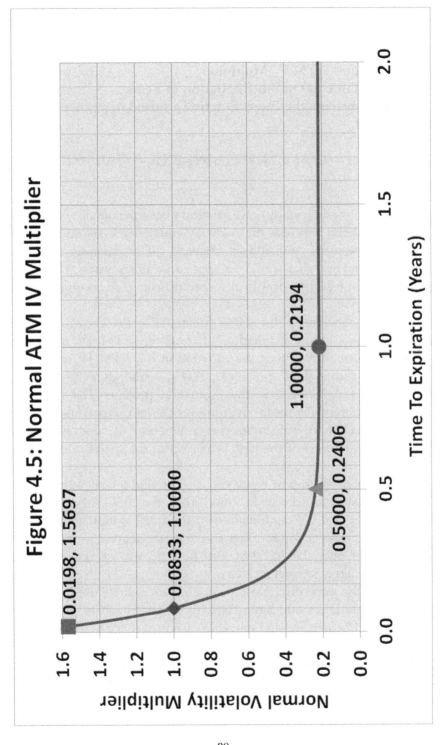

Figure 4.5: Normal ATM IV Multiplier

The formula for the ATM IV multiplier is provided below in Excel format.

Multiplier = ATM IV Multiplier
TTE = Time to Option Expiration in Years
EXP represents the Excel function e raised to a power, e =
2.718281828

Multiplier = 1.0+(-0.780854818)*(1-EXP(-8.629216*(TTE-1/12)))

If I was providing an option analytical platform and all of the data, I would probably estimate the ATM IV multiplier function for each underlying security individually, instead of estimating a single multiplier function that would be applied to all securities. However, that would not be practical in the spreadsheets that accompany the book.

So, how accurate is the above function for the broad range of securities used in the estimation? The above ATM IV multiplier formula explained 96.6% of the variation in the ATM IV regression coefficients across all of the stocks, ETFs, commodities, currencies, bonds, and indices used in the estimation process. The fact that volatility is universally mean reverting results in a remarkably similar pattern of ATM IV sensitivities as a function of time to option expiration, regardless of the type of market or the specific underlying security.

While there will still be some variation around the above ATM IV multiplier estimates, keep in mind that the BSOPM essentially assumes an ATM IV multiplier of 1.0 for all option expirations, which is obviously incorrect. The above model represents a dramatic improvement over the BSOPM. But how do we use the model to calculate the True Normal 30 Vega?

We use the same discrete slope calculation that we used earlier to calculate True Delta and True Earnings Vega. However, instead of assuming a 1% increase and decrease in volatility for all options, we will use the ATM IV multiplier to determine the changes in the normal implied volatility for each option, which will be a function of its time remaining until expiration. We will use the specific changes in the normal implied volatility (positive and negative) for each option to calculate the corresponding discrete changes in the value of each option, which will be used in the slope calculation.

This should be easier to understand by reviewing the table in Figure 4.6. Due to the complexity of these calculations, this is the only example in the chapter that is hypothetical and does not use actual market data. Instead, it uses four hypothetical options with times remaining until expiration of one week, one month, six months, and one year.

All four options assume an underlying stock price of $100, a strike price of $100, a normal implied volatility of 25%, and a risk-free interest rate of 0.25%. In addition, none of the options expire after an earnings event. Using four at-the-money options that are not influenced by earnings greatly simplifies the example by eliminating the effects of the vertical skew and earnings volatility and should make the results more intuitive.

In Figure 4.6, the four options are listed in order of time to expiration, from shortest to longest. The time to expiration in years is provided in the first column, followed by the normal ATM IV multiplier, and the change in the normal ATM IV that will be used to calculate changes in option values. The next two columns report the change in option value for the stated negative and positive changes in the normal ATM IV. The True Normal 30 Vega (TN30 Vega) and the traditional BSOPM Vega values are shown in the next two columns. Finally, the BSOPM error, which represents the difference between BSOPM Vega and the TN30 Vega, is reported in the last column.

Due to the ATM IV multiplier, the BSOPM Vega understates the TN30 Vega of the one-week option by $0.032 per share, which corresponds to $3.20 per contract. This might not sound that significant, but it represents an error of over 36%.

Figure 4.6: True Normal 30 Vega		Change in Option Value		Per Share Values		
Years to Expiration	Normal ATM IV Multiplier	Normal IV Change	- Normal IV Change	+ Normal IV Change	TN30 Vega	BSOPM Vega	BSOPM Vega Error
0.0198	1.5697	1.5697%	-0.088	0.088	0.088	0.056	-0.032
0.0833	1.0000	1.0000%	-0.115	0.115	0.115	0.115	0.000
0.5000	0.2406	0.2406%	-0.068	0.068	0.068	0.281	0.213
1.0000	0.2194	0.2194%	-0.087	0.087	0.087	0.395	0.309

Similarly, the BSOPM Vega understates the TN30 Vega of the one-year option by $0.309 per share, or $30.90 per contract. This is an error of 354%. In other words, the BSOPM Vega is over 4.5 times as large as the TN30 Vega. The traditional Vega metric dramatically overstates the volatility exposure of long-term options and understates the volatility exposure of short-term options by naively assuming that implied volatility changes are constant across the entire term structure of volatilities.

The True Normal 30 Vega formula below is consistent with how all of the True Greek statistics are calculated, with one exception. The instantaneous option price changes are calculated for a 1% change in the 30-day normal at-the-money implied volatility, which results in different and unique changes in the normal volatility for each option in the matrix. The values for the hypothetical one-year option in Figure 4.6 are used in the formula example below:

$N30V_T$ = True Normal 30 Vega
ΔPO_+ = Change in Price of Option for + 1% change in the 30-Day ATM IV
ΔPO_- = Change in Price of Option for - 1% change in the 30-Day ATM IV
$\%\Delta N30IV_+$ = Positive Percentage Change in 30-Day ATM IV (+1)
$\%\Delta N30IV_-$ = Negative Percentage Change in 30-Day ATM IV (-1)

$N30V_T = (\Delta PO_+ - \Delta PO_-)/(\%\Delta N30IV_+ - \%\Delta N30IV_-)$
$N30V_T = (0.087 - (-0.087))/(1 - (-1))$
$N30V_T = (0.174)/(2) = 0.087$

The calculation of True Normal 30 (TN30) Vega in the Integrated spreadsheet accounts for the fact that normal volatility changes are not constant across the term structure of volatilities. Instead, the TN30 Vega models the changes in normal volatility as a function of the time to expiration. It integrates these ATM IV changes with the vertical skew to determine the change in normal volatility for each option. Finally, it uses the aggregate IV formula to calculate the resulting change in aggregate implied volatility, which includes the effects of earnings volatility. Finally, these aggregate IV changes are used to solve for the resulting option prices and the True Greeks.

It is important to understand that all components of volatility are used in the calculation of the True Greeks, which ensures that the resulting values reflect the actual price behavior of all options in the matrix. However, *the Integrated spreadsheet performs all of these calculations automatically and you will not need to use any of the formulas in this book manually.*

True Theta

The traditional Theta formula is a derivative of the continuous BSOPM. As a result, the conventional value of Theta corresponds to (or is scaled to) a *one calendar day decrease* in the time remaining until expiration of each option, but it is actually measured over an infinitesimally small change in time to expiration. Since the BSOPM function is continuous, the traditional measure of Theta completely ignores the existence and effects of discrete earnings announcements, which creates large systematic biases in the Theta calculation.

True Theta eliminates these deficiencies and uses the aggregate IV formula and the comprehensive volatility model to accurately quantify the effect of the passage of time on the value of all options, even those expiring after earnings announcements.

Unlike the other True Greeks, there is no need to calculate the slope of the option price function based on *positive and negative* changes in the explanatory variable. Time only moves in one direction. As a result, True Theta calculates the change in the value of each option for a discrete *one trading day decrease* in time remaining until expiration. Note that Theta is the only Greek that corresponds to a *decrease* in the explanatory variable.

We will now examine the conventional and True Theta values for the option example we used earlier in this chapter: the Under Armor (UA) $60 8/2/2014 call option at the close on July 23, 2014, the last trading day before the earnings announcement. On July 23rd, the option had one earnings trading day and seven normal trading days remaining until expiration.

Since the next UA earnings announcement occurred before the open on July 24th, 2014, the passage of one trading day from the 23rd to the 24th reduced the number of *earnings trading days* from one to zero. The number of normal trading days remained constant at seven.

True Theta used the aggregate IV formula to automatically reduce the earnings volatility weight to zero after the earnings announcement. True Theta also used the comprehensive volatility model to adjust effects of the horizontal skew curve due to the passage of time. The resulting True Theta value for the UA call option at the close on July 23rd, 2014 was -$1.245 per share.

Now, consider the traditional value of Theta for the same option on July 23, 2014. Given the continuous nature of the BSOPM, ask yourself the following question: was the traditional value of Theta higher or lower than the True Theta value of -$1.245?

The continuous BSOPM had no way of accounting for the discrete earnings event that occurred before the open on July 24, 2014. As a result, the traditional Theta formula incorrectly assumed that implied volatility would remain constant until option expiration and that the option value would decay continuously.

On July 23, 2014, the traditional BSOPM Theta value was -$0.115, which understated the magnitude of the one-day time decay by $1.115 per share, or a staggering $111.5 per contract. The value of True Theta was almost eleven times the traditional BSOPM Theta value.

Due to the simplicity of the True Theta calculation, no graph is provided, but here is the formula for True Theta:

T_T = **True Theta**
PO_0 = **Original Price of Option**
PO_- = **Price of Option for one trading day decrease in time to expiration**
ΔPO_- = **Change in Price of Option for one trading day decrease in time to expiration**

$$T_T = \Delta PO_- = (PO_- - PO_0)$$
$$T_T = -1.245$$

The Integrated spreadsheet calculates the value of True Theta directly for all options, so no intermediate values are provided in the above example.

True Rho

Using the True Greek discrete slope calculation framework allowed us to calculate True Delta and True Earnings Vega. The calculation of the True Rho is very similar to the procedure we used earlier to calculate True Delta. However, instead of calculating a linear estimate of the change in the price of an option per one dollar change in the price of the underlying stock, True Rho will calculate the linear estimate of the change in the price of an option per 1% increase in the risk-free interest rate. US T-bill rates are typically used as a proxy for the risk-free interest rate.

Since short-term US T-Bill rates are very near zero as I write this, the discrete risk-free interest rate changes used in the slope calculations are actually plus and minus 0.10%, not plus and minus 1.0%. This has no material effect on the slope calculation or on the value of True Rho, but it is important that the risk-free interest rate be greater than zero when attempting to determine the value of an option. Given the correspondence to the earlier graphical examples for True Delta, I did not include a graph for True Rho.

The True Rho formula below is consistent with how all of the True Greek statistics are calculated, except for the smaller discrete changes in the risk-free interest rate. True Rho is still interpreted as the change in the value of an option for a 1% increase in the risk-free interest rate, regardless of the magnitude of the discrete interest rate changes used in the formula below.

R_T = True Rho
RF = Risk Free Interest Rate
ΔPO_+ = Change in Price of Option for + 0.1% change in RF
ΔPO_- = Change in Price of Option for – 0.1% change in RF
%ΔRF_+ = Positive Percentage Change in IEV (+0.1)
%ΔRF_- = Negative Percentage Change in IEV (-0.1)

$R_T = (\Delta PO_+ - \Delta PO_-)/(\%\Delta RF_+ - \%\Delta RF_-)$
$R_T = (0.0008726 - (-0.0008726))/(0.1 - (-0.1))$
$R_T = (0.0017452)/(0.2) = 0.008726$

The value True Rho for the UA call option in our example is $0.008726 per share, or $0.8726 per contract. The value of True Rho is very small due to the short time to expiration for the UA call option. The impact of a 1% change in the annual risk-free interest rate would have a minimal impact on an at-the-money option with only eight trading days remaining until expiration. As is the case for all of the True Greeks, the True Rho calculation incorporates the aggregate IV formula and the comprehensive volatility model.

Conclusion

Even under normal conditions, the traditional BSOPM Greek values are biased and are inconsistent with actual option price behavior. Earnings announcements magnify these systematic biases and demonstrate the importance of using the aggregate IV formula and the True Greeks to manage risk and to design option strategies.

5 – UA EARNINGS STRATEGY

In this chapter, we will look at the potential payoff from using the tools from this book to identify the option earnings strategy that offers the highest expected return per unit of risk. We will use actual market data for Under Armor (UA) on July 23, 2014 to ensure the trade example is as realistic as possible.

The UA strategy example will display results from both the Basic and Integrated spreadsheets. We covered the Basic spreadsheet in Chapter 3 and we will explore the Integrated spreadsheet in the next few chapters. As a result, our discussion of the Integrated spreadsheet tools in this chapter will be limited to explanations of the screenshots used to illustrate the UA trade.

Trading Edge

Our goal in designing an option earning strategy is to exploit option pricing anomalies related to earnings, which creates an advantage or trading edge. Our new spreadsheet tools now allow us to precisely quantify historical earnings volatility as well as past and current levels of implied earnings volatility (IEV). How could we use this information?

If we determined that the current IEV was too low relative to historical IEV and historical earnings volatility, earnings volatility would be too cheap and options that expired after the earnings announcement would be underpriced. If this occurred several weeks prior to the earnings announcement, we could design a strategy that would profit from the expected increase in IEV.

If we identified the IEV disparity shortly before the earnings announcement, we could design a strategy that would profit from a higher than expected *realized* earnings volatility. In other words, we would bet that *realized* volatility would exceed *implied* earnings volatility.

Instead, if IEV was too high, we could construct the opposite type of strategy - one that would benefit from either a decline in IEV or from a lower than expected level of realized earnings volatility.

Similarly, we can construct strategies that benefit from directional price changes in the underlying stock due to earnings announcements. However, before we can design option strategies to exploit directional biases and IEV anomalies, we must first identify these opportunities. In Chapter 3, I explained how to use the Basic spreadsheet to evaluate historical directional price changes due to earnings announcements and how to calculate all of the earnings volatility metrics.

I will introduce another directional resource in this chapter, but keep in mind that *modeling directional price changes due to earnings announcements is not the main focus or purpose of this book*. The simple directional forecasting examples are only provided as inspiration for your own directional modeling research.

The primary objective of this book is to introduce a theoretically sound framework for quantifying the effects of earnings volatility on all options and to provide tools that will help traders apply that framework in practice.

The framework not only helps us quantify and evaluate earnings volatility, it can also be used to identify the relative value of every option in the matrix. We will discuss volatility modeling in more detail when we explore the Integrated spreadsheet in Chapter 7. For now, just remember that the volatility model simultaneously estimates all of the volatility parameters, including the implied earnings volatility.

The Integrated spreadsheet uses the resulting volatility model to calculate the theoretical price of every option in the matrix, which it then compares to the actual mid-market price to find the precise degree of overvaluation or undervaluation of each option.

The Integrated spreadsheet then uses the volatility model (in conjunction with our custom directional and volatility forecasts) to calculate realistic option prices for a large number of probability-weighed scenarios. The Integrated optimizer then attempts to find the strategy with the highest expected profit per unit of risk. All of these tools help us create a trading edge that we can use to exploit earnings anomalies.

Screening Tools

So where do we begin? There are literally thousands of stocks that we could use to design an option earnings strategy, so first we need to narrow the list to a more manageable number of candidates. I use OptionSlam.com's stock screener for this purpose. OptionSlam provides two versions of the screener: the upcoming earnings stock screener for real-time analysis and the historical stock screener for backtesting or historical analysis. Since we are looking at historical dates, we will be using the historical stock screener in this example. OptionSlam offers many different screening filters, but I will limit my discussion to those used in this example.

Figure 5.1 is a screenshot of OptionSlam.com's historical stock screener with all of the filter settings that I used on June 30, 2014 to find prospective candidates with earning announcements scheduled during the subsequent three months. The "historical running date" (2014-06-30) and the "earnings period from historical date" (Within Three Months) selections are both shown in the top section of the screener.

In the second section of the form, I limited my selection to stocks with weekly options. This served several purposes. First, stocks with weekly options offer much more flexibility in constructing option earnings strategies. As you already know, earnings volatility has a much greater effect on the implied volatility of options expiring shortly after earnings, which makes it more difficult for option traders to evaluate near-term weekly options. This creates pricing anomalies and trading opportunities.

In addition, weekly options are typically available only on liquid stocks with substantial option trading volume. Focusing exclusively on stocks with weekly options should enhance liquidity. In this section, I also limited prospects to stocks with an average daily volume of over one million shares. Maximizing liquidity and reducing transaction costs are crucial to option trading and both of these filters were included to help satisfy these objectives.

In the next section titled "Earnings Statistics," I specified a minimum EVR of 2.0 and a minimum stock price of $20 per share. EVR is OptionSlam's proprietary earnings volatility measure, which is based on the most recent three years of quarterly earnings announcements, with the most recent data weighted more heavily.

EVR ranges between zero and ten, with ten being the most volatile. Therefore, a minimum EVR of 2.0 eliminates the stocks with the lowest level of historical earnings volatility. Why would we do so?

The hypothesis is that stocks with higher levels of earnings volatility would be more difficult for option traders to evaluate, which should increase the frequency and magnitude of earnings-related pricing anomalies. Given our ability to accurately quantify earnings volatility, this should give us an edge that we can use to our advantage.

The minimum stock price of $20 increases the value of options relative to transaction costs and commissions. The commissions are the same on $600 stocks and $6 stocks, but options on $600 stocks control a lot more market value. As a result, setting a minimum stock price prevents us from wasting our time evaluating options on low priced stocks, which would have unacceptably high commissions. Keep in mind that there are no magic numbers. You might prefer to use a minimum stock price of $15 and a minimum daily volume of 500,000 shares. The choice is yours. Relaxing the filters would increase the number of prospective candidates, which has both costs and benefits.

The next section is titled "Tracking Price Change One Day After Previous Earnings Release." I did not use this section in my historical screen, but it allows the user to apply volatility and directional filters to each of the previous one, two, three, or four earnings events.

Instead of the above section, I prefer to screen on the mean and median closing movements of the twelve previous earnings events. The first two filters in this section limit the prospective candidates to stocks that experienced a minimum mean and median *absolute* price change of 5% or more over the past twelve earnings announcements. "Absolute" means the absolute value of the one-day percentage price change experienced from the close immediately preceding earnings to the close on the next trading day. The purpose of this filter is the same as that of the EVR filter used earlier: to limit candidates to stocks with higher levels of earnings volatility.

The last two filters in this section limit the prospective candidates to stocks that experienced a minimum mean and median *raw* price change of 2% or more over the past twelve earnings announcements. The raw price changes include both positive and negative returns. If the mean and median raw returns were above 2%, that indicates a positive return bias due to previous earnings events. In other words, the resulting candidates consistently surprised analysts and traders to the upside, generating mean and median returns in excess of 2% per quarter. We will attempt to use this historical bias to our advantage.

The "Report Format Options" allow us to sort and display the resulting candidates using several different metrics. I chose to sort the results based on the "Average of Earnings Movements – Absolute," which displayed the candidates in descending order of historical earnings volatility. Figure 5.1 is a screenshot of OptionSlam.com's Historical Earnings Screener, with the filter settings described above. Figure 5.2 is a screenshot of the historical screener's results on June 30, 2014.

The filters I used returned 17 stocks, a manageable list of candidates. However, if we look closer, we can immediately eliminate six more candidates. It may be difficult to see in the screen-capture image, but the mean and median closing returns for six of the candidates include a number in parentheses with an asterisk (10*). This indicates that our specified twelve earnings events were not available for these stocks. Given that we are using the historical data to estimate earnings volatilities and directional biases, we will eliminate candidates that do not have sufficient historical data. That leaves us with only eleven prospective candidates for us to consider.

For each of the candidates in Figure 5.2, the symbol, next earnings date, market, sector and EVR are provided on the left side of the table. The right side of the table includes the mean and median *absolute* 1-day percentage price changes over the twelve previous earnings events, followed by the mean and median *raw* 1-day percentage price changes over the twelve previous earnings events. Remember, the absolute percentages are a measure of volatility and the raw percentages indicate directional bias.

A complete examination of all eleven candidates would not be practical here, but I do want to restate our objective: identify a stock with implied earnings volatility (IEV) and option pricing anomalies that we can exploit. After examining the remaining eleven candidates, I selected Under Armor (UA) and chose to implement the option earnings strategy on July 23, 2014, the last trading day before the UA second fiscal quarter 2014 earnings announcement.

Figure 5.1: OptionSlam.com Historical Scan Settings

Please Select A Past Date To Run This Report:

Historical Running Date:	2014-06-30	Required
Earnings Period From Historcial Date:	Within Three Months ▾	
After Market Flag:	N/A ▾	

The Following Descriptive Filters Are Based On Current Market Data:

Stocks List Type	Stocks With Weekly Options	▾
Market	All Markets ▾	Sector	All Sectors ▾
Minimum Average Daily Volume	1000000	

Earnings Statistics Before Each Earnings Event

Optionslam EVR	2 0 ▾	to	N/A ▾
Stock Price	20	to	

Tracking Price Change One Day After Previous Earnings Release:

Max One Day Move	N/A ▾	Movement Percentage	%	to	%
Final One Day Move	N/A ▾	Movement Percentage	%	to	%
Final One Day Direction:	N/A ▾	Directions	N/A ▾	
Weekly Imp Move vs Max One Day Move (Since Jan 2014):	N/A ▾	Inside Or Outside:	N/A ▾	

Mean and Median Calculations: Tracking One Day Price Change After Previous Earnings Release:

Field	Value		Number of Earnings to Calculate	Based On Previous 12 Earnings ▾
Maximum Or Close Movement	Based On Closing Movements ▾			
Average(Mean). absolute value			Min 5 %	Max 5 %
Median: absolute value			Min 5 %	Max 5 %
Average(Mean): raw value			Min 2 %	Max 2 %
Median: raw value			Min 2 %	Max 2 %

Report Format Options:

Sort Report Results By:	Average of Earnings Movement - Absolute ▾	
Records Per Page	All In One Page ▾	

Submit   Download To Excel   Save

Number of Earnings Events Returned: 17

Figure 5.2: OptionSlam.com Scan Results

SYMBOL	EARNING DATE	MARKET	SECTOR	EVR	CLOSING 1 DAY PRICE CHANGE OVER PREVIOUS 12 EARNINGS			
					MEAN	MEDIAN	MEAN (RAW)	MEDIAN (RAW)
GMCR	Aug. 6, 2014 AC	NASDAQ	Consumer Goods	5.8	22.57%	25.03%	6.64%	15.27%
INVN	July 29, 2014 AC	NYSE	Technology	4.7	14.24% (10*)	13.06% (10*)	4.86% (10*)	12.04% (10*)
YELP	July 30, 2014 AC	NYSE	Technology	5.2	13.72% (10*)	15.76% (10*)	8.1% (10*)	13.33% (10*)
AKAM	July 30, 2014 AC	NASDAQ	Technology	3.5	13.36%	14.82%	2.96%	4.85%
EXPE	July 31, 2014 AC	NASDAQ	Services	3.8	12.67%	12.07%	4.07%	3.75%
CIEN	Sept 4, 2014 BO	NASDAQ	Technology	3.5	11.48%	13.93%	6.49%	9.03%
VIPS	Aug. 13, 2014 AC	NYSE	Services	5.8	11.37% (9*)	11.9% (9*)	5.29% (9*)	9.76% (9*)
SPLK	Aug. 28, 2014 AC	NASDAQ	Technology	3.9	10.66% (9*)	14.59% (9*)	2.76% (9*)	10.32% (9*)
TSLA	July 31, 2014 AC	NASDAQ	Consumer Goods	4.3	10.57%	9.32%	2.84%	5.07%
FB	July 23, 2014 AC	NASDAQ	Technology	4.0	10.52% (8*)	16.61% (8*)	7.19% (8*)	16.61% (8*)
SWKS	July 17, 2014 AC	NASDAQ	Technology	2.8	9.49%	9.18%	6.17%	7.86%
KORS	Aug. 4, 2014 BO	NYSE	Consumer Goods	2.9	9.24% (10*)	8.2% (10*)	9.24% (10*)	8.2% (10*)
UA	July 24, 2014 BO	NYSE	Consumer Goods	2.9	7.45%	5.47%	2.79%	3.17%
EA	July 22, 2014 AC	NASDAQ	Technology	3.4	7.4%	6.02%	5.83%	6.02%
SNDK	July 16, 2014 AC	NASDAQ	Technology	2.0	7.09%	9.09%	2.18%	2.83%
ALXN	July 24, 2014 BO	NASDAQ	Healthcare	2.8	6.73%	5.63%	3.83%	3.66%
DHI	July 24, 2014 BO	NYSE	Industrial Goods	2.4	5.67%	5.26%	2.28%	2.24%

UA Historical Earnings Volatility

Clicking on the UA symbol in OptionSlam's historical stock screener brings up the historical earnings statistics as of 2014-07-01. We discussed the historical earnings statistics for UA earlier, when we were exploring how to use the Basic spreadsheet in Chapter 3. Now that we are going to develop a UA strategy, we will need to revisit the historical UA earnings statistics. Rather than searching for the table in Chapter 3, the quarterly UA earnings statistics are shown again in Figure 5.3. Except for the chart title, Figure 5.3 is identical to Figure 3.3.

The 1-day closing percentage returns were calculated from the closing price on the last trade day before earnings to the closing price on the next trading day. You will recall that we entered the 1-day closing percentage changes from Figure 3.3 (5.3) into the Basic spreadsheet, which calculated a series of directional summary statistics and measures of historical earnings volatility. The corresponding UA table from the Basic spreadsheet is reproduced in Figure 5.4.

In Figure 5.4, there are three summary measures of the 1-day log returns. The linear regression, median, and mean log-returns from the twelve previous earnings events were +6.24% (C18), +3.11% (C19), and +2.41% (C20) respectively. When combined with the Root Mean Squared Error (RMSE), the resulting probabilities of a positive earnings return were 77% (E18), 64% (E19), and 61% (E20). This indicates the presence of a positive historical directional bias.

As shown in Figure 5.4, the annualized earnings volatility based on the RMSE for the twelve previous UA earnings events was 136.76% (D22). We will use this historical data for UA to create our own directional and volatility forecasts, which will help us design an option earnings strategy for UA on July 23, 2014.

Reviewing the summary statistics for the past twelve earnings announcements is a good start, but it is now time to revisit the issue that I raised in Chapter 3. Based on a graph of the log-returns for UA, it was clear that the variability of the earnings returns had increased recently. I recreated this graph in Figure 5.5, but I added two rectangles that visually highlight the recent increase in earnings volatility.

Earnings History: Historical Earnings Statistics as of 2014-07-01

Under Armour, Inc. (UA) - NYSE   Next Earnings Date : July 24, 2014 Before Market Open

Figure 5.3: OptionSlam.com Historical EV - UA

UA EVR as of 2014-07-01: 2.9

Earnings Events Available: 26

EARNINGS DATE	PRE EARNINGS CLOSE	AFTER HOURS MOVE	PRICE MOVEMENT WITHIN ONE TRADING DAY						MEAN AND MEDIAN OF ONE DAY CLOSING MOVEMENT OF PREVIOUS 12 EARNINGS			
			OPEN	HIGH	LOW	CLOSE	CLOSING%	MAX%	MEAN	MEDIAN	MEAN RAW	MEDIAN RAW
April 24, 2014 BO	$54.44	-4.66%	$51.88	$52.31	$48.77	$50.42	-7.38%	-10.41%	7.77%	5.47%	2.47%	3.17%
Jan. 30, 2014 BO	$85.22	13.47%	$96.70	$106.65	$96.00	$104.76	22.92%	25.14%	6.77%	5.47%	1.47%	3.17%
Oct. 24, 2013 BO	$83.98	-5.94%	$78.98	$80.84	$77.34	$79.98	-4.76%	-7.9%	6.39%	5.47%	1.88%	3.17%
July 25, 2013 BO	$61.83	5.74%	$65.38	$69.55	$65.34	$69.38	12.21%	12.48%	5.44%	5.23%	0.79%	0.72%
April 19, 2013 BO	$55.67	3.95%	$57.87	$58.44	$55.28	$56.41	1.32%	4.97%	5.73%	5.23%	0.28%	-0.35%
Jan. 31, 2013 BO	$48.13	4.21%	$50.16	$51.94	$50.00	$50.87	5.69%	7.91%	5.75%	5.23%	-0.68%	-2.42%
Oct. 25, 2012 BO	$56.62	-4.52%	$54.06	$55.50	$52.01	$52.93	-6.51%	-8.14%	6.17%	5.23%	-1.1%	-2.42%
July 24, 2012 BO	$48.38	6.86%	$51.70	$55.00	$51.70	$52.79	9.11%	13.68%	5.47%	5.11%	-1.91%	-2.42%
April 20, 2012 BO	$48.25	-1.57%	$47.49	$51.43	$47.06	$50.76	5.2%	6.59%	6.11%	5.14%	-1.27%	-2.42%
Jan. 26, 2012 BO	$38.74	-1.91%	$38.00	$38.63	$36.28	$36.70	-5.26%	-6.35%	5.86%	4.9%	-1.02%	-1.54%
Oct. 25, 2011 BO	$38.15	-2.72%	$37.11	$41.74	$37.03	$40.08	5.03%	9.38%	7.63%	5.39%	0.74%	-1.54%
July 26, 2011 BO	$39.29	0.5%	$39.50	$41.08	$37.35	$37.72	-4.02%	-4.96%	7.84%	6.3%	1.62%	-0.76%

	Earnings Quarter	Post-Earnings % Change (Close to Close)	Post-Earnings LN Return: Next TD	LN Squared	Dev from Mean Squared
1	**Figure 5.4: Historical Earnings Volatility Table**				
3	-1	-7.38%	-7.67%	0.5878%	1.0153%
4	-2	22.92%	20.64%	4.2586%	3.3221%
5	-3	-4.76%	-4.88%	0.2379%	0.5310%
6	-4	12.21%	11.52%	1.3271%	0.8300%
7	-5	1.32%	1.31%	0.0172%	0.0121%
8	-6	5.69%	5.53%	0.3063%	0.0976%
9	-7	-6.51%	-6.73%	0.4531%	0.8356%
10	-8	9.11%	8.72%	0.7601%	0.3980%
11	-9	5.20%	5.07%	0.2570%	0.0707%
12	-10	-5.26%	-5.40%	0.2920%	0.6104%
13	-11	5.03%	4.91%	0.2408%	0.0624%
14	-12	-4.02%	-4.10%	0.1683%	0.4242%
15		Linear Regression	Intercept	Slope	R Squared
16		6.24%	6.24%	0.53%	0.04
17		Earnings Statistics	LN ROR	ROR/RMSE	Pr(ROR>0)
18		Linear Regression	6.24%	0.72	77%
19		Median	3.11%	0.36	64%
20		Mean	2.41%	0.28	61%
21		Earnings Statistics	Earnings ROR	Annualized Volatility	
22		Root Mean Square %Change	8.62%	136.76%	
23		Sigma Around Mean	8.27%	131.30%	

HistoricalEV / ImpliedEV / EVvsTime / Holidays

Note that the height of the rectangle surrounding the first six earnings events is much shorter than the height of the rectangle encompassing the second six earnings events. This is obviously a crude approach, but it does make it easier to see the recent increase in earnings volatility.

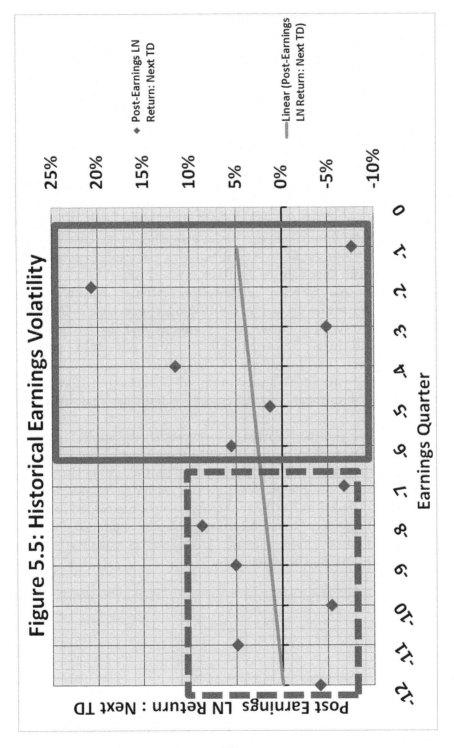

Figure 5.5: Historical Earnings Volatility

It is typically easier to identify patterns visually, but we also need to quantify the recent increase in earnings volatility. Fortunately, if we clear the contents of the six oldest earnings events, the Basic spreadsheet will automatically recalculate all of the summary statistics for the most recent *six earnings events*, including the historical earnings volatility. The UA earnings table from the Basic spreadsheet for the most recent six earnings events is provided in Figure 5.6.

The historical earnings volatility jumped from 136.76% (Figure 5.4 Cell D22) to 168.18% (Figure 5.6 Cell D22), an annualized increase of over 30%. I also used the Basic spreadsheet to recalculate the historical earnings volatility for UA based on the most recent four earnings events. The annualized implied volatility jumped again to 200.98%. I did not include the Basic spreadsheet table based on the data for the four earnings events, but you can easily replicate this calculation with your copy of the Basic spreadsheet.

The dramatic increase in historical earnings volatility from 136.76% over twelve events, to 168.18% over six events, to 200.98% over four 4 events, confirms our hypothesis that the UA earnings volatility had been increasing prior to the July 2014 earnings announcement. The magnitude of the recent increase in earnings volatility increased the likelihood of option pricing anomalies prior to the July 2014 earnings announcement – anomalies that we could exploit.

I will save you the suspense and reveal that the implied earnings volatility (IEV) for UA on July 23, 2014 was only 137.2%. While the market's estimate of IEV was consistent with the historical earnings volatility based on the twelve previous earnings announcements (136.76%), it failed to recognize the large recent increase in earnings volatility. If the recent trend in earnings volatility continued, then the market was grossly underestimating UA's earnings volatility prior to the July 2014 earnings announcement.

	A	B	C	D	E
1	Figure 5.6: Historical Earnings Volatility Table				
2	Earnings Quarter	Post-Earnings % Change (Close to Close)	Post-Earnings LN Return: Next TD	LN Squared	Dev from Mean Squared
3	-1	-7.38%	-7.67%	0.5878%	1.4584%
4	-2	22.92%	20.64%	4.2586%	2.6330%
5	-3	-4.76%	-4.88%	0.2379%	0.8624%
6	-4	12.21%	11.52%	1.3271%	0.5056%
7	-5	1.32%	1.31%	0.0172%	0.0960%
8	-6	5.69%	5.53%	0.3063%	0.0126%
9	-7				
10	-8				
11	-9				
12	-10				
13	-11				
14	-12				
15		Linear Regression	Intercept	Slope	R Squared
16		3.25%	3.25%	-0.50%	0.01
17		Earnings Statistics	LN ROR	ROR/RMSE	Pr(ROR>0)
18		Linear Regression	3.25%	0.31	62%
19		Median	3.42%	0.32	63%
20		Mean	4.41%	0.42	66%
21		Earnings Statistics	Earnings ROR	Annualized Volatility	
22		Root Mean Square %Change	10.59%	168.18%	
23		Sigma Around Mean	9.63%	152.92%	

HistoricalEV / ImpliedEV / EVvsTime / Holidays

UA Directional Confirmation

We have established that UA's IEV was understated on July 23, 2014 and that there had been a persistent positive or bullish directional bias over the previous three years of earnings events. Before we design an option earnings strategy for UA, let's attempt to independently confirm the bullish directional forecast for the July 24, 2014 UA earnings announcement.

Analyzing the 1-day returns from past earnings announcements is the most direct approach to quantifying directional bias, but we can also evaluate earnings per share (EPS) and revenue forecasts. Stocks that beat their consensus EPS and revenue forecasts are more likely to increase in price. If we determine that UA was likely to beat its earnings and revenue expectations on July 24, 2014, then that would support our case for a bullish UA directional forecast.

Consensus revenue and EPS forecasts are widely available, but these forecasts will not help us identify candidates that are likely to beat the consensus. We need another data source that offers insights that go beyond the consensus forecasts.

Estimize.com is a *free* (as I write this) online crowd-sourced platform that aggregates EPS and revenue forecasts from investment professionals, research analysts, statisticians, professors, individual traders, and even finance students. If you are not familiar with the research on the "wisdom of crowds," then you would probably be surprised that aggregate estimates from such a wide range of individuals could offer predictive value over Wall Street's consensus forecasts, but that is exactly the case.

Research studies have demonstrated that aggregate EPS and revenue forecasts from the Estimize community are more accurate than those from sell-side analysts and that it is possible to exploit these differences to generate excess returns.

Estimize enhances their aggregate estimates by weighting each community member's forecast based on the analyst's demonstrated accuracy for that specific company. It is also possible to review the forecast for each analyst and to rank the forecasts in order of the analyst's historical accuracy. Given this data, you could even develop your own EPS and revenue aggregation model. The Estimize EPS and revenue forecasts are exactly what we need to independently confirm our directional forecast.

The Estimize UA EPS and Revenue table from fiscal Q4 2012 through fiscal Q2 2014 is provided in Figure 5.7 (with permission from Estimize). We are interested in the fiscal Q2 2014 earnings data, which is located in the column on the far right side of the table. Estimize does not offer OptionSlam's backtesting feature, so I have whited-out the actual EPS and revenue data for the quarter.

As you can see from the table, the UA Estimize EPS estimate of $0.09 per share exceeds the Wall Street consensus estimate of $0.08 per share. The difference is not large, but the direction is consistent with the bullish historical earnings return bias.

The difference between the UA Estimize revenue estimate and the Wall Street revenue forecast is more significant. The Estimize aggregate estimate of $595.40 million exceeds the Wall Street revenue forecast of $572.54 million by almost 4%. The Estimize EPS and revenue estimates both add support for our bullish directional return forecast.

Figure 5.7: Estimize UA Table

EPS	FQ4 '12	FQ1 '13	FQ2 '13	FQ3 '13	FQ4 '13	FQ1 '14	FQ2 '14
You	-	-	-	-	-	-	-
Estimize	0.24	0.03	0.08	0.34	0.28	0.06	0.09
Wall St.	0.23	0.02	0.07	0.33	0.27	0.04	0.08
Guidance	-	-	-	-	-	-	-
Actual	0.24	0.04	0.08	0.34	0.30	0.06	
YoY Growth	50%	-71%	33%	-37%	-36%	50%	

Revenue	FQ4 '12	FQ1 '13	FQ2 '13	FQ3 '13	FQ4 '13	FQ1 '14	FQ2 '14
You	-	-	-	-	-	-	-
Estimize	505.36	472.08	456.43	711.25	623.85	608.55	595.40
Wall St.	497.52	467.88	448.50	709.11	619.88	597.25	572.54
Guidance	-	-	-	-	-	-	-
Actual	506.00	472.00	454.50	723.15	682.76	642.00	
YoY Growth	26%	23%	23%	26%	35%	36%	

The ability to evaluate the actual numerical values for EPS and revenue in a table is critical, but it is often easier to identify patterns in data visually. Figure 5.8 is a graph of the UA EPS data from fiscal Q4 2012 through fiscal Q4 2014. I apologize if the chart is difficult to read, but it is a screen-capture and I had limited control over the image. Fortunately, it is easy to read online, but less so when reproduced. The solid line represents the actual EPS data, the light dashed line illustrates the EPS estimate, and the dark dashed line depicts the Wall Street EPS estimate. The fiscal Q2 2014 observation is third from the right.

We are interested in evaluating fiscal Q2 2014 for UA, but in this case, I did not white-out the most recent data. We already know from the table in Figure 5.7 that the EPS and revenue estimates for Estimize supported our bullish UA directional forecast for Q2 2014. This is more difficult to see in the chart due to the small difference between the Estimize and Wall Street EPS estimates.

The reason that I included the entire EPS history in the chart is because there is a very prominent pattern in the data. Do you see it? Take a minute to study the UA EPS chart in Figure 5.8.

Do you see the cyclical pattern in the data? UA is a retailer and retail is a very seasonal business. The fiscal Q3 and Q4 EPS data is consistently higher than the fiscal Q1 and Q2 data. This is not a random event. I emphasize this point because it illustrates the potential for creating more sophisticated directional earnings return forecasts that incorporate seasonal patterns. Building a multi-variable directional earnings forecasting model is beyond the scope of this book, but it is an exciting future research avenue that could further expand your trading edge.

You can see from the EPS chart in Figure 5.8 that prior to fiscal Q2 2014, UA had regularly beaten both Wall Street's and Estimize's EPS estimates. In addition, Estimize's estimates had been consistently more accurate than Wall Street's consensus forecasts.

Figure 5.9 is a graph of the UA revenue data from fiscal Q4 2012 through fiscal Q4 2014. The solid line represents the actual EPS data, the light dashed line illustrates the EPS estimate, and the dark dashed line depicts the Wall Street EPS estimate. The fiscal Q2 2014 observation is third from the right.

You will notice the same seasonal pattern in revenue that we saw in EPS. In addition, note that in late 2013 and early 2014, UA's actual revenues were significantly higher than consensus revenue forecasts. Estimize's revenue forecast for fiscal Q2 2014 was significantly higher than the Wall Street consensus and analysts had been consistently underestimating UA's revenues for several consecutive quarters. Both of these factors further strengthened the bullish case for UA's earnings announcement on July 24, 2014.

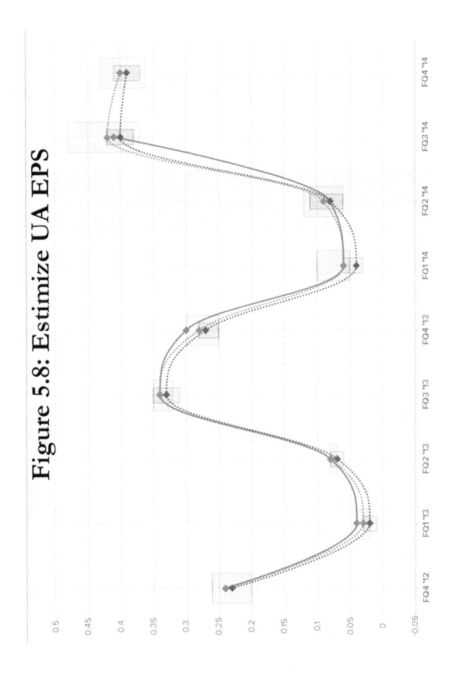

Figure 5.8: Estimize UA EPS

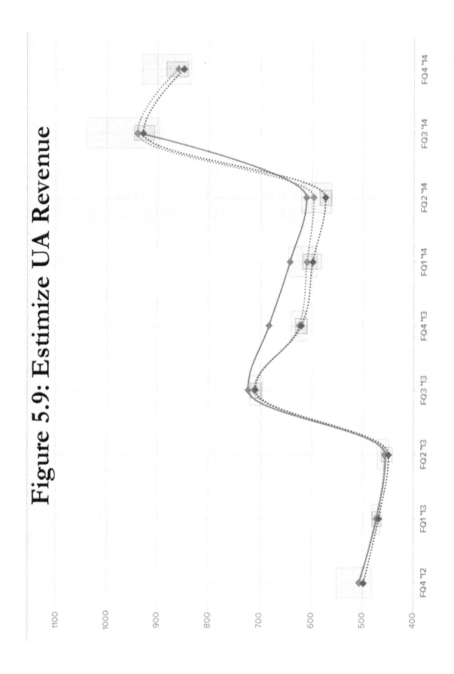

Figure 5.9: Estimize UA Revenue

Scenario Assumptions

We now have enough information to design an option earnings strategy for UA on July 23, 2014. The next step is to enter this information into the Integrated spreadsheet, which will use our forecasts in conjunction with the comprehensive volatility model in an attempt to identify the UA option strategy with the highest expected profit per unit of risk. For this example, I specified a one-day holding period from July 23, 2014 to July 24, 2014 and strategies requiring approximately $10,000 of capital (not shown). The Integrated spreadsheet can accommodate a range of holding periods and capital requirements. In this chapter, our discussion of the Integrated spreadsheet will be limited to a few select screenshots.

Figure 5.10 is a screenshot from the "Specs" Tab of the Integrated spreadsheet that shows the scenario assumptions used in all scenario and optimization calculations. As was the case in the Basic spreadsheet, cells with dark shaded backgrounds represent user inputs. Cells with white or light colored backgrounds represent calculation cells and should not be modified. Let's review several of the most important user inputs.

Relative Value Correction

You will recall that the volatility model is used to identify the relative overvaluation or undervaluation of every option in the matrix. The optimizer will attempt to implement a strategy that exploits our volatility and directional forecasts by buying undervalued options and selling overvalued options. The "Percent UV/OV Correction" (C17) represents the amount of undervaluation or overvaluation *correction* that occurs during the simulation period.

For example, if an option is undervalued (cheap) by $0.20 and the specified UV/OV correction was 100%, then the same option would be fairly priced at the end of the simulation period. In other words, 100% of the initial undervaluation would be realized. Similarly, if the specified UV/OV correction was only 25%, then the same option would be undervalued by $0.15 at the end of the simulation period; 25% of the undervaluation would be realized ((0.20-0.15)/0.20).

This input variable gives the user a tremendous amount of control over the simulation and optimization. When the holding period includes an earnings event, a higher "Percent UV/OV Correction" would be justified. I used 100% in the UA strategy example (C17).

Earnings volatility is arguably the greatest contributor to option pricing anomalies. In addition, large price changes often occur following earnings events, which forces market participants to take a fresh look at option values across the entire matrix. As a result, assuming that 100% of the pre-earnings option pricing anomalies are eliminated after earnings is not unreasonable. If you prefer a more conservative assumption, I would suggest a value between 50% and 100%.

Conversely, if the holding period *does not* include an earnings event, then the "Percent OV/UV Correction" should be much smaller, especially if the holding period is short. When the holding period does not include an earnings event, a value of 0% - 25% would be more appropriate.

Volatility Assumptions

Input cell (C16) represents the change in the 30-day at-the-money (ATM) normal implied volatility (IV) of UA options in response to a 1% increase in the price of the UA stock. The input value of negative 0.15 indicates that the ATM IV will decrease by 0.15% per 1% increase in the price of the UA. For example, if the UA ATM IV was 48% and the UA stock increased by 1%, the UA ATM IV would decline to 47.85%. When scenario inputs are required, the Integrated spreadsheet typically provides reference values to assist in the development of the scenario forecast. In this case, the historical ATM IV/price sensitivity was -0.26% (D16). This value is calculated elsewhere in the spreadsheet. I reduced the magnitude of the forecast to -0.15% due to a recent divergence from the historical value (not shown). We will explore this concept more fully in the next few chapters.

The scenario assumptions also allow the user to specify a change in the *normal* implied volatility for 30-day ATM options (F16). We do not have any justification to forecast a change in the UA normal ATM IV for 30-day options, but if we did, we would enter it here. The volatility model would use the vertical and horizontal skew and the aggregate IV formula to calculate the resulting IV changes for each option in the matrix.

Now it is time to enter our earnings volatility forecasts. The Integrated spreadsheet calculated the historical earnings volatility of 136.76% (F19) over the twelve previous earnings events, which was also calculated in the Basic spreadsheet (Figure 5.4). Earlier in this chapter, we noted the dramatic increase in historical earnings volatility from 136.76% over twelve events, to 168.18% over six events, to 200.98% over four events. Given the recent trend in earnings volatility, I entered 152% (C19) as a conservative estimate of the *realized* annualized earnings volatility, which was between the twelve quarter earnings volatility (136.76%) and the six quarter earnings volatility (168.18%).

The integrated spreadsheet also calculated an implied earnings volatility of 137.2% (E19) using the comprehensive volatility model, which was estimated using every option in the UA matrix. In addition to entering the *realized* earnings volatility above, the Integrated spreadsheet also allows the user to enter a new value for the *implied* earnings volatility (D19).

The realized earnings volatility affects the variability of the UA scenario price changes over our one-day holding period, which will include the effects of the earnings announcement. A user-specified change in implied earnings volatility would affect the valuation of options that include multiple earnings events (those with expiration dates beyond three months). The July 23, 2014 IEV of 137.2% was consistent with historical IEV values, so I used the value of 137.2% in the scenario analysis.

Directional Assumptions

Earlier in this chapter, we discussed the directional bias of previous UA earnings. The regression estimate (+6.237%), median (+3.109%), and mean (+2.410%) log-returns for the twelve previous earnings events are all positive (D21:F21), which indicated a bullish directional bias. We used the Estimize estimates to confirm this directional bias was also present in UA's EPS and revenue forecasts for fiscal Q2 2014. Based on this information, I entered a conservative directional forecast of +2.000% (C21).

Transaction Costs

Let's ignore Row 21 of the Integrated spreadsheet for now and turn to transaction costs, which have a major impact on the performance of all option strategies. The Integrated spreadsheet allows the user to enter two variables for transaction costs. The first value titled "Spread Slippage" represents the difference between the purchase and sales prices relative to the mid-price of a spread.

What is a spread? A spread is the simultaneous purchase and sale of two options of the same type. In other words, a call spread involves buying one call option and selling a second call option with a different expiration date, strike price, or both. The optimization solutions will include some combination of call spreads, put spreads, and straddles or strangles.

I have specified a Spread Slippage of negative $0.10 per spread, per share, per contract (C25). If the mid-point of the spread was $1.25, a spread slippage of negative $0.10 means that we would purchase the spread for $1.35 and sell the spread for $1.15, which would result in a round-trip transaction cost of negative $0.20 per spread. The resulting round trip transaction cost of negative $0.20 would be multiplied by the number of spread contracts and by the number of shares per contract.

For example, our optimal UA strategy will require 62 spread contracts. To find the transaction costs resulting from slippage, we would multiply 62 spread contracts by 100 shares per contract, by negative $0.20. The total round-trip transaction cost due to slippage would be negative $1,240.

Please note that the negative $0.10 spread slippage does not reflect the quoted bid and ask prices for UA options, which would probably be much wider than plus or minus $0.10 from the mid-price. As a rule, options should never be sold at the quoted bid price or purchased at the quoted ask price. Instead, limit orders should be used to execute option transactions near the mid-point between the bid and ask prices.

In addition to spread slippage, the Integrated spreadsheet allows the user to specify a second type of transaction cost: a per contract brokerage commission. I have assumed a per contract commission of negative $0.75 (D25) per contract. The transaction cost calculation assumes that the negative $0.75 per contract cost applies to both purchases and sales on every contract, not on every spread.

The 62 spreads would include a total of 124 contracts. If we incurred a transaction cost of negative $0.75 per contract purchased and negative $0.75 per contract sold, the total commission cost on 124 contracts (62 spreads) would equal negative $186.00. When combined with the spread slippage calculated above, the total round-trip transaction cost for the optimal UA strategy would be negative $1,426.

For a strategy that only requires approximately $10,000 in total capital, a round-trip transaction cost of negative $1,426 has a major impact on the performance of the strategy. That is why it is expressly included in the scenario analysis and optimization process.

	B	C	D	E	F
15	**Figure 5.10: Scenario Assumptions**	Value	Historical	Assumption	Δ ATM IV30
16	Δ ATMIV / 1% Δ Price Increase	-0.15%	-0.26%	Normal IV	0.00%
17	Percent UV/OV Correction	100.00%			
18	Scenario Assumptions	Realized	Implied(U)	Implied(M)	Historical
19	Earnings Volatility	152.00%	137.20%	137.20%	136.76%
20	Scenario Assumptions	Realized	Regression	Median	Mean
21	LN of Earnings Price Return	2.000%	6.237%	3.109%	2.410%
22	Scenario Assumptions	MinROR	MaxROR	Min	Max
23	Min/Max ROR IVPrice	-30.00%	30.00%	-95.82%	44.54%
24	Scenario Assumptions	Spread Slippage	Commission per Contract		
25	Transaction Costs	-0.10	-0.75		

Optimal UA Solution

Figure 5.11 is a screenshot from the "Opt" tab of the Integrated spreadsheet that shows the optimal UA solution found by the Solver optimizer. There are eight columns from left to right: amount (number of contracts), type (call or put), strike price, expiration date (YYMMDD), T-Days (number of trading days until expiration), Mid Price, T-Delta (True Delta), and Rich/Cheap (degree of over or undervaluation).

The call spread is shown in the first two rows, the put spread in the next two rows, and the strangle or straddle in the last two rows. Let's review the call spread first. The optimal solution requires the sale of 11 call options with a strike price of $67.50 and an expiration date of 10/18/2014 and the simultaneous purchase of 11 call options with a strike price of $70.00 and an expiration date of 8/16/2014. The mid-prices are shown for both call options as are the number of trading days remaining until expiration and the True Delta. The more interesting values are the rich/cheap values in the far right column.

Negative values indicate options that were rich or overvalued. Positive values indicate options that were cheap or undervalued. When relative values correct or move toward fair value, rich options underperform and cheap options outperform. The call option sold was rich or overvalued by $0.09 per share, per contract. The call option purchased was cheap or undervalued by $0.19 per share, per contract.

The optimal solution required the sale of 44 put options with a strike price of $64.50 and an expiration date of 8/9/2014 and the simultaneous purchase of 44 put options with a strike price of $62.50 and an expiration date of 8/30/2014. Let's focus again on the rich/cheap values in the far right column. The put option sold was rich or overvalued by $0.34 per share, per contract. The put option purchased was cheap or undervalued by $0.23 per share, per contract.

The final component of the optimal UA strategy was a diagonal strangle, which required the purchase of 7 call options with a strike price of $65.00 and an expiration date of 7/26/2014 and the simultaneous purchase of 7 put options with a strike price of $62.50 and an expiration date of 8/2/2014. In this case, the call option purchased was cheap by $0.32 per share, per contract and the put option purchased was also cheap by $0.09 per share, per contract.

The optimizer will not always be able to purchase undervalued and sell overvalued securities. In addition, the relative value correction is only one component of value added. The optimizer attempts to maximize the probability weighted expected profit of the strategy per unit of risk. The expected profit is also heavily influenced by the volatility and directional assumptions we specified earlier.

	J	K	L	M	N	O	P	Q
5				Figure 5.11: UA Optimal Solution				
6	Amount	Type	Strike	Exp Date	T-Days	Mid Price	T-Delta	Rich/Cheap
7	-11	C	67.50	141018	61	1.675	25.3	-0.09
8	11	C	70.00	140816	17	0.325	7.5	0.19
9	-44	P	64.50	140809	12	5.40	-71.3	-0.34
10	44	P	62.50	140830	27	4.05	-59.9	0.23
11	7	C	65.00	140726	2	0.55	22.3	0.32
12	7	P	62.50	140802	7	3.45	-62.5	0.09

SolveIV2 Greeks TZero CHGTU CHGTX Opt Analysis

The solution may look complicated, but only requires three spread transactions, which makes it relatively easy to manage. However, it would be virtually impossible to find this solution without the optimizer.

P&L Graph

Even for an experienced option trader, the ability to fully appreciate the nature of a strategy by mentally combining the three spreads would be very difficult. That is why we use profit and loss diagrams, which are common to all option analytical platforms. Figure 5.12 is a profit and loss (P&L) diagram for the optimal strategy described in Figure 5.11. You are probably familiar with P&L functions, but the P&L function in figure 5.12 is quite different. The scenario values accurately incorporate the effects of earnings volatility and normal volatility for every option in the matrix, as do the True Greeks.

The independent x-axis represents the UA stock price in dollars. The dependent y-axis on the left side of the diagram denotes the profit and loss of the optimal strategy for three different dates.

The solid upper "P&L 0" represents the P&L at time zero, or the instantaneous profit and loss of the strategy. The solid lower "P&L U" line represents the P&L on the future date specified by the User, which is the date used to optimize the strategy. In this example, the User date was one trading day into the future, or July 24, 2014. The solid lower "P&L X" line represents the P&L on a second future date specified by the User, which is intended to be the expiration date of the option with the shortest-term option.

In this example, the "X" date was two trading days into the future, or July 25, 2014. Given that the "U" and "X" dates are only separated by one day, the lower lines overlap and only appear as a single solid (lower) line in Figure 5.12.

The "U" and "X" probabilities are shown by the faded dashed lines and correspond to the values on the dependent y-axis on the right side of the diagram.

In addition to the P&L graph, I have included summary statistics for the optimal strategy at the top of the diagram.

Let's examine Figure 5.12 and see what we can learn about the strategy. The optimizer always uses the User date, so let's initially focus our attention on the lower P&L line. My first observation was that virtually the entire P&L line was above the break-even or zero profit line. The price of UA before earnings on July 23, 2014 was $60.63.

The optimal strategy would have only underperformed over a very small range of UA prices, centered slightly below the current price. Given that the P&L line included round-trip transaction costs of negative $1,426, the strategy performance was remarkable. This demonstrates the potential power of selling overvalued options and buying undervalued options.

The shape of the P&L function was convex or curved upwards, indicating the strategy would have performed well for large moves up or down in the price of UA. You will recall that Gamma measures the curvature of the option price function, so based on the shape of the diagram, we would expect the optimal strategy to have positive Gamma and it does. The True Gamma was +132.3 and the traditional Black-Scholes (BS) Gamma was +97.2.

The probability function was centered above the UA price of $60.63, which reflects our bullish expected return of 2% (Figure 5.10, cell C21). The width or dispersion of the probability curves is a function of the UA normal and earnings volatility.

What explains the difference between the upper "P&L 0" line and the lower "P&L U" and "P&L X" lines? The difference is quite large, especially near the current UA price. The positive value of Gamma means that the strategy must have had a negative Theta. The True Theta was negative $1,415.5, which fully reflected the volatility crush due to passing the UA earnings date. It is interesting to note that the Black-Scholes (BS) Theta was only negative $74.70, which grossly understated the true cost of the strategy due to the passage of time.

The True Delta was +$24.8 which reflected a small bullish bias, but the BS Delta was actually negative (-$53.6), again misrepresenting the true risk of the strategy. The strategy had a positive True Normal 30 Vega (+$ 19.10) and a positive True Earnings Vega (+$19.3), which is consistent with our forecast of a higher than expected level of earnings volatility.

As stated above, the total transaction costs were negative $1,426. The expected profit (net of transaction costs) was $1,482 and the maximum loss (net of transaction costs) was negative $137. The objective function, which is what the optimizer was attempting to maximize, was the expected profit ($1,482) divided by the *absolute value* of the maximum loss ($137).

The resulting value of the objective function for the optimal strategy was an astounding 10.78, which means the probability-weighted expected profit from the strategy was 10.78 times the maximum loss. The objective function value of 10.78 represents the expected profit per unit or dollar of risk. In this case, risk was defined as the maximum loss (net of transaction costs) of the strategy in any of the discrete scenarios ($137).

So does that mean that the optimal strategy could not have lost more than $137 over the one-day holding period? No, unfortunately the strategy could have lost more than $137. *It is important to remember that the profits and losses for each of the 100 probability-weighted scenarios were based on our input assumptions.*

For example, we assumed that 100% of the undervaluation or overvaluation would correct or be eliminated during the one-day holding period. We also assumed that normal implied volatility and implied earnings volatility values would not change.

All of our input assumptions will affect the profits and losses of each of the discrete scenarios. Fortunately, we have complete control over these input values and we can use the Integrated spreadsheet interactively to examine the sensitivity of the solution to each input assumption. The more you use the spreadsheets, the more you will learn about your strategies.

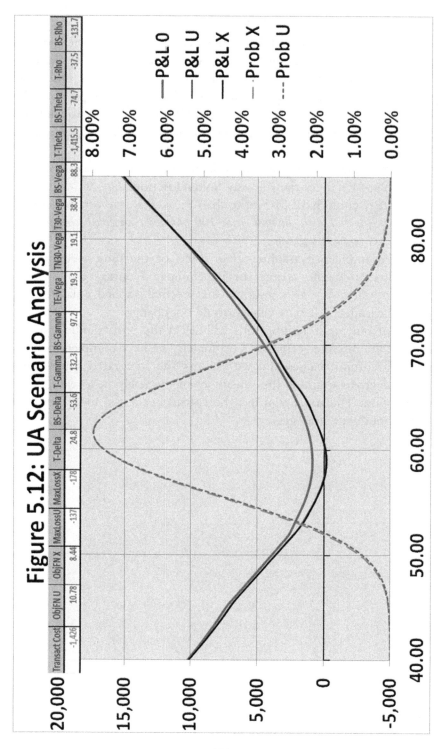

Figure 5.12: UA Scenario Analysis

Confirmation

Just as we used supplemental evidence from Estimize.com to confirm our directional earnings forecasts, it makes sense to corroborate our analytical results as well. Unfortunately, the earnings volatility framework presented in this book is new and is not widely used by the industry.

However, while writing this book I advised OptionVue on how to use and apply the aggregate implied volatility formula to quantify the effects of earnings volatility before and after earnings events. They subsequently integrated my earnings volatility framework into their OptionVue software. The spreadsheets included with this book and OptionVue's software modules are the only commercial tools that I am aware of that currently use my earnings volatility framework.

As a result, I was able to enter the optimal UA solution from Figure 5.11 into the OptionVue software and performed a graphical analysis of the strategy on July 23, 2014. OptionVue's analytical results are depicted in Figure 5.12B. OptionVue's results do not include the directional or earnings volatility forecasts that we developed throughout this chapter.

The UA stock price is shown on the independent x-axis and the strategy profit or loss (in dollars) is shown on the dependent left-vertical axis. The strategy return as a percentage of required capital is shown on the dependent right-vertical axis. The dashed line represents the strategy results for the "T+0" line, which stands for trade date plus zero days (instantaneous P&L). The solid line depicts the strategy results for the "T+1" line, which represents the P&L for a one-day holding period. These two lines are directly comparable to the strategy results shown in Figure 5.12.

OptionVue also includes two horizontal bars at the bottom of the P&L graph. The shorter top line represents a one-standard deviation price move in the common stock of the underlying security for the time horizon selected, in this case one trading day (T+1). The longer bottom line represents a two-standard deviation move for the same holding period. The one and two-standard deviation forecasts both use the aggregate implied volatility formula to accurately incorporate the effects of earnings and non-earnings volatility over the specified holding period.

While the Integrated spreadsheet model and OptionVue's model both use the aggregate implied volatility formula, the other components of the two models are completely independent: estimates of earnings volatility, directional bias, normal volatility, vertical skew, horizontal skew, and the IV/price sensitivity. The Integrated spreadsheet and OptionVue results both include estimated slippage and transaction costs. Despite the model differences, the P&L forecasts are quite similar and both clearly support the transaction.

After publication, I plan to work with OptionVue further to help them integrate any additional analytical concepts from this book that are applicable to their software. Please see the resource section at the end of this book for additional information on OptionVue's products and services, including a discounted subscription offer for *Exploiting Earnings Volatility* readers.

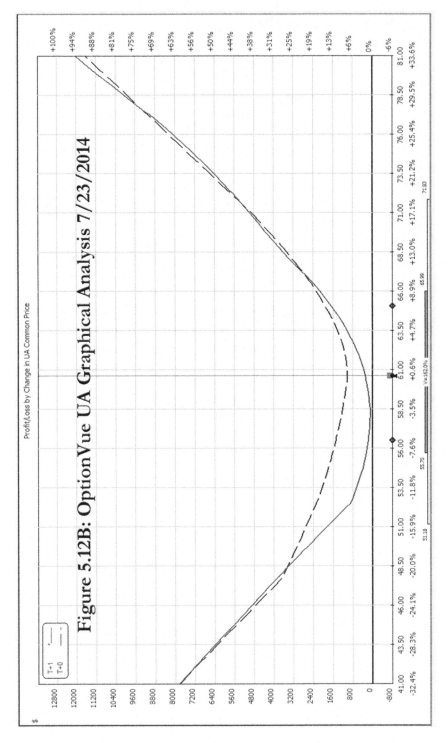

Figure 5.12B: OptionVue UA Graphical Analysis 7/23/2014

Actual Strategy Results

The value of this analytical framework should not be evaluated based on the results from a few strategy examples, but curiosity alone dictates that we ask how the strategy actually performed and how accurately the framework modeled the strategy results for the actual change in the price of UA on July 24, 2014.

Figure 5.13 is the same P&L graph from Figure 5.12 with one addition. The diamond represents the actual profit of the optimal strategy (net of transaction costs) from July 23, 2014 to July 24, 2014. The price of UA increased from $60.63 to $69.53. Our bullish forecast was correct (but understated) and the earnings volatility was also much greater than the implied earnings volatility.

As you would expect, the optimal strategy performed well, earning a total profit of $4,920 (net of transaction costs). The return on required capital of $9,044 (not shown) was 54.40% ($4,920/$9,044), not bad for a one-day holding period. At a price of $69.53, the model forecasted a strategy value of $3,780, meaning that the actual strategy performance exceeded the expected model performance. Given our assumption of a 100% UV/OV Correction, this is a little unusual, but the large change in the price of UA (+14.7%) probably increased the variability of the prices after earnings.

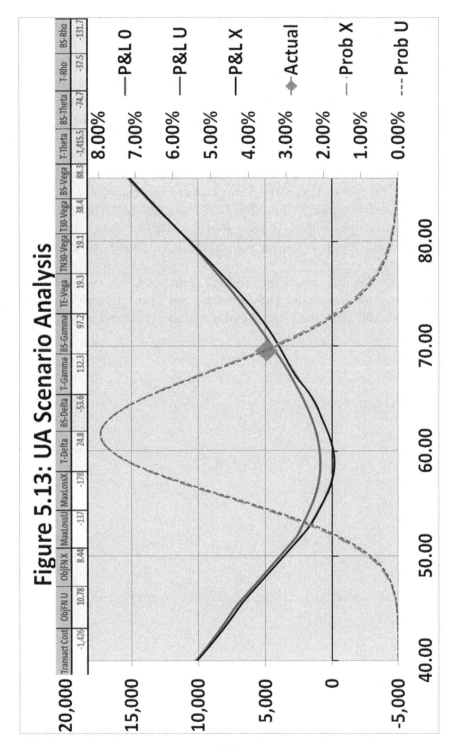

Figure 5.13: UA Scenario Analysis

Conclusion

The purpose of this chapter was to provide a practical example of how to use the *Exploiting Earnings Volatility* analytical approach and toolset to design a realistic earnings strategy, based on actual market prices and actual earnings data. The emphasis in this chapter was on the investment process and the resulting strategy, but we glossed over the mechanics of the Integrated spreadsheet.

In the next three chapters, we will examine the steps required to use the Integrated spreadsheet in practice. We completed a similar exercise in Chapter 3 for the Basic spreadsheet. However, the Integrated spreadsheet is far more complex than the Basic spreadsheet, which is why it will take a few chapters to cover the material.

While the Integrated spreadsheet functions are complex, the functions are automated and accessible via "push-button" macros, which should make the process easier to understand and apply.

6 – INTEGRATED: INPUT & IMPORT

This is the first of three chapters that will provide step-by-step instructions on how to use the second of two spreadsheets that accompany this book: the Integrated spreadsheet. Unlike the Basic Spreadsheet, the Integrated spreadsheet uses macros and requires a more recent version of Microsoft Excel to function properly. As was the case with the Basic spreadsheet, the Integrated spreadsheet is populated with data for Under Armor (UA) as of July 23, 2014.

The purpose of the next three chapters is to explain how to *use* the Integrated spreadsheet, not how to construct the Integrated spreadsheet or how to perform every intermediate calculation. If you have an interest in the intermediate calculations, please review the formulas in the spreadsheet cells.

There are two tabs that are used in both the Integrated and Basic spreadsheets that are very straightforward and will not be discussed in detail. The first is the "Holidays" tab (not shown), where you will enter the dates of exchange holidays (B3:B24) that will be used by the day-count algorithms to calculate the number of trading days throughout the Integrated spreadsheet.

The other self-explanatory tab that will not be discussed is the "Saved" tab (not shown). It is not used directly in any calculations; instead, it is provided as a convenient location to copy and paste data from other tabs that you might want to use again in the future. This will save you a great deal of time if you continue to evaluate the same stocks quarter after quarter.

There is a third tab that is included in both the Basic and Integrated spreadsheets (the "HistoricalEV" tab), but it was already discussed extensively in Chapter 3. As a result, we will not repeat that explanation in this chapter. However, please be aware that the row and column numbers in the "HistoricalEV" tab are slightly different in the two spreadsheets, but the functionality is the same.

As you read the next three chapters, keep in mind that the goal of the Integrated spreadsheet is to provide a practical tool that will help you exploit volatility, directional, and relative value anomalies to develop, optimize, and evaluate option earnings strategies in real-world environments. Before we delve into the minutia of the Integrated spreadsheet, I would like to provide an overview that should help you put the individual steps in the proper context.

Overview

Before we can use the Integrated spreadsheet to design strategies, we must provide information that will allow the Integrated spreadsheet to do all of the required analytical calculations. This information includes user specifications such as analysis dates and filter settings. Filter settings are used to determine which options are used to estimate the volatility model and which options are available as strategy candidates.

In addition, we will also have to provide information that is specific to the underlying security, such as the next earnings and dividend dates, dividend yield, and the multiplier (shares per contract). Finally, we will need to provide historical price and implied volatility data to model the ATM IV/price sensitivity.

After providing the information above, we will use the automated import function (button macro) to pull in all of the required matrix data, apply filters and error checking, and then sort and copy the resulting data to all of the analytical tabs of the Integrated spreadsheet.

We will then use the automated Solver function (button macro) to solve for the volatility parameters (including earnings volatility) that minimize the sum of the squared pricing errors across all of the options in the matrix.

Automated simulation functions (button macros) will use the volatility parameters and user-specific volatility and directional forecasts to calculate scenario-specific values for every option in the matrix, which will be used for optimization, risk management (True Greeks), and graphical analysis.

We will then enter several optimization parameters before using our choice of automated Solver functions (button macros) to identify the option earning strategy that delivers the highest expected return per unit of risk.

Finally, we will evaluate the profit and loss function and the True Greeks of the resulting strategy, which will enhance our understanding of risk and return.

The remainder of this chapter will focus on the steps required to enter data and import the matrix. Chapter 7 will explain how to use the macros to estimate the volatility model and generate the simulation data. Chapter 8 will describe how to use the macros to optimize strategies and analyze the results.

ATM IV / Price Sensitivity

As explained in Chapter 5, normal implied volatility responds to changes in the price of the underlying security. Unfortunately, the magnitude and even the direction of the changes in normal implied volatility vary widely among securities and across time.

As a result, we need to supply a representative value for the ATM IV/price sensitivity that can be used to calculate option values for each of the discrete scenarios. The ATM IV/price sensitivity represents the change in the 30-day at-the-money (ATM) normal implied volatility (IV) of UA options in response to a 1% increase in the price of the UA stock.

Before we can enter an assumed ATM IV/price sensitivity in the Integrated spreadsheet, we need to examine historical ATM IV/price sensitivities for UA, which requires historical data. We enter this data in the "IVPrice" tab of the Integrated spreadsheet, which performs all of the required sensitivity or slope calculations automatically.

Before we copy and paste the implied volatility and price data into the "IVPrice" tab, we need to clear the existing values, which are probably from an earlier analysis. To facilitate this process, I created a button with an assigned macro titled "Clear IV & Price Data (~30 Sec.)" (Figure 6.1). The "30 Sec" indicates that it takes roughly 30 seconds to run the macro, which surprised me the first time it ran. Additional time is required due to the use of Excel's lookup function to align the price and volatility data.

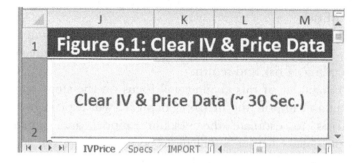

After clearing the data, the next step is to copy and paste the daily historical price and volatility data from your data source into the appropriate cells of the "IVPrice" tab. Your broker may be able to supply this data and it is available from a number of third-party data vendors, including OptionVue.

Figure 6.2 only shows the first few rows of price and IV data from the IV price tab, but thousands of rows are available to store many years of historical data. As is the case throughout the Basic and Integrated spreadsheets, the dark shaded backgrounds with white text indicate input cells. The input data begins in row three. The historical pricing dates are entered in Column O and the *adjusted* closing prices for UA are entered in Column P.

What are adjusted prices? Proportional adjustments should always be made when analyzing historical prices, which will eliminate discrete price changes due to dividends and splits. These large discrete price jumps would create large undesirable and unrealistic changes in the ATM IV/price sensitivities. In addition, please ensure that you correct any data errors and missing data points. The spreadsheet will not do this for you.

The historical IV dates are entered in Column R and the 30-day ATM normal IVs for UA are entered in Column S. If you do not have access to normal IVs, then use implied volatilities. However, the IV values should always be derived from one-month at-the-money (ATM) options. The volatility model will automatically calculate the resulting normal IV changes for all of the options in the matrix based on the estimated horizontal and vertical skew parameters.

The price and IV dates do not need to line up in the spreadsheet. As described above, Excel's lookup function will align the data correctly.

	Symbol	Pricing Date	Adjusted Closing Price		IV Date	30-Day IV
Figure 6.2: IV & Price Historical Data						
3	UA	20080501	17.35500		20080501	57.00%
4		20080502	17.28500		20080502	56.10%
5		20080505	16.86500		20080505	58.30%
6		20080506	17.51500		20080506	55.10%
7		20080507	17.35000		20080507	54.30%
8		20080508	17.25000		20080508	52.40%
9		20080509	17.10500		20080509	52.70%

IVPrice / Specs / IMPORT / SolveIV2

There are two additional user inputs required (Figure 6.3) to calculate the ATM IV/price sensitivities. The first value (D1) represents the number of trading days used to calculate the change in IV and the change in price. The second input value (G1) represents the number of observations used to calculate the ATM IV/price sensitivity or slope. I recommend using 22 for both values, regardless of your holding period.

Calculating price and IV changes over 22 trading days (roughly one calendar month) results in significant changes, which is useful when estimating an ATM IV/price sensitivity that will be applied to pricing scenarios that span a wide range of prices. Using 22 observations to calculate the slope eliminates some of the day-to-day variability that would result from using fewer observations.

Many of the cells in Figure 6.3 are intermediate calculations and therefore do not require further explanation. However, there are a few values that are relevant. The most important is the average slope of -0.263% (I1), which represents the average slope calculation for UA over the entire price and IV history. We saw this value earlier when we designed the option earnings strategy for UA in Chapter 5. You will recall that this value was provided on the "Specs" tab (Figure 5.10 cell D16) to give us a reference point when entering our own ATM IV/price sensitivity assumption.

In addition to the average ATM IV/price sensitivity -0.263% (I1), the ATM IV/price sensitivity is also calculated for every pricing date in the spreadsheet and the daily values are provided in Column G. The ATM IV/price sensitivity for UA on our analysis date of July 23, 2014 was +0.214% (not shown), which was quite different from the historical average of -0.263%. I entered an assumed ATM IV/price sensitivity of -0.15% (Figure 5.1 cell C16) when we designed the UA strategy in Chapter 5. The value of -0.15% was closer to the historical average of -0.263%, but shaded slightly higher to acknowledge the ATM IV/price sensitivity of +0.214% on July 23, 2014.

There are two more relevant values in Figure 6.3. The minimum (A1) and maximum (B1) UA returns over any 22-day (D1) period are also provided on the "IVPrice tab" and again on the "Specs" tab (Figure 5.10 Cells E23:F23). These values will be useful when setting the range of return values where the ATM IV/price sensitivity will apply (Figure 5.10 Cells C23:D23). To avoid unusual implied volatility forecasts (or negative IV values), I always ensure that my specified range is well inside the historical return values. For the UA analysis, I entered a return range of plus and minus 30% (Figure 5.10 Cells C23:D23). We will revisit these assumptions again in the next chapter.

	A	B	C	D	E	F	G	H	I
1	-95.82%	44.54%		22	X Variable	Y Variable	22	Average Slope =	-0.263%
2	Symbol	Date	Adjusted Closing Price	30-Day IV	Log Return	Change in 30-Day IV	Slope = Change in 30-Day IV per 1% increase in Log Return	Log Return (Regression Data)	
3	UA	20080501	17.35500	57.00%					
4	0	20080502	17.28500	56.10%	-0.40%	-0.90%	2.227%	-0.40%	
5	0	20080505	16.86500	58.30%	-2.86%	1.30%	-0.402%	-2.86%	
6	0	20080506	17.51500	55.10%	0.92%	-1.90%	-0.554%	0.92%	
7	0	20080507	17.35000	54.30%	-0.03%	-2.70%	-0.546%	-0.03%	
8	0	20080508	17.25000	52.40%	-0.61%	-4.60%	-0.233%	-0.61%	
9	0	20080509	17.10500	52.70%	-1.45%	-4.30%	0.343%	-1.45%	

Figure 6.3: Price / IV Slope Calculations

IVPrice / Specs / IMPORT / SolveIV2 / Greeks / TZero / CHGTU / CHGTX / Opt / Anal

Dates

The next step in using the Integrated spreadsheet is to enter the required dates. All of these dates are entered in the "Specs" tab (Figure 6.4). The first is the "Analysis Date" of July 23, 2014 (H2), which is also the pricing date. The spreadsheet assumes closing prices and does not calculate fractional days, although this is something that could be implemented in the future and would be particularly beneficial when evaluating short-term options.

The "1st User Date" is the date used for optimization purposes. For UA, I specified a User date of July 24, 2014 (H4). As was the case above, closing prices are assumed, which means the holding period for the UA optimization was one trading day.

The "2nd User Date" was designed to represent the date of the earliest option expiration. It is important to note that the optimizer will not buy or sell any options that expire before the first or second "User Dates." Since we do not yet know which options will be included in the optimal strategy, I recommend entering a "2nd User Date" equal to the "1st User Date" or equal to the first option expiration after that date.

In the UA example, the "2nd User Date" was July 25, 2014 (H5), which corresponds to the expiration date of the first weekly option series. After solving for the optimal strategy, you could always return to the "Specs" tab and enter a different "2nd User Date." As long as the "2nd User Date" falls on or after the option expiration date of the nearest-term option used in the optimal strategy, changing the date will not affect the optimization result. Both "User Dates" should obviously occur after the "Analysis Date."

	G	H	I	J
	Figure 6.4: Analysis Dates		# Trade	# Earnings
1	7/23/2014	Analysis Date	Days	Days
2	Analysis Date (Pricing Date)	7/23/2014	0	1
3	T+1 (<= All Exp Dates)	7/24/2014	1	1
4	1st User Date (<= All Exp Dates)	7/24/2014	1	1
5	2nd User Date (<= All Exp Dates)	7/25/2014	2	1

IVPrice Specs IMPORT SolveIV2 Greeks TZero

In addition to the "Analysis Date" and "User Dates" on the "Specs" tab, we also need to enter the date of the first earnings announcement (July 23, 2014 in Cell H7) and the first dividend date (August 7, 2014 – H16) that fall after the "Analysis Date." *It is extremely important to note that the earnings announcement date must correspond to the date of the close immediately preceding the next earnings announcement, not the date of the actual earnings announcement.*

In this case, the UA earnings were scheduled to be released before the open on July 24, 2014. However, if you entered an earnings date of July 24, 2014, the Integrated spreadsheet would assume the earnings announcement occurs *after* the close on July 24, 2014. *As a result, you must always enter the date of the close immediately preceding the next earnings announcement.*

As of July 23, 2014, UA did not pay dividends, so the first ex-dividend date of August 7, 2014 (H16) was arbitrary and has no effect on the analysis. The next earnings date (H7) and next dividend date (H16) are entered on the "Specs" tab (Figure 6.5).

Figure 6.5: Earnings & Dividend Dates

	G	H	I	J
			# Trade	
6	Est .Earnings Dates (AMC)	Date	Days	Years
7	Next Earnings Date E1	7/23/2014	0	0.0000
8	Next Earnings Date E2	10/22/2014	64	0.2540
9	Next Earnings Date E3	1/21/2015	125	0.4960
10	Next Earnings Date E4	4/22/2015	188	0.7460
11	Next Earnings Date E5	7/23/2015	252	1.0000
12	Next Earnings Date E6	10/22/2015	316	1.2540
13	Next Earnings Date E7	1/21/2016	377	1.4960
14	Next Earnings Date E8	4/21/2016	440	1.7460
15	**Est .Dividend Dates**	Date	# TD	Years
16	Next Dividend Ex-Date D1	8/7/2014	11	0.0437
17	Next Dividend Ex-Date D2	11/6/2014	75	0.2976
18	Next Dividend Ex-Date D3	2/5/2015	136	0.5397
19	Next Dividend Ex-Date D4	5/7/2015	199	0.7897
20	Next Dividend Ex-Date D5	8/7/2015	263	1.0437
21	Next Dividend Ex-Date D6	11/6/2015	327	1.2976
22	Next Dividend Ex-Date D7	2/5/2016	388	1.5397
23	Next Dividend Ex-Date D8	5/6/2016	451	1.7897

Holidays / HistoricalEV / Saved / IVPrice / **Specs** / IMPOR

The Integrated spreadsheet assumes that earnings will be announced quarterly and will automatically populate the subsequent seven quarterly earnings announcement dates. The Integrated spreadsheet will use these dates to determine the number of earnings trading days for each option in the matrix. Unlike the Basic spreadsheet, the Integrated spreadsheet calculates the actual number of earnings trading days for every option.

The Integrated spreadsheet also populates the dates for the subsequent seven ex-dividend dates. These dates are calculated based on the number of dividend payments per year (4), as specified in Cell D2 of the "Specs" tab, which is the first of the General Specs we will discuss (Figure 6.6).

General Specs

Another General Spec is the annual dividend yield (0%), which is entered in Cell F2. As mentioned above, UA did not pay dividends, so the annual dividend yield was 0%. If a company does pay dividends, those future dividends will affect the value of the company's options. When a stock passes its ex-dividend date, the price of the stock declines and this effect must be included when modeling option prices and implied volatilities.

Three additional General Specs are included in Figure 6.6: the annual risk-free interest rate, the option multiplier, and the American option flag. The risk free interest rate (0.25%) is entered in Cell C3 and is used in option valuation and risk analysis. The option multiplier (100) is entered in Cell C5 and is important in the calculation of the True Greeks and scenario values. In the case of UA, the American flag (Y) is entered in Cell E5, which signifies that (Yes) UA options may be exercised prior to expiration. A discrete binomial lattice that models optimal exercise at each node is required to accurately value American options.

Due to the use of Normal and Earnings volatility, which are not constant, the resulting binomial lattice will not recombine, which makes this solution method impractical. The number of nodes in a non-recombining binomial lattice increases exponentially. However, the American flag does impose some crude boundary conditions during the option valuation process.

Please note that many of the user input values in Figure 6.6 will

not change when you evaluate different stocks. Most companies pay
dividends quarterly, the risk free interest rate is not company specific,
the standard option multiplier is 100, and most stock options are
American. All of the remaining values in the table will be calculated
automatically.

	B	C	D	E	F
	Figure 6.6: General Specs		Dividends /	$ Dividend	Dividend
1	User Specifications	Value	Year	Amount	Yield
2	Underlying Price	60.63	4	0.00	0.00%
3	Risk-Free Interest Rate	0.25%			7/26/2014
4	IV	48.04%			7/26/2014
5	Option Multiplier	100	American	Y	

IVPrice | Specs | IMPORT | SolveIV2 | Greeks | TZero | CHGTU | CH

Estimation Filter Specs

We are almost ready to import the file, but we still need to specify
two sets of filters (Figure 6.7). The minimum and maximum values
for the first set of filters (C7:D14) will determine which options will
be included when solving for the volatility parameters.

The maximum number of trading days until expiration is the only
user input required in the second set of filters (F9). The minimum
number of trading days remaining until expiration will also be used as
a candidate filter, but this value will be determined by the second
"User Date" we entered earlier (Figure 6.4 Cell H5). As I mentioned
at that time, the optimizer will only consider options that expire on
or after the "User Dates."

The two sets of filters serve two very different purposes. The
objective in specifying the filters that will determine the options used
in volatility modeling is to be as inclusive as possible, while
preemptively avoiding potential pricing errors that could compromise
the integrity of the volatility model. By definition, any options
excluded from the volatility estimation would not be available as
strategy candidates either.

Let's review the filters used in the UA analysis on July 23, 2014
(Figure 6.7). Columns C and D represent the minimum and
maximum acceptable filter values for the volatility estimation. I have
specified a minimum option price of $0.20 (C7). Low priced options
are typically either very short-term, out of the money, or both. In

such cases, large changes in implied volatility are required to affect the option values. If these options were mispriced, even by seemingly insignificant amounts, the resulting implied volatility errors would be very large, which would compromise the accuracy of our volatility model parameters.

Notice that the maximum filter for the option price is grayed out (D7), which means that it is not applicable and should not be used during the filtering process. This will be true for several of the filter rules. Remember that user input cells are always shown with a dark shaded background with white text.

I have entered two days as the minimum number of trading days (C8) and 504 as the maximum number of trading days (D9) remaining until expiration for the estimation filters. To ensure an accurate volatility model, leaps should be included. I probably could have excluded the maximum number of trading days filter entirely. Unless long-term options are systematically and dramatically mispriced, they should be included in the volatility estimation.

I included liquidity filters for minimum volume (C10) and minimum open interest (C11), but both have zero values and I typically do not recommend filtering on volume or open interest. Even options with zero open interest or volume can be quite liquid. Liquidity is more a function of the total option volume and total open interest than a function of the volume or open interest of an individual option in the matrix. Obviously it would not make sense to apply maximum volume and open interest filters and these values are grayed out.

I entered the minimum and maximum Call Delta (per contract) filters of +4.0 (C12) and +96.0 (D12) respectively. The rationale for these filters is similar to the argument used for the minimum option price. Given an option multiplier of 100, the minimum and maximum possible Call Deltas (per contract) are zero and 100.

By excluding call options with very high or very low Deltas, we eliminate options that are extremely in or out of the money, both of which are impacted little by changes in implied volatility. As a result, if these options were mispriced, the resulting implied volatility errors would be very large, which would compromise the accuracy of our volatility model parameters.

The same argument applies to extreme Put Deltas. Put Deltas are obviously negative and I have filtered out put options with (per contract) Deltas lower than -96.0 (C13) or higher than -4.0 (D13). Finally, I have limited the maximum estimation skew (the vertical skew coefficient) to a value of 1.0 (D14). I will not explore this value here, other than to state that capping the maximum vertical skew coefficient avoids extreme and unusual volatility skew solutions and this value should not be modified. The vertical skew coefficient will be explained further in Chapter 7.

	B	C	D	E	F
	Figure 6.7: Estimation & Scenario Filter Specs				
6		Estimation Min	Estimation Max	Scenario Min	Scenario Max
7	Min Option Price	0.20			
8	Min TDays to Expire	2		2	
9	Max TDays to Expire		504		75
10	Min Volume	0			
11	Min Open Interest	0			
12	Call Delta	4.00	96.00		
13	Max Put Delta	-96.00	-4.00		
14	Max Estimation Skew		1.00		

Holidays / HistoricalEV / Saved / IVPrice / Specs / IMPORT / SolveIV2

Scenario Filter Specs

I specified a maximum of 75 trading days remaining until expiration for the *scenario* filter (Figure 6.7 Cell F9). Why would I exclude all of the option candidates with greater than 75 trading days remaining until expiration? There are three reasons: liquidity, the relative impact of earnings volatility, and practical optimizer considerations.

By limiting strategy candidates to options with fewer than 75 trading days remaining until expiration, the entire weekly series and the first three monthly options should all be included. Near-term options tend to be more liquid and are also disproportionally affected by earnings volatility. Since we are attempting to design option earnings strategies, it makes sense to ensure we use the most liquid options that are most likely to exploit earnings-related mispricing anomalies.

The other argument for eliminating option candidates with greater than 75 trading days remaining until expiration is to make it easier for the optimizer to find a solution. We will discuss strategy optimization extensively in Chapter 8, but I designed the Integrated spreadsheet to work with the free version of Solver, which has significant limitations regarding problem size, speed, and solution algorithms. Limiting the number of candidates makes it easier for the free version of Solver to find good solutions in a reasonable period of time.

The Integrated spreadsheet is complex and has many input fields. However, most if not all of the input fields in Figure 6.7 are not company-specific. In other words, once you enter your desired filter specifications, you could use the same specs for every stock and every option matrix. As you gain more experience with the spreadsheet, you will probably tweak the filter specs from time to time, but you will not need to change them every time you use the spreadsheet.

Import File Settings

I created a convenient import function (button macro) that will pull in all of the required matrix data, apply filters and error checking, and then sort and copy the resulting data to all of the analytical tabs of the Integrated spreadsheet. Before we can use that function, we need to specify the location of the import file and define the file specifications.

It should be no surprise that we will enter the file specifications on the "Specs" tab (Figure 6.8). To open and import the file, the import macro requires a file path and name, which is defined by the following user fields: symbol (UA), file path (C:\Users\Brian2012\Desktop\OVFiles\), pricing date (20140723), pricing time (1600), file type (.CSV).

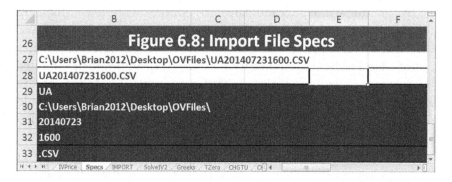

	B	C	D	E	F
26	**Figure 6.8: Import File Specs**				
27	C:\Users\Brian2012\Desktop\OVFiles\UA201407231600.CSV				
28	UA201407231600.CSV				
29	UA				
30	C:\Users\Brian2012\Desktop\OVFiles\				
31	20140723				
32	1600				
33	.CSV				

IVPrice **Specs** IMPORT SolveIV2 Greeks TZero CHGTU O

These user inputs are entered in Cells B29:B33. The Integrated spreadsheet then aggregates the input fields to create a filename (B28) and a complete file path & file name (B27), which is used by the macro.

Your file path will obviously be different, but I suggest placing all of your import files in the same directory to make it easier to use the import function. Since each file is time and date specific, you can even have multiple files for the same symbol in the same directory. The import function reads comma-separated-value or CSV files.

Import File Format

Before we can use the import macro, we must ensure the file is in the proper format and the data fields are in the correct order. I am a paying customer of OptionVue and I use their option platform to export CSV files, which I import directly into the Integrated spreadsheet using the import function (button macro). Trading Insights also has an affiliate relationship with OptionVue; please refer to the Resources section at the end of this book for additional information on OptionVue's discount offer.

Figure 6.9 is a screenshot of OptionVue's ASCII Export dialog box (with permission from OptionVue). Note the selected asset is UA and the OptionVue *export* file path and name exactly matches the *import* file path and name in Figure 6.8 of the Integrated spreadsheet. If you decide to use OptionVue to generate your import files, please use the settings from Figure 6.8.

The good news is that it is quite easy to use the OptionVue file export function in conjunction with the import function in the Integrated spreadsheet. The bad news is that we also need to define the precise format of the OptionVue export file, to ensure that it will work correctly with the import function in the Integrated spreadsheet. Fortunately, this only needs to be done once.

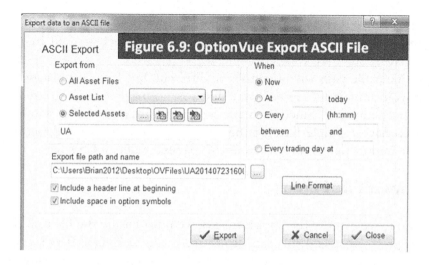

Figure 6.9: OptionVue Export ASCII File

To define the OptionVue export file format, click on the "Line Format" button in Figure 6.9. That will bring up OptionVue's Line Format screen (Figure 6.10). The right hand side (RHS) of the screen provides a list of all available parameters. The left had side (LHS) of the screen includes the list of parameters included in the export file, in the order listed.

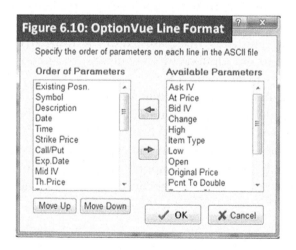

Figure 6.10: OptionVue Line Format

Simply use the buttons to move the desired fields from the RHS to the LHS and move the parameters up and down until they match the order required by the import function. The actual OptionVue parameters (in the correct order) required by the Integrated import function are provided in Figure 6.11.

Figure 6.11: OptionVue Export Field Names	
1	Existing Posn.
2	Symbol
3	Description
4	Date
5	Time
6	Strike Price
7	Call/Put
8	Exp. Date
9	Mid IV
10	Th. Price
11	Bid
12	Asked
13	Percent O/U
14	Volume
15	Open Interest
16	Delta
17	Gamma
18	Vega
19	Theta
20	Rho
21	Prob.Finish.ITM
22	Last

Once you create your desired export file format in OptionVue, all of your export files will automatically be created in this format. You will not need to use the "Line Format" button every time you export a file.

Data Field Formats

If you are using OptionVue to generate these files, you can proceed to the import functions. However, if you are using another vendor or your broker to create these files, then we need to discuss the format further.

Figure 6.12 is a screenshot of the left-hand-side (LHS) of the first 26 lines of the "IMPORT" tab of the Integrated spreadsheet (after importing the UA file). Figure 6.13 is a screenshot of the right-hand-side (RHS) of the first 26 lines of the "IMPORT" tab of the Integrated spreadsheet. The number of fields (columns) made it impossible to include all of the "IMPORT" data fields in a single screenshot. Please refer to the screenshots of the "IMPORT" tab as I review the format requirements for each import field in the CSV file.

The CSV file begins with a header row, with one title for each of the fields or columns. *The first row of actual data must always be for the underlying stock.* If not, then the import function will not work properly.

The first column (existing position) is not imported into the spreadsheet, but must be present in the import file. The next two columns are symbol (Column B) and description (Column C), which should not require a specific format. The analysis date field (Column D) is very important and it must use the YYMMDD format. The accompanying time field (Column E) does not require a specific format.

The strike price field (Column F) is next and should include a decimal place when needed. The next field (Column G) is used to designate a Call (C) or Put (P) option; note the use of capital letters. The expiration date field (Column H) is also very important and must also use the YYMMDD format.

The MID IV field (Column I) represents the implied volatility at the mid-price between the bid and ask prices. Decimals must be included and a value of 0.895 would represent an annualized implied volatility of 89.5%.

The next three fields are Theoretical Price (Column J), Bid Price (Column K), and Ask Price (Column L), all of which should include decimals when necessary. The values in these columns represent option prices per share, not per contract. All of the above fields are shown in Figure 6.12.

	Symbol	Description	Date	Time	Strike Price	Call/Put	Exp.Date	Mid IV	Th.Price	Bid	Asked
0.000	UA	UA Common								60.62	61
IMPORT CSV	UA 14G67.5D25	JulW4 67.5 Calls	140723	16:00:00	67.5	C	140726	0.895	0.19	0.15	0.3
	UA 14G66.5D25	JulW4 66.5 Calls	140723	16:00:00	66.5	C	140726	0.894	0.3	0.2	0.45
	UA 14G66D25	JulW4 66 Calls	140723	16:00:00	66	C	140726	0.902	0.37	0.3	0.5
User Filter	UA 14G65.5D25	JulW4 65.5 Calls	140723	16:00:00	65.5	C	140726	0.901	0.46	0.4	0.55
	UA 14G65D25	JulW4 65 Calls	140723	16:00:00	65	C	140726	0.894	0.56	0.5	0.6
Error Filter	UA 14G64.5D25	JulW4 64.5 Calls	140723	16:00:00	64.5	C	140726	0.924	0.67	0.65	0.75
	UA 14G64D25	JulW4 64 Calls	140723	16:00:00	64	C	140726	0.902	0.8	0.7	0.85
OPT Sort	UA 14G63.5D25	JulW4 63.5 Calls	140723	16:00:00	63.5	C	140726	0.926	0.95	0.85	1.05
	UA 14G63D25	JulW4 63 Calls	140723	16:00:00	63	C	140726	0.928	1.11	0.95	1.25
Copy IMPORT	UA 14G62.5D25	JulW4 62.5 Calls	140723	16:00:00	62.5	C	140726	0.946	1.3	1.2	1.4
	UA 14G62D25	JulW4 62 Calls	140723	16:00:00	62	C	140726	0.943	1.5	1.35	1.6
IMPORT Combo	UA 14G61.5D25	JulW4 61.5 Calls	140723	16:00:00	61.5	C	140726	0.966	1.71	1.6	1.85
	UA 14G61D25	JulW4 61 Calls	140723	16:00:00	61	C	140726	0.981	1.95	1.9	2.05
	UA 14G60.5D25	JulW4 60.5 Calls	140723	16:00:00	60.5	C	140726	0.986	2.19	2.15	2.3
	UA 14G60D25	JulW4 60 Calls	140723	16:00:00	60	C	140726	0.961	2.45	2.3	2.55
	UA 14G59.5D25	JulW4 59.5 Calls	140723	16:00:00	59.5	C	140726	0.971	2.72	2.6	2.85
	UA 14G59D25	JulW4 59 Calls	140723	16:00:00	59	C	140726		3.01	2.95	3.2
	UA 14G58.5D25	JulW4 58.5 Calls	140723	16:00:00	58.5	C	140726		3.32	3.2	3.6
	UA 14G58D25	JulW4 58 Calls	140723	16:00:00	58	C	140726		3.65	3.5	3.9
	UA 14G57.5D25	JulW4 57.5 Calls	140723	16:00:00	57.5	C	140726		4	3.9	4.4
	UA 14G57D25	JulW4 57 Calls	140723	16:00:00	57	C	140726		4.36	4.1	4.6
	UA 14G56.5D25	JulW4 56.5 Calls	140723	16:00:00	56.5	C	140726		4.74	4.3	5.1

Figure 6.12: Import Macro Buttons & Import Data (LHS)

Holidays | HistoricalEV | Saved | Specs | IVprice | IMPORT | SolveIV2 | Greeks | TZero | CHGTU | CHGTX | Opt | Analysis

The remaining fields are shown in Figure 6.13. The Percent O/U field (Column M) represents the percent overvalued or undervalued. The next two fields are Volume (Column N) and Open Interest (Column O). The next five columns represent the Greeks: Delta (Column P), Gamma (Column Q), Vega (Column R), Theta (Column S), and Rho (Column T). All of the Greek values are per contract, not per share. In other words, the per contract Greeks equal the per share Greeks multiplied by the option multiplier. The next field (Column U) is the probability of finishing in the money (ITM) and the last field (Column V) is the last transaction price.

Given that the Integrated spreadsheet calculates the True Greeks, it might seem strange to import Greek values from an outside source, but we have a chicken and an egg problem. It is beneficial to use Delta to filter the data before estimating the volatility model, but we can't calculate the value of True Delta before estimating the volatility model. That is why we need to import this data. The same reasoning applies to the Mid IV data.

In addition, some of the import data is not used by the Integrated spreadsheet. I use the same OptionVue export file format for different option research projects and all of the data in the Export file is not required by the Integrated spreadsheet. However, the column format and order is important, because the Integrated spreadsheet retrieves the required data from specific columns.

The most important data fields are all date fields, all price fields, strike price, call/put, MID IV, Delta, Vega, and volume and open interest (if you plan to filter on those fields). The description and symbol fields are important for identification purposes, but not for analytical purposes.

Percent O/U	Volume	Open Interest	Delta	Gamma	Vega	Theta	Rho	Prob.Finish.ITM	Last
0.184	20115		1	0	0				60.63
0.083	496	23	9.281	3.657	0.889	-13.103	0.043	0.111	0.24
0.081	63	20	13.406	4.644	1.161	-17.053	0.062	0.146	0.27
0.033	47	56	15.837	5.134	1.301	-19.602	0.073	0.167	0.42
-0.018	89	603	18.507	5.605	1.44	-21.827	0.086	0.19	0.4
0.045	1627	40	21.404	6.046	1.575	-23.725	0.099	0.214	0.5
-0.031	226	81	24.511	6.447	1.703	-27.442	0.113	0.241	0.67
0	68	35	27.806	6.799	1.821	-28.498	0.128	0.269	0.76
0	96	3185	31.261	7.092	1.926	-31.625	0.144	0.299	0.93
-0.009	151	58	34.848	7.321	2.015	-33.473	0.161	0.331	1.12
0	356	546	38.533	7.483	2.088	-35.744	0.177	0.365	1.33
-0.017	2285	115	42.2	6.276	2.142	-36.758	0.194	0.4	1.54
0.009	345	683	45.012	5.504	2.176	-38.475	0.211	0.436	1.75
0.013	95	276	47.752	5.482	2.191	-39.427	0.228	0.472	1.98
0.016	155	521	50.479	5.495	2.187	-39.585	0.245	0.51	2.16
-0.01	2267	206	53.219	5.55	2.163	-38.107	0.261	0.547	2.45
0.002	67	545	56.618	7.573	2.12	-37.584	0.277	0.585	2.7
0.022	22	89	60.381	7.486	2.059	-36.254	0.293	0.622	3
0.024	37	3519	64.087	7.331	1.98	-34.559	0.308	0.658	3.38
0.014	156	335	67.702	7.108	1.885	-32.544	0.323	0.693	3.6
0.038	69	187	71.192	6.821	1.777	-30.264	0.337	0.727	3.88
-0.002	60	132	74.527	6.478	1.656	-27.782	0.349	0.759	4.4
-0.008	2		77.681	6.084	1.527	-25.167	0.361	0.789	4.67

Worksheet tabs: Holidays, HistoricalEV, Saved, IVPrice, Specs, IMPORT, SolveIV2, Greeks, TZero, CHGTU

Figure 6.13: Import Data (RHS)

Import Functions

Now that we have an import file in the proper format, we can run the import function. Actually, there are several Import functions (button macros), all of which are located on the LHS of the "IMPORT" tab (Figure 6.12). The good news is that you should only need to use the last import function titled "IMPORT Combo," which performs all of the import functions in the proper sequence.

When I created the spreadsheet, I wrote all of the import-related macros individually. The top five buttons on the LHS of the "IMPORT" tab correspond to the five individual macro functions performed by the "IMPORT Combo" macro discussed above. All of the functions must be performed in the proper sequence before beginning the analytical process. Even though you should not need to use the individual macros, I left the individual macro buttons in the spreadsheet to allow me to identify the source of any errors that might occur during the import process.

Here is a brief explanation of the individual macro functions. The "IMPORT CSV" macro does exactly what its name implies; it imports all of the matrix data from a correctly formatted CSV file into the appropriate columns of the "IMPORT" tab.

The "User Filter" macro function applies the filter settings from Figure 6.7 to the option matrix, eliminating any options that do not meet the user-specified filter criteria.

The "Error Filter" macro applies some basic error-checking procedures to the remaining options and removes any options that are flagged during the process. For example, in order to apply the volatility model, an implied volatility must be calculated for each option. If a large pricing error prevented the option model for solving for implied volatility (due to an option price below the intrinsic value for example), then that option would be excluded. Keep in mind that these error filters can only identify glaring pricing errors and that the user is responsible for ensuring the integrity and accuracy of the data. Inaccurate or incorrectly formatted data will result in errors, invalid results, or both.

The "OPT Sort" function performs a multi-layered sort on all of the options in the matrix that satisfy all of the filters and pass the error-checking process. The options are sorted first by type with calls at the top and puts at the bottom. Within the calls and puts, the options are sorted in ascending order of trading days remaining until expiration (shortest to longest). The final layer sorts the options in descending order of strike price.

All of the analytical tabs in the Integrated spreadsheet require a common dataset. "Copy IMPORT" is the final import-related function, which copies the filtered, error-checked, sorted option matrix from the "IMPORT" tab to each of the analytical tabs of the

Integrated spreadsheet.

All of the import-related macro functions (including the sort) must be performed before beginning the analytical processes. To reduce potential problems with the analytical functions or the optimizer, I suggest that you always run the "IMPORT Combo" macro function and ignore the individual import macro functions. The "IMPORT Combo" macro function runs the individual import-macro functions in the proper order and prepares the Integrated spreadsheet to perform all of the analytical calculations.

Summary

At first glance, the amount of input data required by the Integrated spreadsheet might seem daunting; so let's review the day-to-day input process, assuming that we have already developed procedures to supply the necessary data in the proper format - which is a one-time project.

The first step is to copy and paste the price and IV history. We then need to enter the three analysis dates, the next earnings date, the next dividend date, and the dividend yield. The remaining general specs and filter specifications should be consistent for the vast majority of stock candidates and should require few changes.

To describe the import file name, we need to enter the symbol, the analysis date, and the time. One final step: push the "IMPORT Combo" button. That's it. Once you have developed a procedure to generate the input data, the input process for the Integrated spreadsheet should be fast and efficient.

7 – INTEGRATED: VOLATILITY MODEL & SIMULATION

This is the second of three chapters that provide step-by-step instructions on how to use the Integrated spreadsheet. As a reminder, the Integrated spreadsheet is populated with data for Under Armor (UA) as of July 23, 2014, which is the same stock for which we designed an option earnings strategy in Chapter 5.

In Chapter 6, we entered all of the required input data and imported the UA option matrix. In this chapter, we will review the steps required to use that data to simultaneously solve for all of the parameters of the volatility model, including the implied earnings volatility (IEV). For those of you who would like to learn more about the structure of the volatility model, I will also explain how the volatility model parameters are used to describe the vertical and horizontal skews.

After solving for and explaining the volatility model parameters, we will examine the steps required to generate the simulation results, which will be used to calculate the True Greeks and to optimize earnings strategies.

Volatility Model Estimation

Estimating the parameters of the volatility model is an optimization problem. As was the case for the Basic spreadsheet in Chapter 3, the Integrated spreadsheet uses Solver, which is included with Microsoft Excel as a free Add-in. As I explained in Chapter 3, if you have never used Solver before, then you will first need to enable the Solver Add-in in your version of Excel. This exact procedure will depend on your version of Microsoft Excel. In MS Office 2010, you would use the following button sequence:

File => Options => Add-Ins => Manage Excel Add-ins => Go

This will bring up the Add-in screen we reviewed in Chapter 3 (Figure 3.5), which you can use to enable the Solver Add-in. You may need to browse to find the Solver Add-in.

The optimization problems in the Integrated spreadsheet are more complex than the problems we solved using the Basic spreadsheet. As a result, I created macros that run Solver automatically in the Integrated spreadsheet. However, you will still need to enable the Solver Add-in and may also need to add the Solver VBA reference to allow Solver to be run from Visual Basic (VBA). The macro uses VBA Solver function calls, so these macros may not be compatible with non-Microsoft, out-of-date, or non-English language versions of Excel. Please refer to your Excel documentation for further instructions on managing and enabling Add-ins.

Figure 7.1 is a screenshot of the Solver problem used to estimate the volatility model parameters. We will use the Solver macro to solve this problem, so you will not see this screen in practice, but it is still a convenient way to describe the problem. In this section, I will also refer to Figure 7.2, which is a partial screen capture from the "SolveIV2" tab. Figure 7.2 includes a table with the results of the UA volatility model estimation on July 23, 2014. It also shows the macro buttons that are used to estimate the volatility model. The Solver problem displayed in Figure 7.1 references cells that are depicted in Figure 7.2.

Solver Volatility Model

Every optimization problem requires an objective or goal, typically something that we are attempting to minimize or maximize. In the case of the volatility model (Figure 7.1), we are attempting to minimize the value in Cell S12 (Figure 7.2), which represents the root mean squared error (RMSE) of the prices of every option in the matrix that met our filter criteria. The pricing errors are *approximated* using the errors in implied volatility and the input Vega, adjusted for the percentage of normal trading days.

To meet the objective, an optimizer must systematically change the adjustable or decision variables, which in this case represent the volatility model parameters that quantify the vertical skew, the horizontal skew, and the implied earnings volatility (IEV). The volatility model parameter values are contained in the following Cells: S4, S6:T8, U6:V6, U8:V8. The list of decision variables is shown in Figure 7.1 and the specific adjustable cells can be seen in the table in Figure 7.2.

Notice that the "Make Unconstrained Variables Non-Negative" check-box in Figure 7.1 is *unchecked*, indicating that the unconstrained volatility parameters may be negative. Finally, the solving method shown in Figure 7.1 is "GRG Nonlinear" because the volatility functions are non-linear and Solver uses the Generalized Reduced Gradient (GRG) Algorithm to process these nonlinearities.

I will explain the volatility parameters and the associated constraints in detail later in this chapter. For now, let's continue to focus on running Solver and on the UA volatility model solution's summary statistics.

There are two Solver macro buttons shown in Figure 7.2. The "Randomize Volatility Parms" macro should be run first, followed by the "Estimate Volatility Model" macro. As described earlier, the volatility model contains non-linear functions, which makes it more difficult for an optimizer to solve. Optimizers often get stuck on a local optimal solution of a non-linear function, which may prevent the software from finding the global optimal solution. As a result, the success of a non-linear optimization is dependent on the initial conditions. That is why I included the "Randomize Volatility Parms" macro: to provide different starting points for the optimization procedure.

Unlike a simple linear programming optimization problem, there is no guarantee that an optimizer will be able to identify the best possible solution for non-linear problems. Fortunately, the Solver volatility model estimation runs relatively quickly and you can rerun the optimization with a new set of initial parameter values if you are not satisfied with your results.

So how can we evaluate the estimation results? The first step is to check the Solver return value, which will allow us to verify that Solver ran correctly and did not experience any errors. In the UA estimation, the Solver return value was zero (X4). A list of Solver return values and their descriptions from the Frontline (Solver Vendor) website is shown in Figure 7.3. A return value of zero indicates that "Solver found a solution. All constraints are satisfied."

Now we are interested in evaluating how well the volatility model solution explains the volatility structure of the UA matrix. The Solver solution resulted in an objective function value of $0.175 (S12), which represents the root mean squared pricing error for the 348 (R3) options used in the estimation process. The root mean squared normal volatility error was 12.23% (S10).

You may be familiar with the term "R-Squared" which is often used in linear regression to explain how well a statistical model fit the underlying data. R-Squared represents the percentage of variance in the data explained by the model. As a result, the value of R-Squared must be between zero and one (100%). A value of one or 100% would indicate that 100% of the variance in the data is explained by the model. The R-Squared of the UA model was 0.869 or 86.9% (S3).

	R	S	T	U	V	W	X	Y
1								
2		RSquared	**Figure 7.2: Volatility Model Solver Solution**					
3	348	0.869	C	Min EV	Min A	Max Parm	Solver Result	
4	Implied EV	137.20%	8.64%	1.10%	1.10%	600.00%	0	
5		ATMIV (Call)	ATMIV (Put)	VSlope	VCurve			
6	B	299.78%	-3.81%	-5.74%	-10.14%	Randomize Volatility Parms		
7	C	0.67%	600.00%					
8	A	26.52%	32.34%	2.56%	21.19%			
9	IV Err^2	520.90%						
10	IV Err	12.23%		IV Error	$ Error	Estimate Volatility Model		
11	Price Err^2	10.61	Max Pos	69.95%	0.44			
12	Price Err	0.175	Max Neg	-50.15%	-0.68			

Holidays HistoricalEV Saved IVPrice Specs IMPORT SolveIV2 Greeks TZero CHGT

Figure 7.3: Frontline Solver Return Values

SolverSolve Return Value

If a Solver problem has not been completely defined, **SolverSolve** returns the #N/A error value. Otherwise the Solver runs, and **SolverSolve** returns an integer value corresponding to the message that appears in the Solver Results dialog box:

0   Solver found a solution. All constraints and optimality conditions are satisfied.

1   Solver has converged to the current solution. All constraints are satisfied.

2   Solver cannot improve the current solution. All constraints are satisfied.

3   Stop chosen when the maximum iteration limit was reached.

4   The Objective Cell values do not converge.

5   Solver could not find a feasible solution.

6   Solver stopped at user's request.

7   The linearity conditions required by this LP Solver are not satisfied.

8   The problem is too large for Solver to handle.

9   Solver encountered an error value in a target or constraint cell.

10   Stop chosen when the maximum time limit was reached.

11   There is not enough memory available to solve the problem.

13   Error in model. Please verify that all cells and constraints are valid.

14   Solver found an integer solution within tolerance. All constraints are satisfied.

15   Stop chosen when the maximum number of feasible [integer] solutions was reached.

16   Stop chosen when the maximum number of feasible [integer] subproblems was reached.

17   Solver converged in probability to a global solution.

18   All variables must have both upper and lower bounds.

19   Variable bounds conflict in binary or alldifferent constraint.

20   Lower and upper bounds on variables allow no feasible solution.

When I initially ran the UA volatility model estimation, I was disappointed by the magnitude of the $0.175 (Figure 7.2 Cell S12) pricing error and by the 12.23% (Figure 7.2 Cell S10) normal volatility error. I had used the estimation model many times before and the magnitude of the UA errors was higher than usual. I reviewed the individual pricing errors in Column Q of the "SolveIV" tab (subset shown in Figure 7.5) and determined that there were *systematic pricing anomalies* in the UA matrix. Note, the anomalies were not pricing errors; they represented undervalued and overvalued options. We exploited these pricing anomalies when we designed the optimal option earnings strategy for UA in Chapter 5.

If you are not satisfied with the results of the Solver volatility model estimation and rerunning Solver with different initial parameter values does not resolve the problem, there are two other options that may improve the model results. The first is to modify the parameters Solver uses to run the optimization algorithm (Figure 7.4).

	AB	AC
3	**Figure 7.4: Solver Parameters**	
4	Option Name	Value
5	MaxTime	300
6	Precision	0.000010
7	Derivatives	2
8	IntTolerance	1
9	Convergence	0.0000001
10	AssumeNonNeg	FALSE
11	PopulationSize	1,000
12	RandomSeed	0
13	RequireBounds	FALSE
14	MutationRate	0.25
15	MaxTimeNoImp	60

IMPORT   SolveIV2   Greeks

The Solver macro reads the parameter values from the dark shaded cells in Figure 7.4. If you modify these values, the Solver macro will use your parameter values during the volatility model optimization process. A description of Solver's solution parameters is beyond the scope of this book. Please refer to the Solver documentation for more information on the solution parameters. If you are not a proficient and experienced Solver user, I recommend using the initial Solver solution parameters provided in the Integrated spreadsheet.

If you discover one or two extreme pricing *errors* that are adversely affecting the quality of the volatility model estimation, you could exclude them from the estimation without modifying the filters or reimporting the matrix.

Column D on the "SolveIV2" tab represents an Exclude flag (see Figure 7.5). Normally the Exclude flag is set to zero for every option, which means that it is included in the estimation. However, if you would like to exclude one or more options due to extreme pricing errors, enter the value of one (1) in the appropriate row of Column D. *Before closing and saving the Integrated spreadsheet, remember to reset the Exclude values to zero.* Otherwise, you would exclude the option in that row in all future optimizations.

	A	B	C	D	M	N	O	P	Q
1	**Figure 7.5: Exclude Flag & Error Values**								
2									
3	Description	Call/Put	Include	Exclude	NIV Error	NIVErr SQ	VW Err	VWE SQ	UVAL
4	UA Common		0	0	0.00%	0	0	0	0
5	JulW4 67.5 Calls	C	1	0	-50.15%	0.2515451	-0.22	0.04781	0.22
6	JulW4 66.5 Calls	C	1	0	-50.15%	0.2515451	-0.29	0.081542	0.29
7	JulW4 66 Calls	C	1	0	-48.08%	0.2311842	-0.31	0.094105	0.31
8	JulW4 65.5 Calls	C	1	0	-44.59%	0.1988068	-0.31	0.099142	0.31
9	JulW4 65 Calls	C	1	0	-41.38%	0.1712166	-0.32	0.102143	0.32
10	JulW4 64.5 Calls	C	1	0	-38.46%	0.1479182	-0.32	0.10317	0.32
11	JulW4 64 Calls	C	1	0	-35.84%	0.1284518	-0.32	0.102438	0.32
12	JulW4 63.5 Calls	C	1	0	-33.53%	0.112397	-0.32	0.100269	0.32
13	JulW4 63 Calls	C	1	0	-31.52%	0.0993763	-0.31	0.097036	0.31
14	JulW4 62.5 Calls	C	1	0	-29.84%	0.0890596	-0.31	0.093378	0.31
15	JulW4 62 Calls	C	1	0	-28.49%	0.0811683	-0.30	0.089563	0.30
16	JulW4 61.5 Calls	C	1	0	-5.65%	0.0031883	-0.06	0.003631	0.06
17	JulW4 61 Calls	C	1	0	5.75%	0.0033028	0.06	0.003813	-0.06
18	JulW4 60.5 Calls	C	1	0	9.65%	0.0093165	0.10	0.010716	-0.10
19	JulW4 60 Calls	C	1	0	-9.85%	0.0096935	-0.10	0.010907	0.10
20	JulW4 59.5 Calls	C	1	0	0.52%	2.702E-05	0.01	2.92E-05	-0.01
21	JulW4 59 Calls	C	1	0	15.65%	0.0245007	0.16	0.02498	-0.16
22	JulW4 58.5 Calls	C	1	0	18.07%	0.0326596	0.18	0.030792	-0.18
23	JulW4 58 Calls	C	1	0	9.91%	0.0098146	0.09	0.008387	-0.09
24	JulW4 57.5 Calls	C	1	0	31.47%	0.0990142	0.27	0.075192	-0.27

After editing the Solver solution parameters (Figure 7.4) and/or the Exclude values in Column D (Figure 7.5), rerun the Solver macros to re-estimate the volatility model.

Volatility Model Parameters

We initially used Figure 7.2 to evaluate the Solver UA volatility model solution, but we deferred a discussion of the volatility model parameters until now. To eliminate the need to refer back to Figure 7.2, I created a second copy of the volatility model solution and parameters in Figure 7.6.

The volatility model simultaneously estimates eleven different volatility model parameters: the annualized implied earnings volatility (S4), three horizontal skew coefficients for call options (S6:S8), three horizontal skew coefficients for put options (T6:T8), two vertical skew slope coefficients (U6, U8) and two vertical skew curve coefficients (V6, V8).

We have discussed the implied earnings volatility (IEV) extensively throughout the book, so I will not go into more detail here, except to note that the IEV is estimated simultaneously with all of the other volatility model coefficients. By definition, IEV is an estimate of implied *earnings* volatility, which is the same for all of the options in the matrix. All of the other volatility model parameters are used to explain *normal* volatility, which is different for every option in the matrix. The aggregate implied volatility formula is used to combine earnings volatility and normal volatility.

	R	S	T	U	V	W	X	Y
1								
2		RSquared		**Figure 7.6: Volatility Model Solver Solution**				
3	348	0.869	C	Min EV	Min A	Max Parm	Solver Result	
4	Implied EV	137.20%	8.64%	1.10%	1.10%	600.00%	0	
5		ATMIV (Call)	ATMIV (Put)	VSlope	VCurve			
6	B	299.78%	-3.81%	-5.74%	-10.14%	Randomize Volatility Parms		
7	C	0.67%	600.00%					
8	A	26.52%	32.34%	2.56%	21.19%			
9	IV Err^2	520.90%						
10	IV Err	12.23%		IV Error	$ Error			
11	Price Err^2	10.61	Max Pos	69.95%	0.44	Estimate Volatility Model		
12	Price Err	0.175	Max Neg	-50.15%	-0.68			

Before we can estimate the normal volatility model parameters, we must first define the structure of the volatility model. In other words, we need a set of formulas that can be used to calculate the normal volatility for every option in the matrix. Those formulas must rely exclusively on objective variables that can be calculated or are observable for every option. The resulting formulas will describe two option pricing phenomenon: the horizontal skew and the vertical skew.

The normal horizontal and vertical skew sections that follow are optional material. In other words, you do not need to know the structure of the horizontal and vertical skew calculations to use the Integrated spreadsheet or to create earnings strategies.

However, understanding the horizontal and vertical skew is valuable; the volatility structure has a profound effect on option risk and returns. Gaining insight into the volatility structure will help you design and evaluate all types of option strategies, which will make you a better option trader. The formulas are not overly complicated, but are not required reading.

Unlike the aggregate implied volatility formula presented earlier, which correctly aggregates independent components of volatility and is consistent with option pricing theory, the volatility model presented in the following sections is one of many possible structures that could be used to model option volatility. There is no one definitive volatility structure or model. I designed the model with sufficient power to explain the distribution of normal implied volatilities across time and among strike prices. The model is continuous, which means that it can be used to solve for the normal implied volatility for any strike price and time to expiration, now or in the future.

Normal Horizontal Skew

Normal implied volatility varies as a function of time to expiration, reflecting the market's implied forecast of future volatility. If the current level of normal volatility is perceived as too low, then implied volatilities will increase as a function of time to expiration. If the current level of normal volatility is viewed as too high, then implied volatilities will decrease as a function of time to expiration. The normal horizontal skew function will calculate the at-the-money normal implied volatility (ATM NIV) as a function of the time remaining until option expiration (in years). The number of remaining trading days is used to calculate the time remaining until expiration.

As explained earlier, we will estimate two horizontal skew functions, one for calls and one for puts. Both functions will use the same formula or structure, but will have different coefficients. The normal horizontal skew function has three terms: an intercept, a slope, and a measure of curvature.

Let's begin with the normal horizontal skew function for at-the-money UA call options on July 23, 2014. An actual UA call option with a time to expiration of 0.08730 years (~1-month) will be used in the calculation example below.

ATM NIV_C = At-the-money call option normal implied volatility
EXP represents the Excel function e raised to a power,
e = 2.718281828
a_C = call option intercept = 26.52% (S8)
b_C = call option slope = 299.78% (S6)
c_C = call option curvature = 0.67% (S7)
T = Time to expiration in years = 0.08730 (example value)

ATM NIV_C =a_C+b_C*(1-EXP(-c_C*T))

ATM NIV_C =26.52%+299.78%*(1-EXP(-0.67%*0.08730))
ATM NIV_C =26.52%+299.78%*(1-EXP(-0.000585))
ATM NIV_C =26.52%+299.78%*(0.000585)
ATM NIV_C =26.52%+0.17% = 26.69%

Let's continue with the normal horizontal skew function for at-the-money UA put options on July 23, 2014. An actual UA put option with time to expiration of 0.08730 years (~1-month) will be used in the calculation example below.

ATM NIV_P = At-the-money put option normal implied volatility
EXP represents the Excel function e raised to a power,
e = 2.718281828
a_P = put option intercept = 32.34% (T8)
b_P = put option slope = -3.81% (T6)

c_P = put option curvature = 600.00% (T7)
T = Time to expiration in years = 0.08730 (example value)

ATM NIV_P = a_P+b_P*(1-EXP(-c_P*T))

ATM NIV_P =32.34%+ -3.814%*(1-EXP(-600.00%*0.08730))
ATM NIV_P =32.34%+ -3.814%*(1-EXP(-0.5238))
ATM NIV_P =32.34%+ -3.814%*(0.407734)
ATM NIV_P =32.34%+ -1.56% = 30.78%

The above volatility model formulas and UA coefficients can be used to calculate the at-the-money normal implied volatility for any UA call option or put option, regardless of the amount of time remaining until expiration. The solid line in Figure 7.7 (higher on the left) depicts the modeled ATM NIV for UA put options on July 23, 2014. The solid line (higher on the right) shows the estimated ATM NIV for UA call options on the same date.

We also need to define formulas and estimate the resulting coefficients of the vertical skew model to find the normal implied volatility for every option in the UA matrix. The dotted and dashed lines in Figure 7.7 illustrate the curve and slope coefficients for the vertical skew model as a function of time to expiration. We will discuss the vertical skew model in detail in the next section.

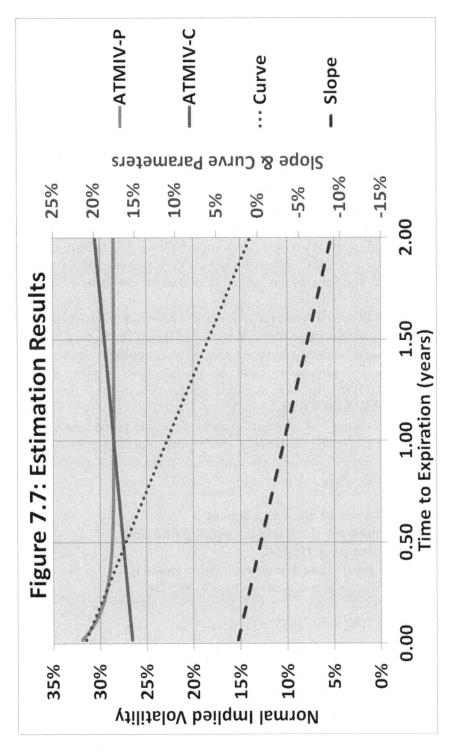

Figure 7.7: Estimation Results

Normal Vertical Skew

Normal implied volatility varies as a function of the strike price of an option in relation to the current underlying stock price. This relationship is called the vertical skew, which is driven by the market's expected magnitude of *directional* price movement. In other words, if the market expects the prices of the underlying security to fall much faster than they rise, options with relatively low strike prices will have higher implied volatilities than options with relatively high strike prices. The implied volatility relationship will be reversed when the market expects prices to rise much faster than they fall.

To model the vertical skew, we must first come up with a metric that quantifies the relative strike price, which we will call the vertical skew coefficient (VSC). We will then create a formula that expresses the normal implied volatility of any option in the matrix as a function of its VSC.

I considered several possible VSC functions, but ultimately decided to use the same function used by OptionVue in their vertical skew modeling. Their metric fit the normal implied volatility data well, and it is consistent with the Black-Scholes Option Pricing Model (BSOPM). In fact, elements of the VSC formula are taken directly from the BSOPM.

The following VSC formula expresses the difference between the strike price and the underlying stock price, adjusted for the time remaining until expiration. The following example uses specific data values for an actual UA put option on July 23, 2014.

VSC = Vertical Skew Coefficient
LN represents the Excel natural log function
K = Strike price ($56.00)
S = Current Underlying Stock Price ($60.63)
T = Time to expiration in years = 0.08730

$$VSC = LN(K/S)/(T^{0.5})$$

$$VSC = LN(56.00/60.63)/(0.08730^{0.5})$$
$$VSC = LN(0.923635)/(0.295466)$$
$$VSC = -0.079438/(0.295466)$$
$$VSC = -0.269$$

Now that we have the calculated the value of the vertical slope coefficient (VSC), we can use the formula below to calculate the normal implied volatility for the one-month (0.08730 years) UA put option with the strike price of $56. In fact, after we calculate the VSC, we have all of the information necessary to calculate the normal implied volatility for any option in the UA matrix. The following example is a continuation of the one-month (0.08730 years) UA put option for which we calculated the ATM NIV earlier in the horizontal skew section.

NIV = Normal Implied Volatility
VSC = Vertical Skew Coefficient
ATM NIV = At-the-money normal implied volatility
(calculated earlier: 30.78%)
T = Time to expiration in years = 0.08730
b_{VS} = **Vertical Skew Slope**
c_{VS} = **Vertical Skew Curvature**

$$NIV = ATM\ NIV + (b_{VS}*(VSC)+c_{VS}*(VSC^2))$$

Unfortunately, we cannot solve for the NIV until we calculate the vertical skew slope and vertical skew curvature values. Just as the ATM NIV varies as a function of the amount of time remaining until expiration (horizontal skew), the vertical skew is not constant across the term structure of volatilities either. In other words, the shape of the vertical skew curve is different for options with different expiration dates. As a result, the values of the vertical skew slope (b_{VS}) and the vertical skew curvature (c_{VS}) are both unique to options with 0.08730 years remaining until expiration.

However, it would not be practical or desirable to estimate independent vertical skew slope and curvature values independently for every option expiration date. We are ultimately interested in calculating the normal implied volatility for any option in the matrix on the initial pricing date and *at our choice of several projected dates in the future*. As a result, we need to model the vertical skew slope and curvature as a *continuous* function of the time remaining until expiration.

The vertical skew slope and curvature functions were depicted earlier in Figure 7.7 estimation results. The dotted and dashed lines in Figure 7.7 illustrate the curve and slope coefficients for the UA vertical skew model respectively. Both the vertical skew slope and vertical skew curve functions are linear, which means that both functions can be explained by slope and intercept coefficients, which are estimated simultaneously with all of the other volatility model parameters.

Below are the formulas used to calculate the vertical skew slope and vertical skew curve coefficients, both of which are expressed as a function of time remaining until expiration. The formulas below are a continuation of our earlier example, which used the one-month UA put option with a $56 strike price.

b_{VS} = **Vertical Skew Slope**
A = **Intercept (Figure 7.6 Cell U8) = 2.556%**
B = **Slope (U6) = -5.742%**
T = **Time to expiration in years = 0.08730**

b_{VS} = A + B*(T)
b_{VS} = 2.556% + -5.742%*(0.08730)
b_{VS} = 2.556% + -0.501%
b_{VS} = 2.055%

c_{VS} = **Vertical Skew Curvature**
A = **Intercept (V8) = 21.192%**
B = **Slope (V6) = -10.136%**
T = **Time to expiration in years = 0.08730**

b_{VS} = A + B*(T)
b_{VS} = 21.192% + -10.136%*(0.08730)
b_{VS} = 21.192% + -0.501%
b_{VS} = 20.307%

To refresh your memory, here is the normal implied volatility calculation that we began earlier for the one-month UA put option with the $56 strike price. The values of the vertical skew slope (2.055%) and curvature (20.307%) for the one-month UA put option were derived above.

NIV = Normal Implied Volatility
VSC = Vertical Skew Coefficient
ATM NIV = At-the-money normal IV (30.78%)
b_{vs} = Vertical Skew Slope (2.055%)
c_{vs} = Vertical Skew Curvature (20.307%)

NIV = ATM NIV + $(b_{vs}*(VSC)+c_{vs}*(VSC^2))$
NIV = 30.78% + (2.055%*(-0.269)+20.307%*(-0.269^2))
NIV = 30.78% + (-0.55%+20.307%*(0.07236))
NIV = 30.78% + (-0.55%+1.7%)
NIV = 30.78% + (0.92%)
NIV = 31.70%

Volatility Model Estimation Summary

Before we continue, let's take a step back and review the preceding volatility model calculations intuitively. The volatility model simultaneously estimates eleven different volatility model parameters: the annualized implied earnings volatility (S4), three horizontal skew coefficients for call options (S6:S8), three horizontal skew coefficients for put options (T6:T8), two vertical skew slope coefficients (U6, U8) and two vertical skew curve coefficients (V6, V8).

After estimating the volatility parameters, the next step is to use the three horizontal skew coefficients to solve for the at-the-money normal implied volatility (IV). Unfortunately, normal implied volatility also varies as a function of the strike price in relation to the current price of the underlying security. As a result, we must calculate the vertical skew coefficient (VSC) to quantify the strike price relationship.

The vertical skew also varies as a function of the time remaining until expiration, so we also need to calculate the vertical skew slope and curvature coefficients for each option. Finally, we can use all of these values to calculate the vertical skew, which can be combined with the ATM NIV to determine the normal implied volatility for each option.

Figure 7.8 shows the normal implied volatility (dependent y-axis) as a function of the vertical skew coefficient (independent x-axis) for expiration dates ranging from one week to two years (RHS legend).

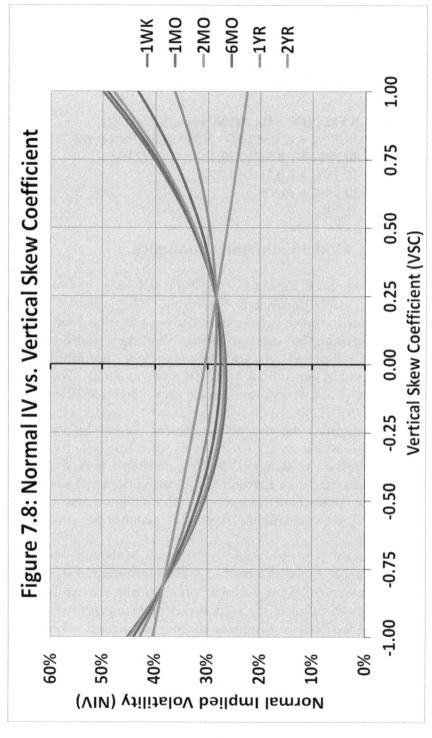

Figure 7.8: Normal IV vs. Vertical Skew Coefficient

Aggregate Implied Volatility Revisited

Now that we have estimated the normal implied volatility, how do we find the aggregate implied volatility? We use the aggregate implied volatility formula from Chapter 2 to combine the normal implied volatility and the implied earnings volatility into a single implied volatility value. Here is the aggregate implied volatility calculation for the one-month UA put option that we have used throughout this chapter.

NTD_E = **Number of Earnings Trading Days**
NTD_N = **Number of Normal Trading Days**
W_E = **Earnings Volatility Weight**
W_N = **Normal Volatility Weight**

$W_E = NTD_E/(NTD_E + NTD_N)$
$W_E = 1/(1 + 21) = 4.5455\%$

$W_N = NTDN/(NTDE + NTDN)$
$W_N = 21/(1 + 21) = 95.4545\%$

IV = Aggregate Implied Volatility (Annualized)
V_E = **Earnings Volatility (Annualized) = 137.20%**
V_N = **Normal Volatility (Annualized) = 31.70%**

$IV = ((W_E*(V_E{}^{\wedge}2))+(W_N)*(V_N{}^{\wedge}2))^{\wedge}0.5$
$IV = ((4.5455\%*(137.20\%^{\wedge}2))+(95.4545\%)*(31.70\%^{\wedge}2))^{\wedge}0.5$
$IV = ((8.5564\%)+(9.5921\%))^{\wedge}0.5$
$IV = (18.1485\%)^{\wedge}0.5$
$IV = 42.60\%$

The volatility model estimated that the annualized implied volatility of the one-month (8/23/2014) UA $56 put option was 42.60% at the close on July 24, 2014. The actual annualized implied volatility of the 8/23/2014 UA $56 put option was 42.23%.

Solver Volatility Model Constraints

The volatility model Solver solution was shown in Figure 7.2 and again in Figure 7.6. We initially focused on the Solver solution statistics and then on the volatility model parameters. In both cases, we ignored the input Cells with the dark shaded background (U4:W4) which we use to constrain the Solver solution. Now that we have reviewed all of the volatility model parameters, we can revisit the Solver constraint cells.

I specified a minimum implied earnings volatility (IEV) of 1.10% (U4), which is only applied to decision variable cell S4. I also set a minimum intercept value of 1.10% (V4), which applies to all four intercept decision variables (S8:V8). Finally, I set a minimum and maximum range of negative 600% to positive 600% (W4) for all of the decision variable cells (S6:V6), which excludes the implied earnings volatility (S4). These values should work well for many Solver problems, but you may modify these values if you would like more control over the Solver solution. *If you find the shape or curvature of the functions too extreme, I suggest reducing the maximum parameter range from plus or minus 600% to plus or minus 300%, or even lower.*

True Greeks & Simulation

Now that we have estimated the volatility model parameters for UA on July 24, 2014, we can use these values to calculate the True Greeks. In Chapter 5, we specified a number of assumptions that were used to simulate price changes for all of the options in the UA matrix. These assumptions were initially shown in Figure 5.10 and are depicted again in Figure 7.9 for easier reference.

	B	C	D	E	F
15	**Figure 7.9: Scenario Assumptions**	Value	Historical	Assumption	Δ ATM IV30
16	Δ ATMIV / 1% Δ Price Increase	-0.15%	-0.26%	Normal IV	0.00%
17	Percent UV/OV Correction	100.00%			
18	Scenario Assumptions	Realized	Implied(U)	Implied(M)	Historical
19	Earnings Volatility	152.00%	137.20%	137.20%	136.76%
20	Scenario Assumptions	Realized	Regression	Median	Mean
21	LN of Earnings Price Return	2.000%	6.237%	3.109%	2.410%
22	Scenario Assumptions	MinROR	MaxROR	Min	Max
23	Min/Max ROR IVPrice	-30.00%	30.00%	-95.82%	44.54%
24	Scenario Assumptions	Spread Slippage	Commission per Contract		
25	Transaction Costs	-0.10	-0.75		

Specs / IMPORT / SolveIV2 / Greeks / TZero / CHGTU / CHGTX / Opt

We will not review the user assumptions again, but these assumptions are used to calculate all of the scenario assumptions, including the discrete option price values used in the True Greek sensitivity calculations.

You will remember from Chapter 4 that the True Greeks represent risk measurements or sensitivities, which are derived from discrete changes in price, time, normal volatility, earnings volatility, etc. As a result, to calculate the True Greeks, we need to re-calculate how the value of each option would change in response to specific changes in each of the independent variables, including any resulting effects on the other dependent variables.

This is nothing more than a succession of price simulations, but one that requires the parameters of the comprehensive volatility model described in this chapter to accurately model normal volatility, earnings volatility, and aggregate volatility. The ability to calculate scenario-specific volatility values for each option allows us to calculate the True Greeks. All of the True Greek calculations were described in detail in Chapter 4.

The True Greek intermediate and final calculations are all stored on the "Greeks" tab of the Integrated spreadsheet, but you may run the True Greek macro from any of the following tabs: "Greeks," "TZero," "CHGTU," and "CHGTX." To run the True Greeks macro from any of these tabs, click on the button titled "T-Greeks."

Figure 7.10 is a screen shot from the "Greeks" tab that shows the location of the "T-Greeks" macro button and the "SIM ALL" macro button. The "SIM ALL" button runs the price simulations for the current pricing date ("SIM 0"), the first user specified pricing date used in the optimization ("SIM U") and the second user pricing date which typically corresponds to the expiration date of the shortest dated option ("SIM X").

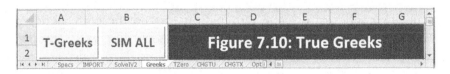

The "TZero" tab represents the current pricing date (zero time elapsed). On the "TZero" tab, you can use the following button macros: "T-Greeks," "SIM ALL," and "SIM 0" (Figure 7.11). The values for the instantaneous price simulation (July 23, 2014) are stored on the "TZero" tab.

Figure 7.11: Simulation 0

The "CHGTU" tab represents the pricing simulation results for the first user simulation date (July 24, 2014) which are used for optimization purposes. On the "CHGTU" tab, you can use the following button macros: "T-Greeks," "SIM ALL," and "SIM U" (Figure 7.12). The values for the price simulation on the first user date are stored on the "CHGTU" tab.

Figure 7.12: Simulation U

The "CHGTX" tab represents the pricing simulation results for the second user simulation date (July 25, 2014), which was intended to represent the expiration date of the nearest-term option considered in the optimization process. On the "CHGTX" tab, you can use the following button macros: "T-Greeks," "SIM ALL," and "SIM X" (Figure 7.12). The values for the price simulation on the second user date are stored on the "CHGTX" tab.

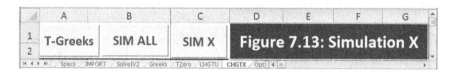

Figure 7.13: Simulation X

The simulation macros apply the user assumptions (Figure 7.9) to generate a series of discrete terminal prices (and the corresponding scenario probabilities) for the underlying stock. For each terminal price, the volatility model parameters are used to calculate the resulting normal and aggregate implied volatilities for every option in the matrix. All of these calculations include the effects of the vertical and horizontal skews, which are different for every option, but are all derived from the same volatility model framework and volatility model parameters. The aggregate implied volatility values are then

174

used to calculate the terminal values of each option on the desired date.

The simulated option values and corresponding probabilities provide the necessary data to help us identify the option earnings strategy with the highest expected profit per unit of risk. The simulated option values are also used to evaluate the most promising strategies graphically. We will explore optimization and graphical analysis in Chapter 8.

Summary

There is a lot going on behind the scenes in the Ingegrated spreadsheet, especially with respect to the volatility model and simulation calculations. Fortunately, all of these functions are automated and are very easy to use.

First push the "Randomize Volatility Parms" and "Estimate Volatility Model" macro buttons on the "SolveIV2" tab to estimate the volatility model. If your data is accurate and you use the appropriate filter settings, it is unlikely that you will need to customize the Solver solution parameters or constraints on a regular basis.

After reviewing the volatility model results, push the "T-Greeks" and "SIM ALL" buttons on any of the following tabs: "Greeks," "TZero," "CHGTU," or "CHGTX." This will generate and save all of the Greek and simulation results for every option in the matrix.

Except in special cases, that's all you will need to do: push four buttons in the proper sequence. That will prepare the spreadsheet for the final steps: optimization and graphical analysis..

8 - INTEGRATED OPTIMIZATION & ANALYSIS

This is the third of three chapters that provide step-by-step instructions on how to use the Integrated spreadsheet. The Integrated spreadsheet is populated with data for Under Armor (UA) as of July 23, 2014.

In Chapter 6, we entered all of the required input data and imported the UA option matrix. In Chapter 7, we solved for the optimal parameters of the volatility model, including the implied earnings volatility (IEV). In this chapter, we will review the steps required to solve for the optimal option earnings strategy and analyze strategy candidates graphically. We will use the "Opt" tab for strategy optimization and the "Analysis" tab for graphical analysis.

Identifying the option strategy with the highest expected profit per unit of risk is an optimization problem. The optimization problem in this chapter uses Solver. As I explained in previous chapters, if you have never used Solver before, then you will first need to enable the Solver Add-in in your version of Excel and you may also need to add the Solver VBA reference.

Introduction to Optimization

A comprehensive explanation of optimization would require one or more college or graduate level courses, which is well beyond the scope of this book. However, a brief introduction to optimization will help you understand how and why the Integrated spreadsheet was constructed; it will also explain how the strategy optimization problem was designed to operate within the strict size constraints imposed by the free version of Solver. This introduction will help you get the most out of the strategy optimizer in the "Opt" tab of the Integrated spreadsheet.

We will start with basic concepts and then examine how additional real-world complexity affects optimization problems. Optimizers attempt to either maximize or minimize an objective function. Finding the optimal option earnings strategy means maximizing the expected profit per unit of risk. Optimizers attempt to identify the best possible combination of values for a group of decision variables, subject to a set of constraints.

The simplest type of optimization problem is called a linear program or LP. In a linear program, the objective is a linear function of the decision variables, which results in a very simple (flat) geometric landscape. Given this simplicity, if *any* linear program with continuous decision variables has an optimal solution, the Simplex algorithm will find that solution – and will do so relatively quickly. That's right; a single algorithm published in 1947 called the Simplex algorithm can find the optimal solution to *any* linear program, provided that the decision variables are continuous.

What if one or more of the decision variables are not continuous and can only take on integer values? Then all bets are off. This seemingly benign integer constraint makes otherwise simple linear problems exceedingly onerous to solve. This type of optimization problem is called an integer linear program. A large linear program might take only a few seconds to solve on a desktop computer. The identical linear program with integer decision variables (integer linear program) might take *a few days* to solve! Unfortunately, the decision variables for many real-world problems can only accept integer values, and the strategy optimization problem in the Integrated spreadsheet is no exception. Since we cannot buy or sell a fractional number of option contracts, our decision variables must be integers.

We now need to add one final layer of complexity. What if the objective function is not linear? In other words, what if the objective that we are trying to maximize or minimize is a non-linear function of the decision variables? As you might expect, this is not going to make our life any easier. Non-linear objective functions are analogous to an n-dimensional geographic landscape, with rolling hills, peaks, mountains, cliffs, and valleys.

If the geometric landscape is smooth and convex over the entire range of solutions, then gradient-based techniques will be able to find the *global* maximum or minimum, which is what we want. How does a gradient-based technique work? At any given point, it evaluates the slope, derivative, or gradient in each direction. To find the global maximum, it takes several small steps in the direction of the steepest gradient, then stops and recalculates a new set of gradients. It repeats the process until it reaches the global maximum. This algorithm is only guaranteed to find the optimal global solution if the entire solution region is smooth and convex. If not, then gradient-based solution algorithms may get stuck at a *local* optimum, when our goal is to find the best possible solution over the entire geometric landscape, which is called the global optimum.

Unfortunately, our geometric solution landscape is not uniformly smooth and convex, so we need a different approach, one that has a better chance of exploring the entire geometric solution landscape and finding the global optimum. That solution technique is called a genetic or evolutionary algorithm.

Genetic algorithms begin with a large population of solutions and repeatedly "breed" parent solutions, taking gene sequences (decision variable values) from both parents, to create child solutions. This is called crossover. Evolution is cruel but effective, only allowing the "fittest" child solutions to survive and populate subsequent generations. Evolution is powerful, but it does take time, and so do genetic algorithms. Fortunately, Moore's law and the consistent increase in processing speeds have made genetic algorithms an invaluable tool in non-linear optimization.

However, there is an obvious problem with genetic algorithms. What if the characteristics of the initial population are inferior and subsequent generations can only inherit the mediocre genes of the initial parent population? Sure, the solution will improve somewhat over time, but it will always be limited by the substandard genes of the initial population. In optimization terms, this means that the global optimal solution will not be found in the geometric landscape represented by the initial parent population.

For maximum effectiveness, geometric algorithms must search the entire solution space. How do geometric algorithms solve this inbreeding problem? Mutation. A user-specified percentage of the parent genes spontaneously and randomly mutate, bringing new genes to the child generations that were not present in either parent's genes. Many gene mutations generate poor solutions and simply die out in the first generation.

However, others open up promising new regions of the geometric landscape that lead to superior objective function values. Once the promising new mutated gene improves the quality of the offspring, it will survive and flourish and the new region of the solution space will be explored in subsequent generations.

Increasing the percentage of mutations helps the geometric algorithm explore the entire geometric landscape, but also makes it more difficult for the algorithm to pass attractive genes on to future generations. Changing the mutation percentage involves tradeoffs between landscape coverage and efficiency of convergence.

Another problem with geometric algorithms is that they abhor constraints and perform much better when the only constraints are simple boundary conditions. When feasible parent solutions repeatedly produce infeasible child solutions due to multiple constraints, it would be very challenging for geometric algorithms to progress toward the optimal solution.

There is one final problem with genetic algorithms: there is no way to know when they have found the optimal solution. Genetic algorithms are really nothing more than a sophisticated version of trial and error and they never give up. They will continue to breed and evaluate new offspring until the power goes out. We literally need to tell them when to stop.

As you probably already guessed, strategy optimization is a non-linear, discontinuous, integer programming problem with hundreds or even thousands of prospective option candidates. As a result, it is the most difficult type of optimization problem to solve. Using the free version of Solver will make it even more challenging.

Free Solver's Limitations

When I wrote this book, I wanted to make the material and spreadsheet tools as accessible and practicable as possible, so forcing the reader to purchase expensive optimization software just to experiment with strategy optimization seemed unreasonable. As a result, I designed the optimization problem to use the free version of Solver that is included with recent versions of Microsoft Excel.

Unfortunately, the free version of Solver is artificially restricted to work with a limited number of decision variables and constraints. In addition, the solution algorithms in the free version of Solver are purposely inefficient and relatively slow. These deliberate deficiencies are intended to induce Solver users to upgrade to one of the premium versions of Solver. While I am an ardent proponent of capitalism and this is an effective marketing technique, it necessitated some compromises and creativity when designing the strategy optimization framework.

Normally, when designing a strategy optimization, I would assign one (or more) decision variables to each investment candidate. In the simplest case, each candidate would have its own decision variable, which would represent the number of contracts purchased or sold for that option. This is a very efficient and intuitive approach, but it requires a large number of decision variables.

Unfortunately, even after using filters to reduce the number of option candidates from the matrix, our UA example had almost 350 candidates, which would have far exceeded free Solver's 200 decision variable limit. As a result, my usual approach would not work with the free version of Solver.

Optimization Design Considerations

Instead, I had to make some compromises. First, I decided to limit solutions to combinations of three spreads: a call spread, a put spread, and a straddle or strangle. This may seem like a significant concession, but combinations of these three spreads can be used to create almost every conventional option strategy: butterflies, broken wing butterflies, condors, calendars, credit spreads, debit spreads, diagonals, straddles, strangles, plus a surprising variety of unusual hybrid combinations.

The call and put spreads both require an offsetting purchase and sale, which is obviously the definition of a spread. This structure helps limit potential losses, which is especially important when trading options over earnings events.

The strategy optimization only permits straddle/strangle purchases. Holding short positions in straddles or strangles when earnings are announced could lead to unlimited losses. Given that earnings are typically announced when the market is closed, there is no way to hedge or manage these losses. As a result, the strategy optimizer only permits long straddles or strangles. However, you may still short volatility by using the put and call spreads to construct butterflies, condors, or similar covered hybrid derivatives.

Given the above structure, there are only six potential option positions: two for the call spread, two for the put spread, and two for the straddle or strangle. The row number in the "Opt" tab of the Integrated spreadsheet will be used to describe the specific options purchased or sold for each spread. This will only require a total of six integer decision variables, each of which will contain the row number of the option purchased or sold to construct the spread.

The values of these six decision variables will describe the positions used to construct each spread, but we still need to know how many contracts to buy or sell. For that we will need three additional integer decision variables, one for each spread. We only need three additional decision variables (not six), because the spreads all require the same number of contracts on both sides of the trade. The resulting integer problem solution only requires nine decision variables, instead of potentially hundreds or even thousands. As a result, this problem structure does not violate free Solver's decision variable limits.

That is the good news. The bad news is that this approach is not nearly as efficient as assigning one or more decision variables to each option candidate. As a result, the Integrated spreadsheet employs a specific sorting algorithm in the "IMPORT Combo" macro to help mitigate some of the inefficiencies resulting from this approach.

Several Solution Methodologies

The success of a genetic algorithm depends heavily on searching the optimal region of the solution landscape, which in turn is governed by the initial starting point/solution. As a result, the initial values of the decision variables used to seed the genetic algorithm are critical to the success of the algorithm.

Many different traders will use the Integrated spreadsheet, all with unique backgrounds, goals, and time constraints. As a result, the spreadsheet was designed to accommodate several different methodologies for searching the solution landscape for the optimal solution. For traders who have a specific strategy solution in mind, the Integrated spreadsheet includes macros that allow them to use their solution as the starting point in a single Solver optimization run.

Keep in mind that starting-point solutions must be expressed as a combination of the spreads described earlier: call spread, put spread, and/or straddle/strangle. One, two, or all three spreads can be used and the user will be able to specify the time to expiration and Deltas for each option in the initial solution.

Unfortunately, strategy optimization is complex and most traders will not have a specific strategy in mind. Given the importance of searching the entire solution space, I created ten pre-set strategies for those traders to use as starting points in the optimization: bull call spread, bear put spread, neutral condor, neutral butterfly, bullish butterfly, bearish butterfly, neutral strangle, neutral straddle, bullish strangle, and bearish strangle. The pre-set strategy names and descriptions are not important. They simply represent ten solutions centered in different regions of the solution landscape with a range of risk characteristics or Greeks.

For users who would like to use the pre-set strategies, but would prefer to identify an attractive strategy as quickly as possible, the Integrated spreadsheet includes a macro that will calculate the values of the objective function for each of the pre-set strategies and a second macro that will use the most promising macro as the starting point for a *single Solver optimization run.*

If you have more time and would like to maximize exploration of the solution set, the Integrated spreadsheet includes a macro that will use the pre-set solutions as starting points for *ten different Solver optimization runs.* In an attempt to improve on the findings of the genetic algorithm, the same macro will then run a second series of Solver optimization runs using the Generalized Reduced Gradient (GRG) nonlinear algorithm, with the initial ten optimal Solver solutions as starting points. The result is twenty Solver runs, from twenty different starting points, using two different solution algorithms. This sounds complicated (and it is), but it can be accomplished by pushing a single macro button and taking a break for a cup of coffee (or two).

It is interesting that the final solutions will often deviate significantly from the starting solutions. In fact, the genetic algorithm is likely to produce different solutions every time you run the optimizer. That probably seems strange if you are used to solving linear programs with the Simplex algorithm, which will always find the single best solution, if one exists.

The genetic and GRG nonlinear algorithms are not guaranteed to locate the single global optimum of a non-linear, discontinuous, integer optimization problem. Fortunately, we do not need the "best" solution to generate a trading edge; we only need to identify solutions with an attractive expected profit per unit of risk.

Objective Function

So what do I mean by expected profit per unit of risk? The expected profit is easy to understand. Expected profit equals the probability-weighted profit across 100 discrete pricing scenarios. The prices and probabilities were derived from a binomial lattice that was generated from the expected normal volatility, the expected earnings volatility, and the holding period used in the optimization.

To calculate the expected profit per unit of risk, we also need to specify a risk measure. I included three different risk measures, one of which must be selected from a drop-down list in Cell A1 of the "Opt" tab of the Integrated spreadsheet (not shown). The first risk measure is sigma, which represents the standard deviation of the expected profit. This measure is used by many traders, which is why I included the risk measure in the spreadsheet. However, I did not use this risk measure in the examples from this book. The reason is that standard deviation or variation in expected profits is only a problem on the loss side. Scenarios with large gains also increase sigma, which would lower the objective function, making those solutions look worse.

As a result, I used the second risk measure (maximum loss) to calculate the objective function for all of the examples in the book. In other words, the resulting objective function would equal the expected or probability-weighted profit divided by the absolute value of the maximum loss. We use the absolute value because the maximum loss is negative and we want to maximize the objective function.

Finally, I included a third risk measure with a value of one (1.0). Using a constant value of 1.0 probably seems strange as well, but if we divide the expected profit by 1.0, the result equals the expected profit. In other words, by including a risk measure of 1.0, this allows users to maximize the expected profit if they desire, with no consideration of risk.

User Input Settings

Before running Solver, the Integrated spreadsheet must translate the user or pre-set strategy descriptions into row numbers, which are used to describe the three spreads. The row numbers are also used to calculate the objective function and various strategy summary statistics. The user and pre-set strategy descriptions both use the section of the "Opt" tab illustrated in Figure 8.1 to translate trading days until expiration and Delta into the row numbers for the corresponding options from the matrix that most closely approximate the desired values.

For now, let's focus on how we use this section of the spreadsheet to enter the user-defined strategy that will serve as the starting point for Solver. You will recall that cells with a dark shaded background and white text represent input cells. The most important of the user input cells indicate whether the three spreads (Call, Put, Straddle/Strangle) will be included in the solution (Q18:S18). A value of one indicates the spread will be included and a value of zero directs the spreadsheet to exclude the spread. The only acceptable values for these three cells are one and zero.

Next, we will need to enter the desired number of trading days until expiration for each of the six options used in the three spreads (K16:P16). The desired number of trading days for the call sale and purchase are entered in Cells K16 and L16. The desired number of trading days for the put sale and purchase are entered in Cells M16 and N16. Finally, we enter the trading days for the call and put components of the straddle/strangle in Cells O16 and P16. In this example, 22 days is approximately equivalent to one month.

Even if a spread is excluded from the initial strategy, as is the case for both the call and put spread in Figure 8.1 (Q18:R18), we still need to enter a plausible number of trading days that is consistent with the range of option candidates used in the optimization.

It is also important to note that the number of trading days entered in Cells K16:P16 will be used for *all strategies*. This includes user-defined strategies as well as the ten pre-set strategies. It would have been too cumbersome to specify a different set of values for every strategy.

In addition to trading days until expiration, we also need to enter the desired Delta for each of the six options used to construct the three spreads (K18:P18). Obviously the calls will have positive Deltas and the Puts will have negative Deltas. The Deltas are expressed per contract, not per share. In the case of UA, the call Deltas will range from zero to 100 and the put Deltas will range from zero to negative 100.

J	K	L	M	N	O	P	Q	R	S	T
13		Figure 8.1: Strategy Optimizer - User Input Settings						ReqCap	RC Loss	
14	C1 Sell	C1 Buy	P2 Sell	P2 Buy	C3 Buy	P3 Buy	RC1	0.00	0.00	
15 Call/Put	C	C	P	P	C	P	RC2	0.00	0.00	Copy User
16 T-Days	40	2	2	40	22	22	RC3	587.50	0.00	
17 Act Tdays	41	2	2	41	22	22	# SP1	# SP2	# SP3	
18 Delta	10.0	50.0	-10.0	-50.0	60.0	-40.0	0	0	1	Opt
19 Act Delta	13.1	48.5	-17.0	-45.5	60.7	-39.4	Size	16	610.50	User
20 Solution	138	17	201	316	106	281	0	0	16	
21 Price	0.70	1.98	0.63	3.15	3.75	2.13				
22 Strike	70.0	61.0	56.0	60.0	59.0	59.0				

The spreadsheet uses Excel's Match function to find option candidates that closely match the desired number of trading days until expiration and the desired Delta. The row numbers for the resulting options are stored temporarily in the solution Cells (K20:P20).

In addition, the Integrated spreadsheet also calculates the number of contracts for each spread (Q20:S20) to be consistent with the user-specified amount of required capital. In all of the strategy examples in the book, I specified a required capital range of $9,000 to $11,000 (not shown), to give the optimizer some flexibility in finding an integer solution. This flexibility is very important.

The spreadsheet calculations of required capital look at each spread individually and are relatively simplistic. In reality, every broker uses their own margin calculation algorithms, which are based on FINRA margin requirements and on their proprietary portfolio margin risk models.

Let's look at the options selected by the spreadsheet for the initial solution. The call and put spreads are excluded, so we will focus on the straddle. The nearest call option candidate was found in row 106 (O20) and the closest put option was located in row 281 (P20). For both the call and put purchase, we specified 22 trading days until expiration (O16:P16). The call and put options found by the spreadsheet for the initial strategy exactly matched our desired number of trading days (O17:P17).

We specified Deltas of 60 (O18) for the call option and negative

40 (P18) for the put option. The call and put options found by the spreadsheet had Deltas of 60.7 (O19) and negative 39.4 (P19) respectively. In addition, the spreadsheet reports the option type (K15:P15), option price (K21:P21), and strike price (K22:P22) for each of the options identified by the spreadsheet.

Once we are satisfied with the initial solution, we can use the user macros to evaluate or optimize the initial strategy. To calculate the objective function value (and other summary statistics) for the initial strategy, use the "Copy User" button macro shown at the right-side of Figure 8.1. The Copy User macro will copy the initial solution from Cells K20:S20 to the calculation region of the spreadsheet shown in Figure 8.2 (C3:K3).

Figure 8.2 shows the initial user-strategy *before* optimization. The value of the objective function (before the strategy is optimized) equals +0.25 (L3), which is not bad, especially for a (non-optimized) starting point. The objective function value of +0.25 represents the expected profit after transaction costs, divided by the absolute value of the maximum loss.

If you are curious, the $1,212 in Cell L2 represents the expected profit before transaction costs and the value of 0.17 in Cell L4 represents an alternative objective function value, which in this case equals the expected profit divided by sigma. The optimizer will always attempt to maximize the value shown in Cell L3. The other values are shown for informational purposes only.

The "MaxLoss" shown in Cell A1 indicates that the objective function (L3) equals the expected profit divided by the absolute value of the maximum loss. The solution (C3:K3) is also used to calculate a number of other summary statistics, which we will review later in this chapter. For now, we will continue to focus on optimization procedures.

	A	B	C	D	E	F	G	H	I	J	K	L
			C1 Sell	C1 Buy	P2 Sell	P2 Buy	C3 Buy	P3 Buy	# SP1	# SP2	# SP3	OBJ FN
1	MaxLoss											
2	10	MAX	152	152	326	326	152	326	300	300	300	1,212
3	0	Solution	138	17	201	316	106	281	0	0	16	0.25
4	Description	MIN	5	5	179	179	5	179	0	0	0	0.17

Figure 8.2: User Strategy Before Optimization

If you are satisfied with the initial objective function value (L3), use the "Opt User" push-button macro (Figure 8.1) to optimize the user-defined strategy. The optimized strategy results are shown in

Figure 8.3. The objective function value increased from 0.25 (Figure 8.2 cell L3) to 0.63 (Figure 8.3 cell L3), which is a very good solution. You will also notice that the expected profit excluding transaction costs (L2) and the expected profit divided by sigma also increased.

If we look a little closer, there is another very interesting observation: the optimized solution includes a 14-contract put spread (J3), which was not even part of the initial solution. The initial solution only used a straddle.

	B1		f_x									
					Figure 8.3: User Strategy After Optimization							
	A	B	C	D	E	F	G	H	I	J	K	L
1	MaxLoss		C1 Sell	C1 Buy	P2 Sell	P2 Buy	C3 Buy	P3 Buy	# SP1	# SP2	# SP3	OBJ FN
2	10	MAX	152	152	326	326	152	326	300	300	300	2,633
3	0	Solution	137	17	202	315	104	281	0	14	12	0.63
4	Description	MIN	5	5	179	179	5	179	0	0	0	0.33

Saved / IVPrice / Specs / IMPORT / SolveIV2 / Greeks / TZero / CHGTU / CHGTX / Opt / Analysis

This was the best solution found by Solver based on the initial user solution. If we ran Solver again, it might even improve upon this value. When we use the ten pre-set solutions later in this chapter, Solver will be able to find a strategy solution with a much larger expected profit per unit of risk. As a result, we will delay our discussion of the optimal solution until then.

Before we explore the pre-set optimization macros, let's take another look at the Solver settings (Figure 8.4). The Solver settings used by the strategy optimizer are located in the Cells V10:V20 on the "Opt" tab. As was the case when using Solver to identify the optimal volatility model parameters, you should review the Solver documentation before modifying these values. However, modifying these settings might improve Solver's performance.

Before continuing, I want to explain a few of the Solver settings in Figure 8.4. The "MaxTime" value of 300 (V10) indicates that Solver will run for a maximum of 300 seconds (five minutes) per optimization run. Obviously increasing this value will give Solver more time to explore the solution space, but keep in mind that the Solver macro uses both the genetic algorithm and the GRG algorithm.

The "MaxTimeNoImp" value of 60 (V20) instructs Solver to stop an optimization if the objective function value has not improved in the past 60 seconds. This setting will prevent Solver from wasting additional time when its search algorithm is ineffective.

The "PopulationSize" of 1000 (V16) is a relatively large initial population, which will diversify the "gene pool" and help Solver explore the entire solution space. However, increasing the population will also increase the run-time.

I mentioned the mutation rate before. The initial "MutationRate" of 0.25 (V19) will allow Solver to consider solutions that were not represented in the initial population, but should not compromise Solver's ability to converge on a solution. Varying this setting could improve or degrade Solver's performance.

Finally, the "RandomSeed" of zero (V17) instructs Solver to generate a different population every time it runs the analysis. This allows you to re-run Solver in an attempt to improve upon your initial solutions. Solver only retains improved solutions, so re-running Solver cannot reduce your objective function.

	U	V
8	**Figure 8.4: Solver Settings**	
9	Option Name	Value
10	MaxTime	300
11	Precision	0.000100
12	Derivatives	2
13	IntTolerance	0.00
14	Convergence	0.000100
15	AssumeNonNeg	FALSE
16	PopulationSize	1,000
17	RandomSeed	0
18	RequireBounds	TRUE
19	MutationRate	0.25
20	MaxTimeNoImp	60

CHGTX | Opt | Analysis

Pre-Set Strategy Optimization

As explained earlier, the "Opt" tab includes ten pre-set strategies to use as starting points in the optimization: bull call spread, bear put spread, neutral condor, neutral butterfly, bullish butterfly, bearish butterfly, neutral strangle, neutral straddle, bullish strangle, and bearish strangle. The strategies shown in Figure 8.5 represent the ten pre-set solutions, which are centered in different regions of the solution landscape.

The strategy descriptions use the same framework we used earlier to enter the user strategy. The number of trading days entered in Cells K16:P16 (Figure 8.1) are used for *all strategies*, so we do not need to enter these values again. However, the pre-set strategy descriptions do include the desired Delta values (Figure 8.5 Cells AA25:AF34) as well as the include/exclude values (Figure 8.5 Cells AG25:AI34) for each spread. The values in the last row of Figure 8.5 (AA35:AI35) are automatically populated with the user settings from Figure 8.1 (K18:S18). The user strategy is not used by the pre-set strategy optimization macros.

	Z	AA	AB	AC	AD	AE	AF	AG	AH	AI
23		Figure 8.5: Pre-Set Strategy Settings								
24	Strategy	C1 Sell	C1 Buy	P2 Sell	P2 Buy	C3 Buy	P3 Buy	# SP1	# SP2	# SP3
25	Bull CS	10.0	50.0	-10.0	-50.0	50.0	-50.0	1	0	0
26	Bear PS	10.0	50.0	-10.0	-50.0	50.0	-50.0	0	1	0
27	Condor	20.0	10.0	-20.0	-10.0	50.0	-50.0	1	1	0
28	BFly	50.0	10.0	-50.0	-10.0	50.0	-50.0	1	1	0
29	Bull BFly	35.0	25.0	-50.0	-30.0	40.0	-60.0	1	1	0
30	Bear BFly	50.0	30.0	-35.0	-25.0	60.0	-40.0	1	1	0
31	Strangle	10.0	50.0	-10.0	-50.0	50.0	-50.0	0	0	1
32	Straddle	10.0	50.0	-10.0	-50.0	40.0	-40.0	0	0	1
33	Bull S	10.0	50.0	-10.0	-50.0	40.0	-60.0	0	0	1
34	Bear S	10.0	50.0	-10.0	-50.0	60.0	-40.0	0	0	1
35	User Input	10.0	50.0	-10.0	-50.0	60.0	-40.0	0	0	1

CHGTX Opt Analysis

The easiest, most exhaustive (and most time consuming) way to search for the optimal strategy is to use the "Opt All" push-button macro (Figure 8.6).

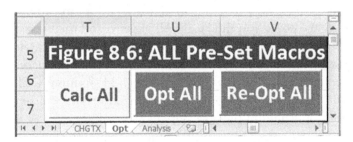

Figure 8.6: ALL Pre-Set Macros

Calc All   Opt All   Re-Opt All

CHGTX Opt Analysis

The "Opt All" macro copies the Delta and include/exclude spread values for the first pre-set strategy (AA25:AI25) to the Delta row of the user matrix described earlier (Figure 8.1 K18:S18). The user matrix finds the appropriate row numbers for each option (Figure 8.1 K20:S20) and the macro then copies these values to the calculation region of the "Opt" tab (C3:K3). The macro then uses these values as the starting point to run the Solver optimization. The results for the first pre-set strategy are then copied to the first row of the strategy results section of the "Opt" tab (Figures 8.7 & 8.8, Cells K25:Y25).

The "Opt All" macro then repeats the same procedure for the remaining nine pre-set strategies. The optimized results for all of the pre-set UA strategies are shown in Cells K25:Y34 of Figures 8.7 & 8.8. The results were split into Figures 8.7 & 8.8 due to the width of the region. This macro requires twenty different optimization runs, which takes a lot of time.

If you are not satisfied with the results, you could use the "Re-Opt All" push button macro (Figure 8.6) to re-optimize all of the strategies. However, instead of starting from the pre-set strategy definitions, Solver would start with the results from the previous optimization runs (K25:S25). The "Re-Opt All" macro would then copy the results from the re-optimization to Cells K25:Y34, replacing the original optimization results. This macro also requires twenty different optimization runs and will probably take nearly as much time as the "Opt All" macro.

The "Calc All" push-button macro in Figure 8.6 follows the exact same procedure as the "Opt All" macro, *except it does not optimize the initial strategies*. Instead, it calculates the objective function and summary statistics for each pre-set strategy (before optimization) and copies the non-optimized results to Cells K25:Y34. Why would we want to do this? Because the "Calc All" macro is very fast and we might not have enough time to run 20 different optimization runs.

Instead, we could run the "Calc All" macro and then use the "Opt (Nth)" push-button macro in Figure 8.7 to optimize the single pre-set strategy with the highest (pre-optimization) objective function value. Simply enter the desired solution number (1-11) in input Cell J24 and push the "Opt (Nth)" button. The optimized results will replace the initial solution values in the appropriate row in Figure 8.7 & 8.8.

In addition to the "Opt (Nth)" macro, there are three additional macros that only use one user-specified pre-set solution at a time. The "Re-Opt (Nth)" push-button macro uses the original optimization results for the pre-set strategy of our choice to re-optimize the strategy. It then copies the results to the corresponding row of Figures 8.7 & 8.8.

The "Calc (Nth)" macro calculates the (pre-optimization) objective function and summary statistics for the pre-set strategy of our choice and copies the results to the appropriate row of the results section of the "Opt" tab.

Finally, the "Copy (Nth)" push-button macro copies the solution of our choice back to the calculation region of the "Opt" tab (C3:K3), which recalculates the objective function and all of the summary statistics. The solution in the calculation region of the "Opt" tab is also used to generate the values for the graphical analysis, which will be discussed later in this chapter.

The row numbers for each option and the number of contracts for each spread are shown in Figure 8.7, as are the four macros that run one of the pre-set strategies at a time.

	Figure 8.7: Calc/Opt/Copy Nth Strategy Results			Calc (Nth)	Opt (Nth)	Re-Opt (Nth)	Copy (Nth)		
23									
24	1	C1 Sell	C1 Buy	P2 Sell	P2 Buy	C3 Buy	P3 Buy	# SP1	# SP2	# SP3
25	1	148	71	228	298	9	207	11	44	7
26	2	128	60	267	295	143	271	44	129	4
27	3	95	55	191	259	102	277	36	36	0
28	4	138	9	198	303	93	280	21	15	15
29	5	92	121	266	315	143	260	53	6	21
30	6	141	12	195	317	106	281	24	24	0
31	7	152	136	205	205	78	267	156	83	0
32	8	56	79	292	236	113	286	0	63	12
33	9	37	74	228	212	19	299	0	25	9
34	10	138	17	202	316	105	281	0	3	14
35	11	137	17	202	315	104	281	0	14	12

Figure 8.8 is a continuation of Figure 8.7. Each row in Figure 8.8 corresponds to the same strategy from the same row in Figure 8.7. Figure 8.8 shows the objective function (T), average profit after transaction costs (U), standard deviation of the profit (V), maximum loss (W), the required capital (X), and the Solver result (Y).

As you can see in Figure 8.8, the ten pre-set strategies produced a wide range of optimal solutions, which illustrates the advantage of using the "Opt All" macro whenever possible. The first pre-set strategy generated the optimal solution with the highest objective function value, a remarkable 10.78 (T25). The expected profit for the optimal solution derived from the first pre-set strategy was 10.78 times the absolute value of the maximum loss. Both the expected profit and maximum loss were calculated net of assumed transaction costs. This was an unusually large objective function value and was only possible due to the optimizer's ability to exploit large systematic pricing anomalies in the UA matrix.

	J	T	U	V	W	X	Y
23				**Figure 8.8: Strategy Results**			
24	1	OBJ FN	Avg Profit	σProfit	Max Loss	Req Cap	Result
25	1	10.78	1,482	1,894	-137	9,044	0
26	2	1.36	2,986	5,900	-2,203	10,982	0
27	3	-0.08	-822	4,152	-9,940	10,663	0
28	4	-0.05	-306	5,492	-6,302	10,551	0
29	5	-0.05	-204	4,289	-4,466	10,215	14
30	6	-0.20	-964	3,286	-4,746	10,070	0
31	7	0.32	3,102	9,221	-9,670	9,670	0
32	8	0.34	2,495	10,486	-7,290	10,893	0
33	9	0.40	1,653	5,748	-4,088	9,236	0
34	10	0.31	984	5,000	-3,201	9,166	0
35	11	0.63	2,035	6,257	-3,254	9,508	0

H ◀ ▶ H   CHGTX   Opt   Analysis   ♩

Solver Strategy Optimization Problem

All of the optimizations generated return values of either zero or fourteen. To refresh your memory, the Frontline Solver return values are shown again in Figure 8.9.

A return value of zero indicates that "Solver found a solution. All constraints and optimality conditions are satisfied." A return value of fourteen indicates that "Solver found an integer solution within tolerance. All constraints are satisfied." In this case, all of the optimizations returned feasible solutions, but the first solution was clearly the best. Always remember to check the Solver return values for each solution before proceeding.

Figure 8.9: Frontline Solver Return Values

SolverSolve Return Value

If a Solver problem has not been completely defined, **SolverSolve** returns the #N/A error value. Otherwise the Solver runs, and **SolverSolve** returns an integer value corresponding to the message that appears in the Solver Results dialog box:

0	Solver found a solution. All constraints and optimality conditions are satisfied.
1	Solver has converged to the current solution. All constraints are satisfied.
2	Solver cannot improve the current solution. All constraints are satisfied.
3	Stop chosen when the maximum iteration limit was reached.
4	The Objective Cell values do not converge.
5	Solver could not find a feasible solution.
6	Solver stopped at user's request.
7	The linearity conditions required by this LP Solver are not satisfied.
8	The problem is too large for Solver to handle.
9	Solver encountered an error value in a target or constraint cell.
10	Stop chosen when the maximum time limit was reached.
11	There is not enough memory available to solve the problem.
13	Error in model. Please verify that all cells and constraints are valid.
14	Solver found an integer solution within tolerance. All constraints are satisfied.
15	Stop chosen when the maximum number of feasible [integer] solutions was reached.
16	Stop chosen when the maximum number of feasible [integer] subproblems was reached.
17	Solver converged in probability to a global solution.
18	All variables must have both upper and lower bounds.
19	Variable bounds conflict in binary or alldifferent constraint.
20	Lower and upper bounds on variables allow no feasible solution.

If you have a recent version of Microsoft Excel, you should be able to use the push-button macros to run Solver automatically, provided you have enabled the Solver Add-in and the visual basic component. In the event that you are unable to run the Solver macros or you would like to modify the Solver problem, you would need to run Solver manually. To help you get started, I have included Figure 8.10, which is a screen-shot of the Solver problem used during the strategy optimization process.

Solver attempts to maximize the expected profit per unit of risk, which is located in Cell L3. It does this by systematically modifying the decision variables, which are located in Cells C3:K3. As you will recall, these are the same cells the macros populated with the initial starting point solutions.

As explained earlier, genetic algorithms do not function as efficiently with constraints, so they were kept to a minimum. However, some constraints were necessary. Here is a brief description of the most important constraints. There are three constraints related to the decision variables, which restrict the decision variables (C3:K3) to integer values with row numbers that correspond to the appropriate option type (call or put) for each spread component.

The required capital (P3) is bounded by a user-specified minimum (P4) and a user-specified maximum (P2). For all of the strategy examples in the book, I specified a range of $9,000 (P4) to $11,000 (P2).

I also included constraints that allow the user to force the time to expiration for the call spread and put spread purchases to exceed the time to expiration for the call spread and put spread sales. If you want to enforce this limit, enter the value of zero in Cell AG1.

Cell AG1 represents the maximum difference between the trading days to expiration for spread purchases minus sales. In other words, the trading days to expiration for spread purchases, minus the trading days to expiration for spread sales, must be greater than or equal to the value of Cell AG1. If the time to expiration for spread purchases is greater than or equal to the time to expiration for spread sales, the Financial Industry Regulatory Agency (FINRA) considers the spread "covered," which results in reduced margin requirements.

I use portfolio margin in my trading account, which allows much greater flexibility in option trading. As a result, the value of Cell AG1 in the UA example was negative 75, which permitted spreads that did not meet the FINRA requirements. The optimal UA solution used this flexibility and identified a solution that would not have been possible within the FINRA covered spread requirements.

Be careful not to equate this flexibility with excessive risk. For the call and put spreads, the number of options purchased will always equal the number of options sold. The time to expiration of the option purchased might be shorter than the time to expiration of the option sold, but the strategy would only be held until the expiration date of the shorter-term option. It would not be appropriate to hold the naked short position.

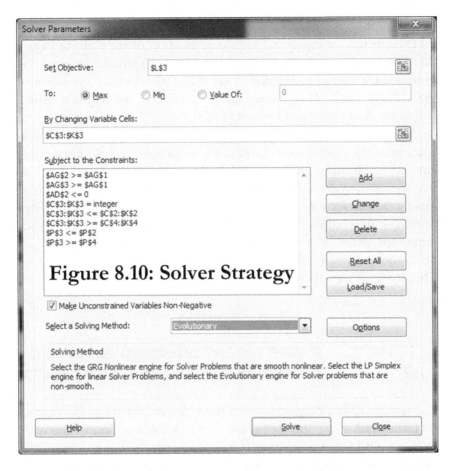

Figure 8.10: Solver Strategy

After running the "Opt All" push-button macro, it was obvious that the first pre-set strategy produced the optimization solution with the highest objective function. To reevaluate this solution, we enter the value of one into Cell J24 (indicating the first strategy solution) and execute the "Copy (Nth)" push-button macro to copy the first solution into the calculation region of the "Opt" tab. Columns A through L of the UA solution are shown in Figure 8.11. This section shows the row numbers for each option, the number of spread contracts, and the objective function value.

Figure 8.11: UA Optimal Strategy Solution (L)

	A	B	C	D	E	F	G	H	I	J	K	L
			C1 Sell	C1 Buy	P2 Sell	P2 Buy	C3 Buy	P3 Buy	# SP1	# SP2	# SP3	OBJ FN
1	MaxLoss											
2	10	MAX	152	152	326	326	152	326	300	300	300	2,908
3	0	Solution	148	71	228	298	9	207	11	44	7	10.78
4	Description	MIN	5	5	179	179	5	179	0	0	0	0.78

Figure 8.12 is a continuation of the UA solution shown in Figure
8.11. Each row of Figure 8.12 is a continuation of the rows in Figure
8.11. Row three represents the UA solution. Figure 8.12 shows the
average profit after transaction costs (M3), the standard deviation of
the average profit (N3), the maximum loss (O3), the required capital
(P3), and all of the True Greeks(Q3:W3).

As discussed earlier, input Cells P2 and P4 represent the user-
specified maximum and minimum required capital constraints
entered by the user and imposed by Solver. The other cells in row
two and row four with the dark shaded background are also user
inputs, *but are not used in the optimization.* Instead, they provide visual
warnings (red shaded background) if the maximum (Row 2) or
minimum (Row 4) values are violated. We already examined the
profitability statistics and True Greeks for the optimal UA strategy in
Chapter 5, so we will not revisit the results again here.

	Figure 8.12: Optimal UA Strategy Solution (M)									
M	N	O	P	Q	R	S	T	U	V	W
Avg Profit	σProfit	Max Loss	Req Cap	T-Delta	T-Gamma	TE-Vega	TN30-Vega	T30-Vega	T-Theta	T-Rho
-1,426	40,000		11,000	5,000.0	1,000.0	2,500.0	2,500.0	2,500.0	5,000.0	5,000.0
1,482	1,894	-137	9,044	24.8	132.3	19.3	19.1	38.4	-1,415.5	-37.5
0			9,000	-5,000.0	-1,000.0	-2,500.0	-2,500.0	-2,500.0	-2,500.0	-5,000.0

Figure 8.13 is a continuation of the UA solution shown in Figures
8.11 and 8.12. Each row of Figure 8.13 is a continuation of the rows
in Figures 8.11 and 8.12. Row three represents the UA solution. The
Deltas of the options in the optimal UA solution are shown on the
left-side of Figure 8.13 in row three (X3:AC3). The cells with the
dark shaded background in rows two and four are warning cells only
and are *not used to constrain the optimal Solver solution.* In this case, they
are designed to warn the user about solutions that contain deep in-
the-money options.

The remaining dark shaded input cell (AG1) was discussed earlier.
Cell AG1 represents the maximum difference between the trading
days to expiration for spread purchases minus sales. If you want to
enforce this limit, enter the value of zero in Cell AG1. If you want to
relax this constraint, enter a large negative number in Cell AG1. The
remaining cells all contain intermediate calculations and are not
directly applicable to our discussion of the optimization process.

Figure 8.13: Optimal UA Strategy Solution (R)

	X	Y	Z	AA	AB	AC	AD	AE	AF	AG	AH	AI
	SP1 Sell Δ	SP1 Buy Δ	SP2 Sell Δ	SP2 Buy Δ	SP3 Buy Δ	SP2 Buy Δ						
1							0	-11,550	4,625	-75	9,044	
2	90.0	90.0	90.0	90.0	90.0	90.0	0	-2,750	1,485	-44	1,958	1,958
3	25.3	7.5	-71.3	-59.9	22.3	-62.5		-8,800	5,940	15	2,860	2,394
4	-90.0	-90.0	-90.0	-90.0	-90.0	-90.0		0	-2,800	0	2,800	0
5							ExpD < AD	Max Payout	Proceeds	Net Tdays	ReqCap	RC Loss

Looking at row numbers is not the easiest way to visualize a complex strategy. Figure 8.14 reproduces the table that we used in Chapter 5 (Figure 5.11) to summarize the options used to construct the optimal UA strategy. For each component of the three spreads, the number of contracts, option type, strike price, expiration date, trading days until expiration, mid-price, True Delta, and the degree of undervaluation (Rich/Cheap) are provided in columns J through Q respectively.

	J	K	L	M	N	O	P	Q
5	Figure 8.14: Optimal UA Strategy Solution - Positions							
6	Amount	Type	Strike	Exp Date	T-Days	Mid Price	T-Delta	Rich/Cheap
7	-11	C	67.50	141018	61	1.675	25.3	-0.09
8	11	C	70.00	140816	17	0.325	7.5	0.19
9	-44	P	64.50	140809	12	5.40	-71.3	-0.34
10	44	P	62.50	140830	27	4.05	-59.9	0.23
11	7	C	65.00	140726	2	0.55	22.3	0.32
12	7	P	62.50	140802	7	3.45	-62.5	0.09

I personally prefer to examine the P&L graph before implementing any option strategy. Figure 8.15 reproduces the P&L graph that we used in Chapter 5 to examine the optimal UA strategy. All of the macro buttons, tables, and data discussed in this chapter are located on the "Opt" tab of the Integrated spreadsheet. The P&L graph in Figure 8.15 is located on the "Analysis" tab.

The Integrated spreadsheet will automatically generate the P&L graph *for the solution in the calculation region of the "Opt" tab (C3:K3)*. The only user requirement is to execute the "Scale Axes" push-button macro located near the top-left of the P&L graph (not shown). The "Scale Axes" macro automatically scales the vertical and horizontal axes based on the range of the scenario data. If you forget to use the "Scale Axes" macro, the P&K graph may not be readable.

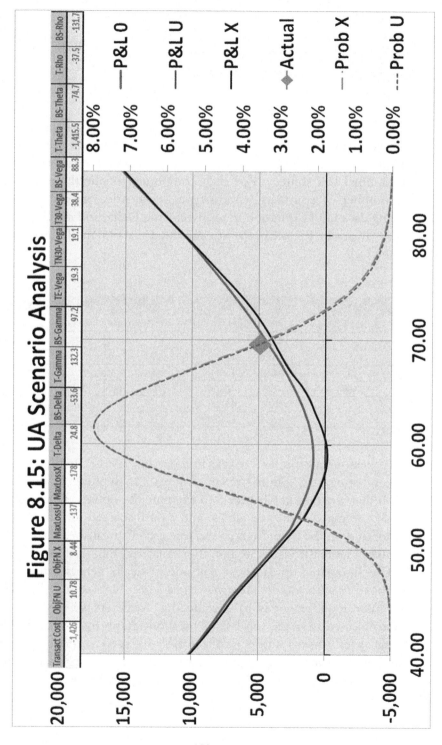

Figure 8.15: UA Scenario Analysis

Summary

The strategy optimization process is complex and I have included a lot of detail to help you understand the process. However, the optimization procedure is almost entirely automated. The easiest way to use the strategy optimizer is to enter a constant number of trading days (that exceeds your desired holding period) in Cells K18:P18. Then push the "Opt-All" button and let Solver search for the strategy with the highest expected profit per unit of risk.

If you would like to use a more interactive (and faster) approach, feel free to use your own custom solution or pick the most promising of the pre-set solutions as the starting point for the optimization.

Regardless of the optimization process you choose, once you find an attractive solution, examine the P&L graph on the "Analysis" tab to ensure that you understand every aspect of the profit distribution before implementing any option earnings strategy.

9 - CREE EARNINGS STRATEGY

In Chapter 5, I demonstrated how the tools in this book could be used to create a trading edge by exploiting earnings-related pricing anomalies in Under Armor (UA) options on July 23, 2014. In that chapter, we first used OptionSlam.com to screen the entire database of stocks for candidates with high levels of historical earnings volatility and a demonstrated directional earnings return bias.

We used OptionSlam.com's earnings return data to evaluate UA's historical earnings volatility and we also calculated past and current levels of implied earnings volatility. This analysis allowed us to forecast the expected level of *realized* earnings volatility for UA's upcoming earnings announcement (before the open on July 24, 2014).

Similarly, we studied UA's historical one-day returns immediately following the previous twelve quarterly earnings announcements and identified a systematic bullish earnings directional bias. We confirmed that bullish directional bias by reviewing the Estimize.com consensus revenue and EPS forecasts relative to Wall Street's revenue and EPS estimates.

The Integrated spreadsheet employed Solver in an attempt to identify the UA option earnings strategy with the highest expected profit per unit of risk. The expected risk and return calculations for every option in the UA matrix were derived from the comprehensive volatility model parameters, our specific volatility and directional forecasts, and from the expected corrections in each option's relative value during the holding period. Finally, we examined the profit and loss diagram and the True Greeks for the optimal strategy.

In Chapters 6, 7, and 8, we examined how to use the Integrated spreadsheet to perform all of the above functions. We have now covered all of the concepts, formulas, definitions, and procedural steps required to evaluate, optimize, and trade option earnings strategies. In this chapter, we will apply the same investment process that we used in Chapter 5 (described above) to design one more real-world option earnings strategy. Since we have covered all of this material in previous chapters, this chapter will focus more on the investment process and trade strategy and less on definitions, data sources, and spreadsheet mechanics.

The objective of this exercise is to reinforce your understanding of the concepts that we have used throughout this book and to gain some additional practical insights into trading option earnings strategies. As we proceed, keep in mind that our goal is to use our tools and resources to identify and exploit a trading edge.

Screening Earnings Candidates

Figure 9.1 is a screenshot of OptionSlam.com's historical stock screener with all of the filter settings that I used on September 25, 2014 to find prospective candidates with earning announcements scheduled during the subsequent three months. I limited my selection to stocks with weekly options and an average daily volume of over one million shares. I specified a minimum EVR of 2.0 and a minimum stock price of $20 per share.

EVR is OptionSlam's proprietary earnings volatility measure, which is based on the most recent three years of quarterly earnings announcements, with the most recent data weighted more heavily. EVR ranges between zero and ten, with ten being the most volatile.

I further restricted prospective candidates to stocks that experienced a minimum mean and median *absolute* price change of 5% or more and a median *raw* price change of negative 4% or less over the past twelve earnings announcements. The resulting candidates experienced excess earnings volatility and consistently surprised analysts and traders to the downside, generating median returns of less than negative 4% per quarter.

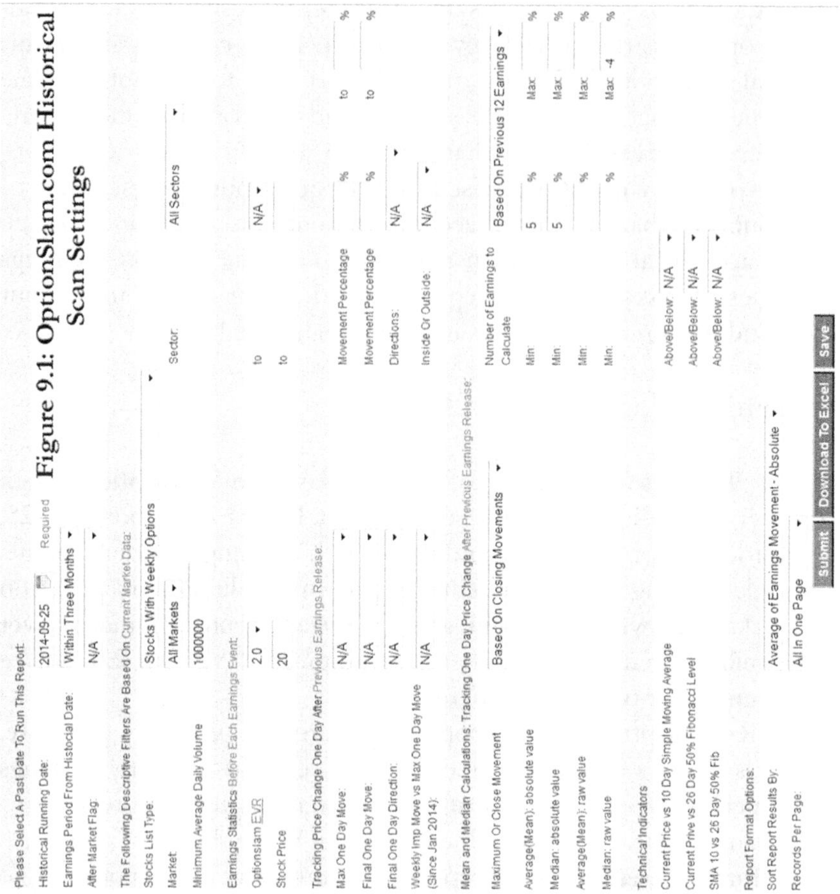

Figure 9.1: OptionSlam.com Historical Scan Settings

Please Select A Past Date To Run This Report: Required

- Historical Running Date: 2014-09-25
- Earnings Period From Historical Date: Within Three Months
- After Market Flag: N/A

The Following Descriptive Filters Are Based On Current Market Data:

- Stocks List Type: Stocks With Weekly Options
- Market: All Markets
- Minimum Average Daily Volume: 1000000
- Sector: All Sectors

Earnings Statistics Before Each Earnings Event:

- OptionSlam EVR: 2.0   to   N/A   %
- Stock Price: 20   to   N/A   %

Tracking Price Change One Day After Previous Earnings Release:

- Max One Day Move: N/A   Movement Percentage   to   %
- Final One Day Move: N/A   Movement Percentage   to   %
- Final One Day Direction: N/A   Directions: N/A
- Weekly Imp Move vs Max One Day Move (Since Jan 2014): N/A   Inside Or Outside: N/A

Mean and Median Calculations: Tracking One Day Price Change After Previous Earnings Release:

- Maximum Or Close Movement: Based On Closing Movements   Number of Earnings to Calculate   Based On Previous 12 Earnings
- Average(Mean): absolute value: Min 5 %   Max %
- Median absolute value: Min 5 %   Max %
- Average(Mean): raw value: Min %   Max %
- Median: raw value: Min %   Max: -4 %

Technical Indicators:

- Current Price vs 10 Day Simple Moving Average: Above/Below N/A
- Current Price vs 26 Day 50% Fibonacci Level: Above/Below N/A
- SMA 10 vs 26 Day 50% Fib: Above/Below N/A

Report Format Options:

- Sort Report Results By: Average of Earnings Movement - Absolute
- Records Per Page: All In One Page

Submit | Download To Excel | Save

Figure 9.2 is a screenshot of OptionSlam.com's historical screener's results on September 25, 2014. The filters I used returned only nine stocks. For each of the candidates in Figure 9.2, the symbol, next earnings date, market, sector and EVR are provided on the left side of the table.

The right side of the table includes the mean and median *absolute* 1-day percentage price changes over the twelve previous earnings events, followed by the mean and median *raw* 1-day percentage price changes over the twelve previous earnings events. The absolute percentages are a measure of volatility and the raw percentages indicate directional bias.

Number of Earnings Events Returned: 9   Figure 9.2: OptionSlam.com Historical Scan Results

| SYMBOL | EARNING DATE | MARKET | SECTOR | EVR | CLOSING 1 DAY PRICE CHANGE OVER PREVIOUS 12 EARNINGS | | | |
					MEAN	MEDIAN	MEAN (RAW)	MEDIAN (RAW)
NFLX	Oct. 15, 2014 AC	NASDAQ	Services	4.8	17.99%	15.18%	0.67%	-4.53%
P	Oct. 23, 2014 AC	NYSE	Services	4.7	12.7%	12.59%	-5.34%	-10.19%
CSIQ	Nov. 12, 2014 BO	NASDAQ	Technology	4.8	12.23%	12.77%	-1.97%	-9.3%
RAX	Nov. 10, 2014 AC	NYSE	Technology	4.5	11.66%	8.72%	-4.11%	-5.25%
CRUS	Oct. 29, 2014 AC	NASDAQ	Technology	3.5	11.39%	10.75%	-1.83%	-8.06%
CREE	Oct. 21, 2014 AC	NASDAQ	Technology	4.3	10.68%	9.66%	-2.79%	-4.09%
FSLR	Nov. 6. 2014 AC	NASDAQ	Technology	3.8	10.17%	9.02%	-2.73%	-7.58%
COH	Oct. 28. 2014 BO	NYSE	Consumer Goods	2.9	8.25%	7.43%	-3.7%	-5.17%
GT	Oct. 29, 2014 BO	NYSE	Consumer Goods	3.0	6.68%	6.7%	-0.89%	-4.21%

Page 1 of 1

203

After examining the nine candidates, I selected Cree, Inc. (CREE) and chose to implement the option earnings strategy on September 26, 2014, *several weeks before* the next scheduled CREE earnings announcement on October 21, 2014.

Why attempt to initiate an option earnings strategy several weeks before an earnings announcement? Option traders know that short-term options decay faster than long-term options. They also know from experience that the implied volatility of options expiring after earnings announcements will increase as time passes and the earnings date nears.

Many traders presume that we could sell short-term options that expire *before* the earnings announcement and buy options that expire *after* the earnings announcement and profit from the rapid decay of the short-term options *and* from the increasing implied volatility of the long-term options. This strategy is called an earnings calendar spread.

If this hypothesis is true, then we should be able to use our tools to identify a candidate with an unusually low level of implied earnings volatility (IEV), which would further enhance the returns of this strategy. The ideal candidate's current IEV would be lower than both previous levels of implied earnings volatility and historical earnings volatility. This would increase the probability that the IEV would rise approaching the date of the earnings announcement, which would enhance the value of our long option position.

Let's test this hypothesis. To do so, we will need to evaluate CREE's implied earnings volatility and historical earnings volatility. The short option positions would expire before the earnings announcement, so we could not own the calendar spread strategy past the earnings date, but we might want to modify the earnings calendar strategy before the earnings announcement or even employ a different strategy. As a result, to ensure that we are fully prepared to design strategies for *any holding period*, we will research both CREE's historical earnings volatility and directional bias.

CREE Historical Earnings Volatility

Figure 9.3 is OptionSlam.com's historical earnings volatility table for CREE as of September 26, 2014. The 1-day closing percentage returns were calculated from the closing price on the last trade day before earnings to the closing price on the next trading day. You will recall that we need to enter the 1-day closing percentage changes from Figure 9.3 into the Basic or Integrated spreadsheet, which will calculate a series of directional summary statistics and measures of historical earnings volatility.

In Figure 9.4, there are three summary measures of the 1-day log returns. The linear regression, median, and mean log-returns from the twelve previous earnings events were -8.28% (C18), -4.20% (C19), and -3.61% (C20) respectively. When combined with the Root Mean Squared Error (RMSE), the resulting probability of a positive earnings return were 26% E(18), 37% (E19), and 39% (E20). This indicates the presence of a negative or bearish directional bias. As shown in Figure 9.4, the annualized earnings volatility based on the RMSE for the twelve previous CREE earnings events was 206.37% (D22).

Earnings History: Historical Earnings Statistics as of 2014-09-26

Cree, Inc. (CREE) - NASDAQ

Next Earnings Date : Oct. 21, 2014 After Market Close

CREE EVR as of 2014-09-26: 4.3

Earnings Events Available: 27

Figure 9.3: OptionSlam.com Historical EV - CREE

EARNINGS DATE	PRE EARNINGS CLOSE	AFTER HOURS MOVE	PRICE MOVEMENT WITHIN ONE TRADING DAY						MEAN AND MEDIAN OF ONE DAY CLOSING MOVEMENT OF PREVIOUS 12 EARNINGS			
			OPEN	HIGH	LOW	CLOSE	CLOSING%	MAX%	MEAN	MEDIAN	MEAN RAW	MEDIAN RAW
Aug 12, 2014 AC	$49.20	-8.84%	$44.85	$45.51	$44.11	$44.82	-8.9%	-10.34%	11.23%	11.24%	-0.75%	0.39%
April 22, 2014 AC	$58.05	-8.61%	$53.05	$53.40	$50.85	$51.04	-12.07%	-12.4%	10.46%	8.78%	0.02%	0.39%
Jan. 21, 2014 AC	$62.83	2.33%	$64.30	$67.98	$62.78	$67.33	7.16%	8.19%	11.07%	11.45%	-1.78%	-2.44%
Oct 22, 2013 AC	$74.31	-16.14%	$62.32	$63.35	$59.02	$61.77	-16.88%	-20.58%	10.12%	8.23%	-0.83%	-2.44%
Aug 13, 2013 AC	$75.76	-18.5%	$61.74	$62.85	$58.55	$58.83	-22.34%	-22.71%	9.36%	8.23%	-0.07%	-2.44%
April 23, 2013 AC	$57.69	-6.77%	$53.78	$58.00	$52.44	$56.46	-2.13%	-9.1%	9.79%	8.83%	-0.5%	-4.13%
Jan. 22, 2013 AC	$33.47	14.66%	$38.38	$41.20	$38.27	$40.85	22.04%	23.09%	9.39%	8.83%	-0.89%	-4.13%
Oct 16, 2012 AC	$26.19	7.9%	$28.26	$29.71	$27.85	$28.92	10.42%	13.44%	9.48%	9.36%	-0.8%	-4.13%
Aug. 7, 2012 AC	$26.34	2.42%	$26.98	$27.30	$25.62	$27.11	2.92%	3.64%	9.82%	9.36%	-0.47%	-4.13%
April 17, 2012 AC	$31.90	-8.21%	$29.28	$30.39	$28.81	$29.97	-6.05%	-9.68%	9.39%	9.36%	-0.04%	-1.84%
Jan. 17, 2012 AC	$23.33	-3.12%	$22.60	$24.49	$22.45	$24.45	4.8%	4.97%	10.14%	11.99%	0.7%	-1.84%
Oct 18, 2011 AC	$27.78	-3.88%	$26.70	$26.75	$24.04	$24.31	-12.49%	-13.46%	9.24%	9.36%	1.59%	-1.34%

	A	B	C	D	E
1		Figure 9.4: Historical Earnings Volatility Table			
2	Earnings Quarter	Post-Earnings % Change (Close to Close)	Post-Earnings LN Return: Next TD	LN Squared	Dev from Mean Squared
3	-1	-8.90%	-9.32%	0.8689%	0.3256%
4	-2	-12.07%	-12.86%	1.6545%	0.8553%
5	-3	7.16%	6.92%	0.4782%	1.1089%
6	-4	-16.88%	-18.49%	3.4182%	2.2122%
7	-5	-22.34%	-25.28%	6.3923%	4.6950%
8	-6	-2.13%	-2.15%	0.0464%	0.0214%
9	-7	22.04%	19.92%	3.9672%	5.5379%
10	-8	10.42%	9.91%	0.9825%	1.8298%
11	-9	2.92%	2.88%	0.0828%	0.4216%
12	-10	-6.05%	-6.24%	0.3895%	0.0689%
13	-11	4.80%	4.69%	0.2198%	0.6894%
14	-12	-12.49%	-13.34%	1.7800%	0.9461%
15		Linear Regression	Intercept	Slope	R Squared
16			-8.28%	-0.84%	0.06
17		Earnings Statistics	LN ROR	ROR/RMSE	Pr(ROR>0)
18		Linear Regression	-8.28%	-0.64	26%
19		Median	-4.20%	-0.32	37%
20		Mean	-3.61%	-0.28	39%
21		Earnings Statistics	Earnings ROR	Annualized Volatility	
22		Root Mean Square %Change	13.00%	206.37%	
23		Sigma Around Mean	12.49%	198.23%	

HistoricalEV / ImpliedEV / EVvsTime / Holidays

Figure 9.5 is a chart of the log-returns for CREE's previous twelve earnings events. As you can see from the graph, only one of the last six earnings returns was positive, indicating that the directional bias (descending solid trend line) might have worsened recently.

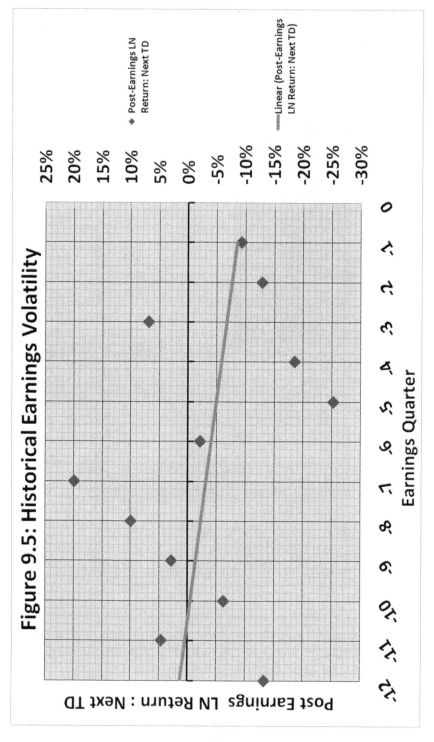

Figure 9.5: Historical Earnings Volatility

As we did when we evaluated UA in Chapter 5, it would be useful to re-calculate the earnings summary return statistics using only the past six observations, which will allow us to gain further insight into recent changes in directional bias and earnings volatility.

Figure 9.6 is the Historical Earnings Volatility Table using only the previous six CREE earnings events. The linear regression, median, and mean log-returns from the *six* previous earnings events were -7.09% (C18), -11.09% (C19), and -10.20% (C20) respectively. The resulting probabilities of positive earnings returns were 31% (E18), 22% (E19), and 24% (E20).

The linear regression returns for the two sets of earnings events were similar, but the mean and median returns were almost 7% lower for the past six earnings events, suggesting an increasing bearish trend. The probabilities of a positive return derived from the mean and median of the past six earnings events both declined by 15%. The market had been consistently disappointed by CREE's recent earnings announcements. If we ultimately decide to create an option earnings strategy that we will hold over the earnings date, we will need to incorporate our directional earnings forecast into the optimization.

The annualized earnings volatility based on the RMSE for the *six* previous CREE earnings events was 232.39% (D22), which was approximately 26% higher than the annualized earnings volatility for the twelve previous earnings events (206.37% in Cell D22 of Figure 9.4). This suggests that not only were the results increasingly bearish, the magnitude of the market's reaction to CREE's earnings announcements had increased as well. We will factor the recent increase in CREE's earnings volatility into our volatility forecasts during the strategy optimization process.

	A	B	C	D	E
1		**Figure 9.6: Historical Earnings Volatility Table**			
2	Earnings Quarter	Post-Earnings % Change (Close to Close)	Post-Earnings LN Return: Next TD	LN Squared	Dev from Mean Squared
3	-1	-8.90%	-9.32%	0.8689%	0.0077%
4	-2	-12.07%	-12.86%	1.6545%	0.0710%
5	-3	7.16%	6.92%	0.4782%	2.9290%
6	-4	-16.88%	-18.49%	3.4182%	0.6872%
7	-5	-22.34%	-25.28%	6.3923%	2.2753%
8	-6	-2.13%	-2.15%	0.0464%	0.6474%
9	-7				
10	-8				
11	-9				
12	-10				
13	-11				
14	-12				
15		Linear Regression	Intercept	Slope	R Squared
16		-7.09%	-7.09%	0.60%	0.01
17		Earnings Statistics	LN ROR	ROR/RMSE	Pr(ROR>0)
18		Linear Regression	-7.09%	-0.48	31%
19		Median	-11.09%	-0.76	22%
20		Mean	-10.20%	-0.70	24%
21		Earnings Statistics	Earnings ROR	Annualized Volatility	
22		Root Mean Square %Change	14.64%	232.39%	
23		Sigma Around Mean	10.50%	166.71%	

HistoricalEV / ImpliedEV / EVvsTime / Holidays

CREE Historical Implied Earnings Volatility

While it is imperative to know CREE's historical earnings volatility, we also need to review how the market has priced past levels of CREE's earnings volatility. If we do not hold our earnings strategy past the earnings announcement, the realized earnings volatility will not affect our strategy. The change in CREE's *implied earnings volatility* over the holding period will affect the strategy through the True Earnings Vega.

In Chapter 3, we examined how the "ImpliedEV" tab of the Basic spreadsheet uses the aggregate IV formula and implied volatility data immediately before and after earnings to solve for the implied earnings volatility (IEV). Figure 9.7 shows the Historical Market Implied Earnings Volatility analysis for CREE's 8/12/2014 earnings announcement. Solver found that CREE's IEV immediately before the 8/12/2014 earnings announcement was 170.5% (C3).

I repeated this analysis for the preceding two earnings announcements as well. CREE's IEV immediately preceding the 4/22/2014 and 1/21/2014 earnings announcements were 179.6% and 227.6% respectively (not shown). The average CREE IEV for the three earnings announcements prior to our current analysis date was 192.5% (C1). All three of the IEV values exceeded 170% and the average of 192.5% was slightly less than the actual historical earnings volatility experienced over the previous twelve (206.37%) and six (232.39%) earnings events.

Figure 9.7: Historical Market Implied Earnings Volatility (Dynamic)

Mean & σ	192.5%	25.1%			1.18%	0.1531%
Analysis Date	8/12/2014	This analysis is ALWAYS performed using the closing IV data immediately before and after earnings announcements				
Market Implied EV	170.5%	10.7%	Solver Estimation of Historical Market Implied Earnings Volatility	Min=>	1.18%	0.1531%

Option Expiration Date	Total Calendar Days	Total Trade Days	Total Normal Days	Aggregate IV of ATM Option	Implied Earnings Volatility	Implied Normal ATM IV	Estimated Post Earnings ATM IV	Actual Post Earnings ATM IV	Estimated Post Earnings ATM IV Change	Actual Post Earnings ATM IV Change	ATM IV Change Error	ATM IV Change Error Squared
8/16/2014	4	3	2	101.0%	170.5%	27.7%	27.7%	27.0%	-73.3%	-74.0%	0.7%	0.0051%
8/23/2014	11	8	7	65.2%	170.5%	26.6%	26.6%	29.0%	-38.6%	-36.2%	-2.4%	0.0591%
8/30/2014	18	13	12	54.6%	170.5%	28.4%	28.4%	28.1%	-26.2%	-26.5%	0.3%	0.0010%
9/6/2014	25	17	16	48.8%	170.5%	26.7%	26.7%	27.5%	-22.1%	-21.3%	-0.8%	0.0062%
9/13/2014	32	22	21	45.8%	170.5%	28.5%	28.5%	28.5%	-17.3%	-17.3%	0.0%	0.0000%
9/20/2014	39	27	26	43.6%	170.5%	29.3%	29.3%	29.4%	-14.3%	-14.2%	-0.1%	0.0002%
10/18/2014	67	47	46	40.1%	170.5%	31.8%	31.8%	31.5%	-8.3%	-8.6%	0.3%	0.0009%
12/20/2014	130	91	90	40.8%	170.5%	36.9%	36.9%	35.5%	-3.9%	-5.3%	1.4%	0.0191%
1/17/2015	158	109	108	39.7%	170.5%	36.4%	36.4%	35.2%	-3.3%	-4.5%	1.2%	0.0133%
3/20/2015	220	152	151	42.0%	170.5%	39.8%	39.8%	37.8%	-2.2%	-4.2%	2.0%	0.0396%
1/15/2016	521	360	359	40.1%	170.5%	39.1%	39.1%	38.2%	-1.0%	-1.9%	0.9%	0.0087%

HistoricalEV / EVvsTime / ImpliedEV / Holidays / Saved

CREE Directional Confirmation

Before we proceed to strategy optimization, we will use one additional source in an attempt to confirm the bearish directional bias that we discovered in CREE's historical earnings return data. As we did in Chapter 5 for UA, we will review the Estimize.com consensus EPS and revenue forecasts for CREE and compare those forecasts to the Wall Street estimates.

We are interested in the 10/21/2014 CREE earnings announcement, which corresponds to the first fiscal quarter of 2015 (FQ1'15) in the Estimize.com EPS table in Figure 9.8 and the Revenue table in Figure 9.9 (the far right-hand-side columns).

The FQ1'15 Estimize.com EPS consensus of $0.33 per share was below the Wall Street estimate of $0.34 per share. Similarly, the Estimize.com Revenue consensus of $431.71 million was also below the Wall Street estimate of $434.55 million. This confirms the bearish directional forecast. However, if we investigate the data further, the bearish implications are even more significant. FQ1'15 was the first time in the last six quarters that the Estimize.com EPS or Revenue consensus was below the Wall Street estimate. This represents a significant change in the direction of CREE's EPS and Revenue consensus estimates for the Estimize.com community, further supporting the likelihood of a bearish directional surprise from CREE's 10/21/2014 earnings announcement.

Figure 9.8: Estimize.com CREE EPS Table

EPS	FQ3 '13	FQ4 '13	FQ1 '14	FQ2 '14	FQ3 '14	FQ4 '14	FQ1 '15
Estimize	0.35	0.38	0.41	0.41	0.43	0.42	0.33
Wall St.	0.34	0.37	0.39	0.39	0.39	0.41	0.34

Figure 9.9: Estimize.com CREE Revenue Table

Revenue	FQ3 '13	FQ4 '13	FQ1 '14	FQ2 '14	FQ3 '14	FQ4 '14	FQ1 '15
Estimize	349.23	379.75	393.62	415.79	418.88	445.25	431.71
Wall St.	345.55	377.36	392.72	412.57	408.14	444.75	434.55

Scenario Assumptions

We now have enough information to design an option earnings strategy for CREE on September 26, 2014. For this strategy example, I specified a holding period from September 26, 2014 to October 17, 2014. The ending date was selected to coincide with the last option expiration date before the CREE earnings announcement on October 21, 2014. I also specified that the resulting strategies should require between $9,000 and $11,000 of capital. We reviewed the input procedures and Integrated spreadsheet images for these specifications in the last few chapters and they are not shown here. In this chapter, our discussion of the Integrated spreadsheet will be limited to a few select screenshots.

Figure 9.10 is a screenshot from the "Specs" Tab of the Integrated spreadsheet that shows the assumptions used in all scenario and optimization calculations. Cells with dark shaded backgrounds and white text represent user inputs. Cells with white or light colored backgrounds represent calculation cells and should not be modified. Let's review several of the most relevant user inputs.

I entered a value of 10.00% (C17) for the CREE "Percent UV/OV Correction," which represents the amount of undervaluation or overvaluation correction that occurs during the simulation period. You may recall that I used 100% in the UA strategy example, which was justified because the UA holding period *included* the earnings event, which is the principal source of pricing anomalies in individual stocks. The CREE holding period *did not* include an earnings event, which warrants the much lower "Percent OV/UV Correction" of 10%.

At the close on September 26, 2014, the comprehensive volatility model used all of the options in the CREE matrix (that passed the input filters) to estimate an implied earnings volatility of 168.27% (E19). As you will recall, CREE's historical earnings volatility over the past twelve earnings events was 206.37% (F19) and was even higher for the past six earnings events (232.39% in Cell D22 of Figure 9.6). Earlier in this chapter, we also calculated the average historical *implied earnings volatility* for the three preceding earnings events: 192.5% (Figure 9.7 Cell C1). Based on the historical values, I assumed (conservatively) that the implied earnings volatility would increase from 168.27% (Figure 9.10 Cell E19) to 180% (D19) during the holding period. In other words, the implied earnings volatility would increase toward CREE's historical actual and implied earnings volatility.

The 190% (C19) realized earnings volatility will not affect the simulation because the holding period does not include an earnings event. Similarly, the assumed 0% (C21) directional earnings price return will not affect the simulation either, because the return bias is only realized after an earnings announcement.

Finally, I assumed slippage of negative $0.10 (C25) per spread trade and negative 0.75 per contract (D25). This slippage estimate is conservative for CREE, but slightly overestimating slippage increases the probability that optimal solutions can be implemented in practice. It should be possible to execute a very high percentage of CREE spreads within $0.05 of the spread mid-point.

	B	C	D	E	F
15	Figure 9.10: Scenario Assumptions	Value	Historical	Assumption	Δ ATM IV30
16	Δ ATMIV / 1% Δ Price Increase	-0.16%	-0.16%	Normal IV	0.00%
17	Percent UV/OV Correction	10.00%			
18	Scenario Assumptions	Realized	Implied(U)	Implied(M)	Historical
19	Earnings Volatility	190.00%	180.00%	168.27%	206.37%
20	Scenario Assumptions	Realized	Regression	Median	Mean
21	LN of Earnings Price Return	0.000%	-8.278%	-4.197%	-3.615%
22	Scenario Assumptions	MinROR	MaxROR	Min	Max
23	Min/Max ROR IVPrice	-35.00%	35.00%	-44.80%	37.77%
24	Scenario Assumptions	Spread Slippage	Commission per Contract		
25	Transaction Costs	-0.10	-0.75		

H ◀ ▶ H | HistoricalEV / Saved / IVPrice / **Specs** / IMPORT / SolveIV2 / Greeks / ◀

Optimal CREE Solutions

I executed the "Opt All" macro, which ran twenty different optimization runs, from twenty different starting points, and used two different solution algorithms. The results for each of the pre-set starting points are shown in Figure 9.11. Figure 9.11 shows the objective function (T), average profit after transaction costs (U), standard deviation of the profit (V), maximum loss (W), the required capital (X), and the Solver result (Y).

The objective function represents the expected return divided by the absolute value of the largest loss incurred in any of the discrete

holding period scenarios. The largest objective function value was
0.01 (T26 & T29) and the largest expected profit (net of transaction
costs) was $125 (U29). The standard deviation of profits (Column V)
and the maximum losses (Column W) incurred were all significant.
The required capital amounts for all solutions (Column X) were
within the specified range of $9,000 to $11,000 and the Solver
solutions were all feasible (Column Y).

The Solver solutions were clearly not as impressive as the UA
optimal solution. So what do we do now? Nothing!

*This is probably the single most important observation in the book and it is
not limited to option strategies: when we do not have a trading edge, we should not
trade.* There are no exceptions to this rule. If we trade without a
demonstrated probabilistic edge, it would be gambling and we would
be destined to lose money as the odds played out against us over
time.

	J	T	U	V	W	X	Y
23		\multicolumn{6}{c}{**Figure 9.11: Strategy Optimization Results**}					
24	5	OBJ FN	Avg Profit	σProfit	Max Loss	Req Cap	Result
25	1	-0.05	-312	4,736	-6,562	10,425	0
26	2	0.01	90	5,213	-9,964	9,965	14
27	3	-0.09	-740	1,180	-8,456	10,710	0
28	4	-0.08	-551	1,461	-7,063	10,566	0
29	5	0.01	125	5,148	-10,556	10,564	0
30	6	-0.03	-222	2,679	-6,536	10,852	0
31	7	-0.07	-280	3,524	-4,111	10,192	0
32	8	-0.09	-574	6,785	-6,549	10,980	0
33	9	-0.09	-366	3,232	-4,043	10,017	0
34	10	-0.11	-521	4,128	-4,757	10,063	0
35	11	-0.04	-339	2,934	-7,814	10,979	0

HistoricalEV Saved IVPrice Specs IMPORT SolveIV2 Greeks

What have we learned from this exercise? This was only one
example, but we assumed that implied earnings volatility would
increase as the earnings date approached and we also had the
supposed advantages of accelerating time decay on short option
positions expiring before earnings and increasing implied volatility of
long option positions expiring after earnings. Even with those
supposed advantages, Solver could not construct a single option
earnings strategy that was able to cover transaction costs, even by
buying overvalued options and selling undervalued options.

This should cause us to seriously question the hypothesis that earnings calendar spreads *inherently* offer positive expected returns. Our example does not imply that earnings calendar spreads will *never* offer attractive risk-adjusted returns, but the above analysis does suggest that those opportunities will probably be case-specific, not systematic.

So what do we do now? We invested all of our time and effort into researching CREE and we have nothing to show for it. Well, that is not exactly true. We analyzed CREE on September 26, 2014, but we still have several weeks before the CREE earnings announcement on October 21, 2014.

The historical actual and implied earnings volatility data for CREE will not change, so neither should our directional and earnings volatility forecasts. In fact, very few of the user specifications in the spreadsheet will change. Simply save a copy of the spreadsheet in a CREE directory and re-run the analysis as often as time permits.

The Integrated spreadsheet provides an automated macro that makes it quick and easy to import CSV files from the CREE matrix at any time before the next earnings event. The "Estimate Volatility Model" macro is also automated, as are the strategy optimization macros. Option prices are not constant and neither are option pricing anomalies, especially approaching earnings.

As our OptionSlam.com historical scan indicated, CREE has experienced a high degree of earnings volatility and a bearish directional bias in the past and our ability to precisely calculate CREE's implied earnings volatility gives us an advantage when evaluating and constructing option earnings strategies, especially when holding a strategy over an earnings event. We only have to wait for an opportunity that we can exploit.

CREE Revisited

For the second CREE strategy optimization example, I specified a one-day holding period from October 21, 2014 to October 22, 2014, which was selected specifically to include the earnings event. I again specified that the resulting strategies should require between $9,000 and $11,000 of capital. The Integrated spreadsheet images for these specifications are not shown here.

Figure 9.12 is a screenshot from the "Specs" Tab of the Integrated spreadsheet that shows the scenario assumptions used in all scenario and optimization calculations on October 21, 2014. Let's review several of the most significant user inputs.

I entered a value of 100% (C17) for the CREE "Percent UV/OV Correction," which represents the amount of undervaluation or overvaluation correction that occurs during the simulation period. This assumption is the same as the 100% "Percent UV/OV Correction" used in the UA strategy example. The 100% correction is plausible because the holding periods include the earnings event.

At the close on October 21, 2014, the comprehensive volatility model used all of the options in the CREE matrix (that passed the input filters) to estimate an implied earnings volatility of only 135.46% (E19). This is much lower than CREE's IEV that we estimated on September 26, 2014 (168.27% in Figure 9.10, Cell E19) and is significantly below CREE's historical actual earnings and implied earnings volatility, which should offer attractive strategy solutions.

CREE's historical earnings volatility over the past twelve earnings events was 206.37% (F19) and was even higher for the past six earnings events (232.39% in Figure 9.6, Cell D22). In addition, the average historical implied earnings volatility (IEV) for the three preceding earnings events was 192.5% (Figure 9.7 Cell C1).

Based on the historical values, I assumed that the implied earnings volatility would increase from 135.46% (Figure 9.12 Cell E19) to 160% (D19) during the holding period. The value of 160% was still well below previous IEV levels for CREE, but the length of the holding period was only one day. However, earnings price shocks can result in material changes in implied earnings volatility.

This time, the 200% (C19) realized earnings volatility *will* affect the simulation because the holding period now includes an earnings event. Likewise, the assumed negative 4% (C21) directional earnings price return will also affect the simulation results, because the return bias is realized after an earnings announcement.

The 200% (C19) realized earnings volatility assumption is consistent with the realized earnings volatility over the previous twelve earnings events (206.37% in Cell F19), but is still lower than the historical earnings volatility over the past six events (232.39%). The negative 4% (C21) directional earnings price return assumption is conservative, especially relative to the mean and median earnings returns over the past six earnings events. The actual earnings return could be substantially worse than negative 4%, but it is wise not to use extreme assumptions when generating optimization scenarios.

As was the case in the first CREE example, I assumed slippage of negative $0.10 (C25) per spread trade and negative 0.75 per contract (D25). Again, this slippage estimate is conservative for CREE, but slightly overestimating slippage increases the probability that optimal solutions can be implemented in practice.

	B	C	D	E	F
15	Figure 9.12: Scenario Assumptions	Value	Historical	Assumption	Δ ATM IV30
16	Δ ATMIV / 1% Δ Price Increase	-0.16%	-0.16%	Normal IV	0.00%
17	Percent UV/OV Correction	100.00%			
18	Scenario Assumptions	Realized	Implied(U)	Implied(M)	Historical
19	Earnings Volatility	200.00%	160.00%	135.46%	206.37%
20	Scenario Assumptions	Realized	Regression	Median	Mean
21	LN of Earnings Price Return	-4.000%	-8.278%	-4.197%	-3.615%
22	Scenario Assumptions	MinROR	MaxROR	Min	Max
23	Min/Max ROR IVPrice	-35.00%	35.00%	-44.80%	37.77%
24	Scenario Assumptions	Spread Slippage	Commission per Contract		
25	Transaction Costs	-0.10	-0.75		

K ◀ ▶ ▶l Holidays / HistoricalEV / Saved / IVPrice / Specs / IMPORT / SolveIV2 / Gr◀

Optimal CREE Solution

Figure 9.13 is a screenshot from the "Opt" tab of the Integrated spreadsheet that shows the optimal CREE solution found by the Solver optimizer. There are eight columns from left to right: amount (number of contracts), type (call or put), strike price, expiration date (YYMMDD), T-Days (number of trading days until expiration), Mid Price, T-Delta (True Delta), and Rich/Cheap (degree of over or undervaluation).

The call spread is shown in the first two rows, the put spread in the next two rows, and the strangle or straddle in the last two rows. The number of contracts in the call spread was zero (J7:J8), so let's review the put spread first.

The optimal solution required the sale of 2 (J9) put options with a strike price of $28.00 (L9) and an expiration date of 11/01/2014 (M9) and the simultaneous purchase of 2 (J10) put options with a strike price of $37.50 (L10) and an expiration date of 12/20/2014 (M10). The put option sold was rich or overvalued by $0.05 (Q9) per share, per contract. The put option purchased was cheap or undervalued by $0.09 (Q10) per share, per contract.

The final component of the optimal UA strategy was a diagonal strangle, which required the purchase of 18 (J11) call options with a strike price of $33.50 (L11) and an expiration date of 11/01/2014 (M11) and the simultaneous purchase of 18 (J12) put options with a strike price of $35.00 (L12) and an expiration date of 12/20/2014 (M12). In this case, the call option purchased was cheap by $0.01 (Q11) per share, per contract and the put option purchased was also cheap by $0.11 (Q12) per share, per contract. The solution only requires two spread transactions, which makes it relatively easy to manage and to execute.

	J	K	L	M	N	O	P	Q
5				Figure 9.13: CREE Optimal Solution				
6	Amount	Type	Strike	Exp Date	T-Days	Mid Price	T-Delta	Rich/Cheap
7	0	C	38.00	141101	8	0.205	11.5	-0.07
8	0	C	35.00	141220	42	1.515	42.3	0.01
9	-2	P	28.00	141101	8	0.21	-7.8	-0.05
10	2	P	37.50	141220	42	5.03	-75.5	0.09
11	18	C	33.50	141101	8	1.26	49.3	0.01
12	18	P	35.00	141220	42	3.23	-58.7	0.11

P&L Graph

The ability to fully appreciate the nature of a strategy by mentally combining multiple spreads would be very difficult. That is why we use profit and loss diagrams, which are common to all option analytical platforms. Figure 9.14 is a profit and loss (P&L) diagram for the optimal strategy described in Figure 9.13. The scenario values accurately incorporate the effects of earnings volatility and normal volatility for every option in the matrix, as do the True Greeks.

The independent x-axis represents the CREE stock price in dollars. The dependent y-axis on the left side of the diagram denotes the profit and loss of the optimal strategy for three different dates.

The solid upper "P&L 0" represents the P&L at time zero, or the instantaneous profit and loss of the strategy. The solid lower "P&L U" line represents the P&L on the future date specified by the User, which is the date used to optimize the strategy. In this example, the User date was one trading day into the future, or October 22, 2014.

The solid lower "P&L X" line represents the P&L on a second future date specified by the User, which is intended to be the expiration date of the option with the shortest-term option.

In this example, the "X" date was also one trading day into the future, or October 22, 2014. Given that the "U" and "X" dates are the same, the lower lines overlap and only appear as a single solid (lower) line in Figure 9.14.

The "U" and "X" probabilities are shown by the faded dashed lines and correspond to the values on the dependent y-axis on the right side of the diagram. In addition to the P&L graph, I have included summary statistics for the optimal CREE strategy at the top of the diagram.

The optimizer always uses the User date, so let's focus our attention on the lower P&L line. The majority of the P&L line was above the break-even or zero profit line except for a narrow region of the diagram centered between the prices of $31 and $37. The maximum simulated strategy loss of negative $1,855 (including transaction costs) occurs at the lowest point in the diagram, which corresponds to a post-earnings price of $33.49. The price of CREE before earnings on October 21, 2014 was $33.15.

The optimal hybrid strategy would have performed very well for price declines in CREE, which should be no revelation. Our research indicated that the price of CREE was likely to decline due to a bearish earnings surprise and we used a negative 4% price shock to create our simulated price distribution. This explains why the probability distributions (dashed lines) are centered below the pre-earnings price of $33.15. The optimizer recognized our bearish forecast and designed a strategy to profit from the expected price decline. Delta measures the directional exposure to price and the True Delta of the strategy was -305.80, reflecting a strategy that would perform well when the price of CREE declines.

The shape of the P&L function was convex or curved upwards, indicating the strategy would have performed well for large moves up or down in the price of CREE. You will recall that Gamma measures the curvature of the option price function, so based on the shape of the diagram, we would expect the optimal strategy to have positive Gamma. The True Gamma was +355.3.

The difference between the upper "P&L 0" line and the lower "P&L U" and "P&L X" is due to the effects of the passage of time, which is measured by Theta. The positive value of Gamma means that the strategy must have had a negative Theta. The True Theta was -$1,579.3, which fully reflected the volatility crush due to passing the CREE earnings date. The Black-Scholes (BS) Theta was only -$136.6, which grossly understated the true cost of the strategy due to the passage of time.

The strategy had a positive True Normal 30 Vega (+$83.4) and a positive True Earnings Vega (+$19.9), which is consistent with our forecast of a higher than expected level of earnings volatility.

The total transaction costs were -$460. The expected profit (net of transaction costs) was $1,803 and the maximum loss (net of transaction costs) was -$1,855. The objective function, which is what the optimizer was attempting to maximize, was the expected profit ($1,803) divided by the *absolute value* of the maximum loss ($1,855). The expected profit can be found on the "Opt" and "Analysis" tabs, but was not shown in Figure 9.14.

The resulting value of the objective function for the optimal strategy was an attractive 0.97, which means the probability-weighted expected profit from the strategy was 0.97 times the maximum loss. The objective function value of 0.97 represents the expected profit per unit or dollar of risk. In this case, risk was defined as the maximum loss (net of transaction costs) of the strategy in any of the discrete scenarios ($1,855).

The optimal objective function value of 0.97 for CREE was appealing, but much lower than the remarkable 10.78 for UA. The CREE option matrix was much more efficiently priced than the UA matrix. As a result, we could not exploit undervalued and overvalued CREE options as effectively as we could when we designed the UA strategy. The average pricing error for the CREE option matrix was $0.099 (not shown), which was much less than the $0.175 (Figure 7.2 Cell S12) average pricing error for the UA option matrix.

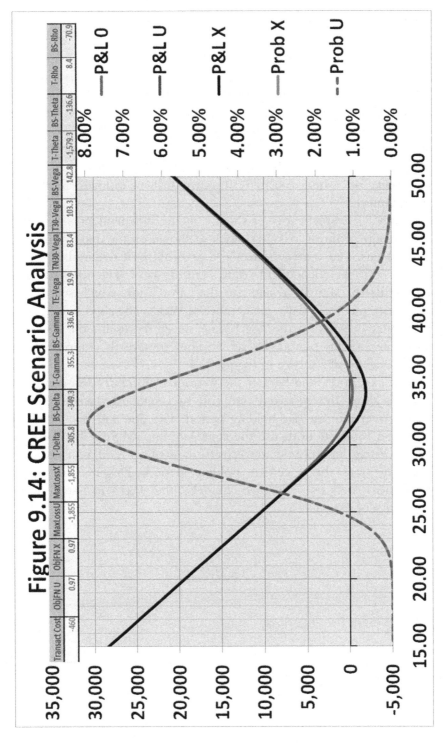

Figure 9.14: CREE Scenario Analysis

Confirmation

As we did earlier when we created the UA option earnings strategy, we will use OptionVue's graphical analysis to look for any major disparities in the strategy results that would warrant further research. I entered the optimal CREE solution from Figure 9.13 into the OptionVue software and performed a graphical analysis of the strategy on October 21, 2014. OptionVue's analytical results are depicted in Figure 9.14B. OptionVue's results do not include the directional or earnings volatility forecasts that we estimated earlier in this chapter.

The CREE stock price is shown on the independent x-axis and the strategy profit or loss (in dollars) is shown on the dependent left-vertical axis. The strategy return as a percentage of required capital is shown on the dependent right-vertical axis. The dashed line represents the strategy results for the "T+0" line, which stands for trade date plus zero days (instantaneous P&L). The solid line depicts the strategy results for the "T+1" line, which represents the P&L for a one-day holding period. These two lines are directly comparable to the strategy results shown in Figure 9.14.

The two horizontal bars at the bottom of OptionVue's graphical analysis show the expected one and two-standard deviation price moves over the one-day holding period. The one and two-standard deviation forecasts both use the aggregate implied volatility formula to accurately incorporate the effects of earnings and non-earnings volatility over the specified holding period. Despite the many differences between the two models, the P&L forecasts were generally consistent.

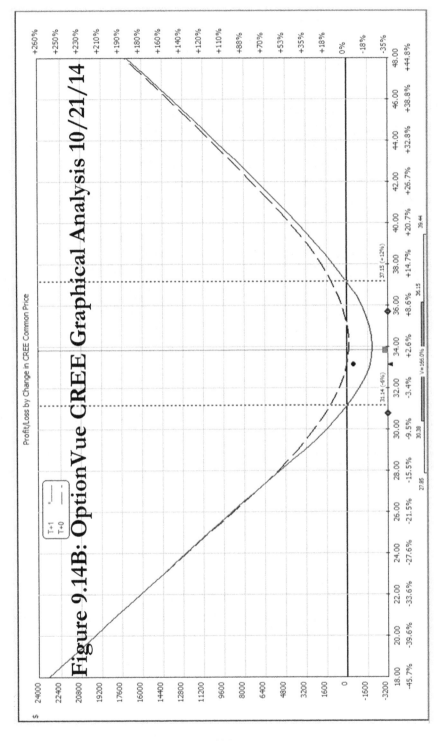

Figure 9.14B: OptionVue CREE Graphical Analysis 10/21/14

Actual Strategy Results

So how did the optimal hybrid CREE strategy actually perform? Figure 9.15 is the same P&L graph from Figure 9.14 with one addition. The diamond represents the actual profit of the optimal strategy (net of transaction costs) from October 21, 2014 to October 22, 2014. The actual price of CREE decreased from $33.15 to $27.28. Our bearish forecast was correct and the realized earnings volatility was also greater than the implied earnings volatility.

As you would expect, the optimal strategy performed well, earning a total profit of $6,482 (net of transaction costs). The return on required capital of $9,488 (not shown) was 68.32% ($6,482/$9,488) over the one-day holding period. At a price of $27.28, the model forecasted a strategy value of $6,344, meaning that the actual strategy performance was almost identical to the modeled strategy performance.

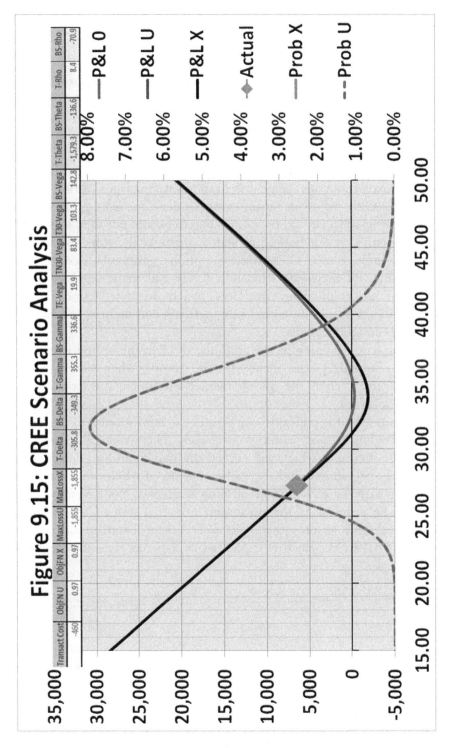

Figure 9.15: CREE Scenario Analysis

Conclusion

The purpose of this chapter was to provide another practical example of how to use the *Exploiting Earnings Volatility* analytical approach and toolset to design a realistic option earnings strategy, based on actual market prices and actual earnings data.

The first pre-earnings CREE example taught us a very important lesson: we do not always have a trading edge. When we do not have a trading edge, we should not trade. When we do have an edge, we should exploit our advantage, but must always manage our risk.

I normally advocate using stop orders to exit positions at predetermined levels and position sizing to ensure our total losses are small relative to our trading capital. Unfortunately, stop loss orders are of limited use when trading options, primarily due to the importance of managing execution levels and minimizing slippage. Even if we could place stop loss orders for our hybrid option spreads, they would be completely ineffective in limiting risk during earnings announcements.

First, earnings are typically announced when the option market is closed. Second, prices make discrete jumps when earnings are announced. Even if the option market was open, the stop orders would not work.

As a result, it is critical to use positing sizing formulas to limit risk when trading option earnings strategies. The maximum loss that could be incurred (which will exceed the maximum loss depicted in the P&L diagram) should always be considered when calculating the position size for your option earnings strategies. Your position size should be reduced as the maximum potential loss of the strategy increases. This ensures that your total loss will remain below the desired threshold, which is expressed as a percentage of your total capital.

10 - PRACTICAL CONSIDERATIONS

The purpose of this final chapter is to provide some practical suggestions on how to get the most out of the tools and concepts introduced in this book. We will examine how to use these tools efficiently to exploit earnings volatility, and we will also explore how this framework could be applied to improve volatility research and to generate new profit opportunities.

Efficient Use of Tools

One important benefit of option earnings plays is that we have hundreds of new trade opportunities every quarter. We know that earnings will be announced every quarter and we even know the exact timing of the announcement in advance. Given that we now have the ability to calculate actual historical earnings volatility, historical implied earnings volatility, and real-time implied earnings volatility, we have a material advantage over the typical retail option trader. To fully exploit our trading edge on the full spectrum of earnings candidates, we have to use our new tools efficiently.

The first step is to automate the data collection process. To calculate historical earnings volatility, we need historical earnings return data. I use OptionSlam.com, which also provides extensive screening tools to help identify prospective trading candidates. Analyzing earnings volatility requires a lot of data and it would be impractical to gather this data manually, especially for a number of different candidates. It would also increase the likelihood of data errors, which would compromise the integrity of our analytical results and could lead to erroneous trades.

To make full use of the input macros in the Integrated spreadsheet, we also need a source of current and historical option data. I use OptionVue, which can export the option matrix data in a format that is compatible with the import macros in the Integrated spreadsheet. The import macros read CSV files in a specific format, which could potentially be generated from other sources. Regardless, we will want to use the tools in the Integrated spreadsheet often, so it is critical to find a reliable source of option matrix data in the designated CSV format.

The next step is to generate and monitor earnings candidates with a history of volatile or directionally biased earnings returns. I use OptionSlam.com's custom screening tools to identify earnings candidates and regularly calculate each candidate's implied earnings volatility and normal volatility. OptionVue also has an "Earnings Plays" subscription service (see Resources section) that could be used to identify earnings strategy candidates.

The best way to develop your earnings volatility intuition is to frequently use the Basic and Integrated spreadsheets to calculate implied earnings volatility and normal volatility. If possible, calculate these values daily for all of your earnings candidates. At a minimum, begin one month before the earnings announcement and end shortly after the announcement.

Save this data in a database or spreadsheet for further research. Once you have saved the historical actual and implied earnings volatility values in your database, you will only need to add new data to the database every quarter; the historical values never change. This data will be invaluable as you create option earnings strategies in the future.

I also recommend saving the data you use in the Integrated and Basic spreadsheets in a separate spreadsheet. Simply copy and paste the values into the separate spreadsheet or tab for future use. When you want to re-run the analysis on a previous candidate, copy and paste the saved data back into the Basic or Integrated spreadsheet and add the most recent data before re-running the analysis.

During earnings season, regularly calculate the implied earnings volatility for each candidate and look for large anomalies that you can exploit. If the anomalies are small, there is no need to waste your time by running an optimization. However, if the anomalies are large, run the strategy optimizer in the Integrated spreadsheet and evaluate the expected profit per unit of risk for the resulting strategies.

If the risk-adjusted expected profits are attractive, examine the actual market prices and confirm that execution at the desired prices is likely. If so, enter limit orders for the option spreads. If executed, manage your strategy using the P&L graph, expected profit, maximum loss, and other strategy summary statistics from the Integrated spreadsheet to make informed exit and risk management decisions.

That may sound like a lot of work -- which is why we get paid for it. Exploiting market inefficiencies takes time and effort, which is why the inefficiencies exist. If you only have time to track a few candidates, then become an expert in those candidates and only execute trades when your strategies' expected risk-adjusted profits are attractive.

Volatility Research

I primarily trade algorithmic strategies and many of my strategies use volatility-based indicators for decision rules and filters. The volatility-based indicators use historical volatility, implied volatility, volatility skews, and option volume in a variety of interesting ways, which include the use of trends, oscillators, and divergences. These volatility-based tools work extremely well for strategies that are based on equity indices and futures, but on not individual stocks. Why? Because the discrete effects of earnings events on the underlying prices, implied volatility, and realized volatility of individual stocks compromise the effectiveness of actual and implied volatility indicators.

As we have discussed throughout this book, implied volatility equals the weighted-average of earnings and non-earnings volatility, and the weighting is a function of the relative number of earnings and non-earnings trading days remaining until option expiration. As a result, implied volatilities of options on individual stocks are not comparable across time or among different candidates. Implied volatility represents the aggregation of two independent sources of volatility, both of which should be analyzed independently.

Until now, it had not been possible to separate earnings and non-earnings volatility. The aggregate implied volatility formula and the spreadsheet tools introduced in this book allow us to isolate and quantify implied earnings volatility, normal implied volatility, and all of the components of normal volatility.

If we are interested in building a forecasting model for realized or implied earnings volatility, we have to evaluate historical earnings volatility and historical levels of implied earnings volatility directly. It will not help us to study implied volatility, which includes the effects of both earnings and non-earnings volatility.

Similarly, if we want to build volatility-based indicators to help us make timing decisions on individual stocks, we need to use historical and current levels of normal or non-earnings volatility. We could go even further and study the historical volatility model parameters derived by the comprehensive volatility model solutions in the Integrated spreadsheet.

The key is to isolate and quantify implied earnings volatility, normal implied volatility, and all of the components of normal volatility *before* attempting to develop volatility-based indicators or strategies. The components of volatility are comparable across time and among individual stocks, while implied volatility is not.

Trading Edge

Separating and quantifying volatility components and saving the resulting data is a great beginning, but our ultimate goal is to use our volatility insights to improve our trading edge. How could we go further?

We have already examined the basic technique of evaluating historical earnings volatility statistically to identify directional biases. We could also use more sophisticated tools to forecast directional price moves due to earnings events: linear regression, non-linear regression, multiple regression, time series analysis, or even neural network models. In addition to evaluating past earnings events for each company, we could also evaluate the earnings volatility for each sector.

This would allow us to answer some interesting questions. How does the earnings volatility for each sector change over time? Is it a function of the economic environment? Is the relative earnings volatility of each company in a sector stable over time? Could the relative ranking of each company within the sector be used to forecast the earnings volatility of each company more accurately?

How do the directional earnings returns for each sector compare over time? Are there observable patterns in the sector directional earnings returns? Could the directional earnings returns for other companies in the sector (that have already reported) help us forecast directional returns for companies in the same sector that have yet to report?

Are the earnings volatilities of some sectors chronically mispriced? Which sectors have offered the best directional and non-directional earnings opportunities historically? Why? Will these trends continue? The spreadsheet tools provided with this book allow us to generate the required data to answer all of these questions, which should greatly enhance our trading edge.

We used the Estimize.com consensus EPS and Revenue estimates to confirm our directional earnings return forecasts in Chapter 5 and Chapter 9. Could we use this data directly to identify trading opportunities? In discussing this book with Euan Sinclair, a proprietary option trader and author of *Volatility Trading*, Sinclair suggested that when the dispersion of earnings estimates is low, earnings surprises are larger. In other words, realized earnings volatility is inversely correlated with the dispersion of earnings estimates. This is an interesting hypothesis and one that we could confirm and exploit by downloading and analyzing the Estimize.com data.

Before we explore other potential applications of this framework, I wanted to pass along a practical insight from a professional option trader with decades of experience. Frank Fahey is a former floor trader and still trades options professionally. In addition, he is a mentor for Discover Options, the educational arm of OptionVue. Fahey recommended contacting the investor relations department of the company and confirming the time and date of the earnings announcement *before* implementing any option earnings strategy.

Most earnings databases are reasonably accurate, but there will be errors. Think about the cost of using the wrong earnings date in our analysis. If our earnings date was off by a single day, it could change the implied volatility of short-term options by 25% or more. It would compromise our entire analysis. All of our volatility model, valuation, risk, and optimization results would be wrong. Learning from experienced and successful traders is one of the best ways to ensure our investment process will work in practice.

New Applications

We have applied the aggregate implied volatility formula specifically to earnings events, but the concept and formula are not limited to earnings announcements. We could use the same conceptual framework and aggregate implied volatility formula to quantify the implied volatility of *any discrete event that provides material new information to market participants.* The only requirement is that we know the expected time and date of the release of that information in advance.

One example would be FDA drug approvals, which obviously have the potential to create extreme price moves in the underlying stock. If we know the approximate FDA announcement date, we could use that date and the aggregate implied volatility formula to solve for the IEV.

Throughout this book the abbreviation "IEV" signified implied *earnings* volatility. In this case, IEV would represent the implied *event* volatility. The framework, formulas, and spreadsheet tools that we used to evaluate earnings volatility could be used to analyze the volatility associated with any discrete event. If the exact announcement date was not known in advance, we could study the term structure of volatility to determine the market's expected distribution of possible announcement dates.

There is only a single FDA announcement for any drug, so it would be impossible to compare past actual event volatilities or historical IEV levels to current IEV levels. However, it would be possible to analyze actual event returns and historical IEV levels for similar classes of drugs or drugs that had similar potential impact on a company's future revenue. We could compare these values to the current IEV for the new prospective drug to identify potential event volatility anomalies.

We could even perform a similar set of IEV calculations for corporate legal judgments and Supreme Court rulings. Obviously the scope of these legal rulings would be limited to specific companies in certain industries, but for these companies, the impact could be dramatic. Our ability to calculate the IEV and evaluate it in the context of a wide range of other market moving events gives us an advantage. The framework and aggregate implied volatility formula are applicable to any discrete event that provides material new information to market participants.

What about releases of economic data? These releases move the market and the release dates are known in advance. Non-Farm Payroll (NFP) is one of the major monthly economic releases. We could use index options to calculate the IEV associated with the monthly NFP report. We could analyze the historical index returns on past NFP dates and we could even calculate historical IEV values. This would give us the appropriate context to evaluate the IEV associated with the current NFP report.

We could solve for the NFP IEV for several equity indices. What if they were materially different? Could that create a trading opportunity? What if the NFP IEV was the same as the normal volatility, but the historical NFP volatility was greater than the norm. That would suggest that the NVP IEV was too low and index options did not reflect the additional volatility associated with the NFP report.

We could calculate similar IEVs for other major economic releases, Fed meetings, etc. All of the resulting IEVs would be analogous. In other words, they would all be expressed as annualized standard deviations, which are directly comparable. This analysis might give us additional insight into optimal timing of initiating our market-neutral option income strategies. The number and type of potential applications are almost limitless.

In our analysis of earnings volatility, we implicitly assumed that the implied earnings volatilities for all future company earnings announcements were equal. This is probably a reasonable assumption. However, if we use the aggregate implied volatility formula to calculate the IEV for multiple independent events, then we would need separate variables for each IEV and each event would have its own weight. The logical extension of the aggregate implied volatility formula to multiple independent events is straightforward.

NTD_{E1} = **Number of Event-1 Trading Days**
NTD_{E2} = **Number of Event-2 Trading Days**
NTD_{EN} = **Number of Event-N Trading Days**
NTD_{N} = **Number of Normal Trading Days**
NTD_{T} = **Total Number of Trading Days**

W_{E1} = Event-1 Volatility Weight
W_{E2} = Event-2 Volatility Weight
W_{EN} = Event-N Volatility Weight
W_N = Normal Volatility Weight

$W_{EN} = NTD_{EN}/(NTD_T)$
$W_N = NTD_N/(NTD_T)$

IV = Aggregate Implied Volatility (Annualized)

V_{E1} = Event-1 Volatility (Annualized)
V_{E2} = Event-2 Volatility (Annualized)
V_{EN} = Event-N Volatility (Annualized)
V_N = Normal Volatility (Annualized)

$$IV = ((W_{E1}*(V_{E1}{}^2))+(W_{E2}*(V_{E2}{}^2)) \ldots (W_{EN}*(V_{EN}{}^2))+ (W_N)*(V_N{}^2))^{0.5}$$

As you can see from the general aggregate implied volatility formula above, we can use this version of the formula to solve for aggregate implied volatilities that are influenced by any number of independent discrete events. We could even use this formula to estimate the forward volatilities implicit in the term structure of volatilities, otherwise known as the horizontal skew. As was the case with the aggregate implied volatility formula presented earlier, all of the weights in the general aggregate implied volatility formula must sum to one (100%).

A thorough exploration of the new topics introduced in this chapter is beyond the scope of this book. Nevertheless, I wanted to share with you some ideas to get you started on your own research projects and to help convey the potential for this innovative new analytical framework.

Conclusion

Exploiting Earnings Volatility has introduced a wide range of concepts and practical tools:

- Two versions of the aggregate implied volatility formula, one for earnings announcements and a second for multiple independent discrete events.

- An analytical framework with practical tools that simultaneously estimated IEV, normal implied volatility, and all components of normal implied volatility including vertical and horizontal skews.

- A calculation methodology with practical tools that calculate True Greeks for every option in the matrix and for option earnings strategies.

- A non-linear integer strategy optimization tool that attempts to identify the option earnings strategy with the highest expected profit per unit of risk.

- A graphical framework to evaluate the resulting strategies.

- Real-world examples with actual market data that demonstrate how to use this analytical framework and tool set to evaluate, optimize, and trade option earnings strategies.

- Suggestions for applying this approach in new ways to further expand your trading edge.

The primary objective of this book was to introduce a theoretically sound framework for quantifying the effects of earnings volatility on all options and to provide tools that will help traders apply that framework in practice.

I also strived to present the material in a way that would be accessible and educational for new traders, while still offering some interesting challenges and insights for experienced option professionals. The diversity in readers' backgrounds was the principal reason that I provided two separate spreadsheets.

I recognize that very few readers will immediately apply all of the concepts and tools included in the book and spreadsheets, but trading is a journey, not a destination. Our goals should be to continuously expand our knowledge and investigate new opportunities to achieve and maintain our trading edge. The concepts and tools presented here were designed to help you pursue those goals – now and in the future.

Thank you for investing your time and effort to review the many new and challenging concepts presented in this book. I hope you found the earnings volatility framework and the insights in this book to be helpful and I hope they greatly enhance your ability to evaluate, construct, and manage your option earnings strategies. Good luck in your trading.

ABOUT THE AUTHOR

Brian Johnson designed, programmed, and implemented the first return sensitivity based parametric framework actively used to control risk in fixed income portfolios. He further extended the capabilities of this approach by designing and programming an integrated series of option valuation, prepayment, and optimization models.

Based on this technology, Mr. Johnson founded Lincoln Capital Management's fixed income index business, where he ultimately managed over $13 billion in assets for some of the largest and most sophisticated institutional clients in the U.S. and around the globe.

He later served as the President of a financial consulting and software development firm, designing artificial intelligence-based forecasting and risk management systems for institutional investment managers.

Mr. Johnson is now a full-time proprietary trader in options, futures, stocks, and ETFs primarily using algorithmic trading strategies. In addition to his professional investment experience, he also designed and taught courses in financial derivatives for both MBA and undergraduate business programs.

His first book, *Option Strategy Risk / Return Ratios: A Revolutionary New Approach to Optimizing, Adjusting, and Trading Any Option Income Strategy*, was published in 2014 and has received outstanding reviews. He has also written articles for the *Financial Analysts Journal*, *Active Trader*, and *Seeking Alpha* and he regularly shares his trading insights and research ideas as the editor of www.TraderEdge.Net.

Mr. Johnson holds a B.S. degree in finance with high honors from the University of Illinois at Urbana-Champaign and an MBA degree with a specialization in Finance from the University of Chicago Booth School of Business.

Email: BJohnson@TraderEdge.Net

RESOURCES

I write a wide range of free, informative articles on www.TraderEdge.Net. The goal of Trader Edge is to provide information and ideas that will help you enhance your investment process and improve your trading results. The articles cover many different topics: economic indicators, technical analysis, market commentary, options, futures, stocks, exchange traded funds (ETFs), strategy development, trade analysis, and risk management. You will find educational articles that appeal to the beginner, as well as advanced tools and strategies to support more experienced traders.

Trader Edge also offers a subscription to one of the proprietary strategies that I developed and trade in my own account. The Trader Edge Asset Allocation Rotational (AAR) Strategy is a conservative, long-only, asset allocation strategy that rotates monthly among five large asset classes: large-cap U.S. stocks, developed country stocks in Europe and Asia, emerging market stocks, U.S. Treasury Notes, and commodities. The strategy was inspired by the "Ivy League portfolio" and uses trend and technical filters to reduce downside risk. The AAR strategy has generated approximately 20% annual returns over the 20+ year combined back and forward test period. Please use the following link to learn more about the AAR strategy: http://traderedge.net/order/aar-strategy/.

During the course of my research for this book, I collaborated with the owners of OptionSlam.com on several enhancements for their site that will help all traders who use option strategies to trade earnings announcements. Examples from the OptionSlam.com site were used throughout this book; many thanks to OptionSlam.com for their permission to use these screenshots.

Given the strong synergies between OptionSlam.com and the tools in this book, OptionSlam.com has agreed to offer an exclusive 15% discount on annual INSIDER Memberships to readers who purchased this book.

OptionSlam.com INSIDER Membership

The following benefits are provided to all INSIDER
OptionSlam.com Members:
- View Earnings History of Individual Stocks
- View Volatility History of Individual Stocks
- View Straddle Tracking History of Individual Stocks
- View and Customize the Upcoming Earnings Filter
- View and Customize the Earnings Calendar
- View Weekly Implied Volatility Report
- View and Customize the Best Trending Stocks Report
- View and Customize the Current Monthly and Weekly Straddles
Report
- View and Customize the Historical Straddles Report
- View Trades from All Members
- Customize and Schedule Email Alerts of Personalized Reports
- Export Earnings Statistics to Excel

OptionSlam.com's historical earnings data provides all of the
return and volatility data necessary to evaluate past earnings
performance. The "Upcoming Earnings Filter" is a powerful and
flexible tool that will help you efficiently identify both directional and
non-directional trading candidates.

I encourage you to visit the Optionslam.com referral page:
https://www.optionslam.com/partner_info/traderedge and take
advantage of the exclusive 15% Trader Edge referral discount. Note
the underscore ("_") between "partner" and "info" in the above link.

OptionVue

Several of the graphs in this book represent screenshot images
captured from OptionVue's software; many thanks to Len Yates and
OptionVue for their permission to include these images. Trading
options without a comprehensive option analytical platform is not
advisable and the OptionVue software is one of the most powerful
tools available. Unlike most broker platforms, OptionVue evaluates
both the horizontal and vertical volatility skews, resulting in much
more realistic calculations and more accurate risk and valuation
metrics. In addition, I worked with OptionVue to help them apply
the aggregate implied volatility formula to quantify the effects of

earnings volatility before and after earnings events in the OptionVue software.

The OptionVue software also includes a very powerful "Trade Finder" module, which is similar to the strategy optimization tool in the Integrated spreadsheet. Trade Finder allows the user to specify an objective, strategy candidates, filters, and forecast adjustments and uses those inputs to search for the best possible strategy. Most important, *Trade Finder uses the aggregate implied volatility formula to accurately incorporate the effects of earnings volatility in its analysis.*

OptionVue also recently released a new subscription service specifically designed for "Earnings Plays." OptionVue's description of the five Earnings Play's strategies follows:

- Prime Movers: Stocks that make big moves - options tend to be undervalued.

- Prime Non-Movers: Stocks that make smaller-than-expected moves, options tend to be overvalued.

- Earnings Pairs: Two stocks in the same industry, only one of which is announcing earnings.

- Echoes - Two stocks in the same industry, with one announcing 1-18 days after the other.

- Runners - Stocks that tend to "run" in price after the earnings announcement.

This system is based on the hypothetical results actual trades would have experienced in the past and shows you a quality ranking for each trade along with its past success rate.

OptionVue also offers real-time and historical option prices, which can be used to backtest option strategies, even with adjustments. Finally, DiscoverOptions, the educational arm of OptionVue, offers one-on-one personal option mentoring from professional option traders with decades of experience.

Through our referral agreement, OptionVue is offering an exclusive 15% discount on the initial purchase of any annual subscription of any OptionVue product and on all DiscoverOptions educational products. However, the discount is not available to current OptionVue clients with an active OptionVue subscription. Please use the coupon code "traderedge" (*lower case with no spaces or quotation marks*) to receive your 15% discount when ordering applicable products from OptionVue online or over the phone.

I encourage you to visit the OptionVue referral page: http://www.optionvue.com/traderedge.html and take advantage of the exclusive 15% Trader Edge referral discount. If you would prefer to evaluate the OptionVue software before placing an order, the above link will also allow you to enroll in a free 14-day trial of OptionVue's option analytical platform.

CSI

Reliable prices are essential for developing and implementing systematic trading strategies. Commodity Systems Inc. (CSI) is one of the leading providers of market data and trading software for institutional and retail customers. Please use the following link to learn more about CSI's pricing subscriptions: https://csicheckout.com/cgi-bin/ua_order_form_nw.pl?referrer=TE.

Note the underscore ("_") between "ua" and "order" and between "order" and "form" and between "form" and "nw" in the above link.

I am a paying customer of OptionSlam.com, OptionVue, and CSI. My company, Trading Insights, LLC, has an affiliate referral relationship with OptionSlam.com, OptionVue, and CSI.

Spreadsheet Tools

Purchasing this book entitles you to an individual user license to download and use the associated risk/return Excel spreadsheets for your own research. However, you may not transfer or share the copyrighted spreadsheet, passwords, or download links with others.

There are two Excel spreadsheets that accompany this book. The name of the first spreadsheet is EEVBasic.xls. The Basic spreadsheet uses some simplifying assumptions to reduce the amount of input data required from the user, but still estimates current and historical earnings volatility and uses those estimates to forecast future levels of implied volatility around earnings announcements. The Basic spreadsheet does not use macros and should be compatible with many different versions of Excel.

The name of the second spreadsheet is EEVIntegrated2.xlsm. The Integrated spreadsheet requires more data, but is far more sophisticated and powerful than the Basic spreadsheet. It does not use simplifying assumptions. Instead, it simultaneously estimates all of the volatility parameters required to model every option in the matrix. These parameters completely describe the vertical and horizontal skews as well as level of earnings volatility implied by option prices.

The Integrated spreadsheet uses this comprehensive volatility model to calculate "True Greeks" and accurate simulated option values. Excel's integrated "Solver" optimization tool is then used by the spreadsheet to identify optimal strategies to maximize risk-adjusted returns. The Integrated spreadsheet uses push-button macros to perform all functions. Due to the extensive use of macros and other functions, the Integrated spreadsheet may only be fully compatible with the latest versions of Microsoft Excel.

The spreadsheets are included in an encrypted, self-extracting, zip file. Many cells in the spreadsheet are protected or validated to ensure the formulas function correctly. However, you may still use the worksheets interactively.

To download the zip file, go to the following page on Trader Edge: http://traderedge.net/eev-spreadsheets-2/ and follow the download instructions.

You will need the following *case-specific password* to unencrypt the zip file: UnlockEEVZip891254

You will also need a separate *case-specific password* to open the Excel files. The password is the same for both Excel files:

OpenEEV245887

If the Trader Edge website is not accessible, please send me an email with an explanation of the error received to BJohnson@TraderEdge.Net. *Include your copy of the electronic receipt* for the purchase of this book and I will send you a copy of the zip file as an email attachment.

Given the complexity of the spreadsheets and macros, it is possible that a few coding or formula errors survived the debugging process. If so, it is likely that these will be discovered after publication. Please send me an email with a detailed description of any coding or formula errors that meet *ALL of the following criteria*:

1. IS reproducible in the *latest version of Microsoft Excel*.

2. IS NOT a function of a specific set of user data or input values.

3. IS NOT due to Solver's inability to find an optimal or feasible

solution.

I do not offer user spreadsheet support, but if I can replicate and correct the error, I will upload a corrected copy of the spreadsheet to the Trader Edge download page and I will update the file origination date on the same page. Please check the download page periodically for the latest versions of the spreadsheets.

I hope you enjoy these tools and find them useful in your option trading and research.

Made in the USA
Las Vegas, NV
21 February 2021